BUILDING A CHAMPION

BUILDING A CHAMPION

On Football and the Making of the 49ers

BILL WALSH

with Glenn Dickey

ST. MARTIN'S PRESS   NEW YORK

Design by Judith A. Stagnitto

Library of Congress Cataloging-in-Publication Data

Walsh, Bill, 1931–
    Building a champion / Bill Walsh with Glenn Dickey.
        p. cm.
    ISBN 0-312-04969-2
     1. Walsh, Bill, 1931–   2. Football—United States—Coaches—
Biography. 3. San Francisco 49ers (Football team) I. Dickey,
Glenn. II. Title.
GV939.W325A3 1990
796.332'092—dc20   90-37273
[B]   CIP

10 9 8 7 6 5 4

To all the men who wore the 49er uniform, however briefly; your sacrifice made this book worthwhile.

Table of Contents

	Acknowledgment	ix
	Introduction by Glenn Dickey	xi
1	Scripting the Game	1
2	The Care and Feeding of Quarterbacks	10
3	The Cutting Edge	32
4	Disappointment in Cincinnati	45
5	Planning the Season	56
6	Worse than Expansion	63
7	Hollywood Henderson and My Drug Education	74
8	The First Breakthrough	83
9	Building an Organization	93
10	Drafting for Success	112
11	Putting It Together	128
12	The First Champion	144
13	Dealing with the Genius Label	161
14	The Repeating Problem	170
15	Good-bye to the Veterans	185
16	The Triumphal Parade	198
17	Triumph and Tragedy: The 1987 Season	211
18	The Quarterback Controversy	229
19	Our Two Greatest Games	247
20	Retiring on a High Note	255
	Appendix	267

Acknowledgments

Acknowledgment to Guy Benjamin, for his assistance in preparing this book.

To Nicole Langerak, my personal secretary, for tolerating endless hours and total unpredictability. Thank you for your Herculean efforts to make things work.

To Proverb Jacobs, my lifelong friend and confidant. Thank you for being there during the tough times.

Introduction

Bill Walsh is the most unusual football coach I've known in my thirty-two years of sportswriting.

I realized this the first time we met, which was over lunch shortly after he was hired as head coach at Stanford in 1977. The meeting itself was not unusual; as sports columnist for *The San Francisco Chronicle*, I always meet with coaches and managers who are new to the Bay Area. But the atmosphere at those meetings is usually filled with clichés. Not with Walsh. He talked of his football philosophy and background, and then we exchanged thoughts on a variety of subjects away from the sport, ranging from world politics to the advantages of living in California.

That, I learned later, was typical of Walsh, a man who is simultaneously an integral part of football and yet apart from it.

Certainly, he is intensely involved with the sport, even now that he is in the broadcast booth rather than on the sidelines.

While we were working on this book, we played in a charity golf tournament in the Napa Valley. The night before the tournament, we were at a dinner for celebrity participants. Cal football coach Bruce Snyder was sitting at a table with me when Walsh came by. Snyder asked a football question and borrowed my pen; immediately, Walsh took a napkin and started diagramming a play. For several minutes, the two were engrossed in discussion of the play, totally unaware of what was happening around them.

I was not surprised because there have been times I've been interviewing Walsh when he has suddenly interrupted the conversation because he'd thought of a play he had to diagram.

And yet the man has an ability to go beyond football that few coaches possess. Most football coaches talk to other football coaches. Walsh has a variety of friends from outside the profession, including such diverse personalities as Nobel Prize winner Dr. Glenn Seaborg and playwright Neil Simon. Former Illinois coach Mike White is one of his closest friends, but otherwise he spends the most time with those from the academic and business communities.

His creative approach to football attracts even those who would otherwise be bored by talk of X's and O's, and his organizational abilities make him much sought after as a speaker for business groups.

But primarily he is the most successful football coach of his time, and his success began with his first year in coaching; at Washington High in Fremont, in the southeast corner of the San Francisco Bay Area, he took a team that had won only one game in three years and guided it to a 9–1 season.

As an assistant in Cincinnati, he made quarterbacks Greg Cook, Virgil Carter, and Ken Anderson passing leaders, as he did with Dan Fouts at San Diego.

In his first collegiate head-coaching assignment, he took a Stanford team to two straight bowl games; Stanford had not been to a bowl in the seven years before Walsh, and has not been to one once since he left.

By the time he came to the San Francisco 49ers in 1979, Walsh was ready. There have been many excellent coaches in the NFL's history, but only a handful of men who have put together a team and then coached it to multiple championships—George Halas, Paul Brown, Vince Lombardi, Chuck Noll. Now, we can add a fifth: Bill Walsh.

Walsh took over a franchise that was the laughingstock of the NFL. Joe Thomas had stripped the team of talent and traded away its No. 1 draft pick—which would have been the very first pick in the draft that year.

In only three years, Walsh built a team that won a Super Bowl. In the last eight years of his 49er coaching career, he had three World Champions, and the 49ers became known as the "Team of the Decade."

For his accomplishments, Walsh was named the "Coach of the Eighties" by the twenty-six member selection committee of the Pro Football Hall of Fame, which based its selection on voting by the

Associated Press and Pro Football Writers Association during the decade.

Walsh's teams were quite different from the dynasties of the past. Typically, the great teams were collections of players who reached their peak together; when they fell off, the team plunged dramatically in the standings.

Lombardi's Green Bay Packers won the first two Super Bowls, but were 6–7–1 after the second one and haven't returned to that championship level since. The Pittsburgh Steelers won four Super Bowls in six seasons, culminating with the 1980 Super Bowl, but fell to third in their division the next season, as their stars grew old and were not replaced.

In contrast, Walsh kept changing, rebuilding as he was winning, with six divisional championships and seven playoff appearances in his last eight years. Each Super Bowl team was quite different; only five 49ers played in all three Super Bowls, and only three of them— quarterback Joe Montana, center Randy Cross, and defensive back Ronnie Lott—played key roles in all three games.

Walsh did it his way. Whether it was his offensive system or his method of evaluating players, he was a step ahead of his competitors.

He baffled and infuriated his coaching rivals, but he also elicited great admiration from those who really understood the game. Former coach Hank Stram, now a TV/radio analyst, often said that watching Walsh's teams was like watching a seminar; whenever Stram covered a 49er game, he and I would talk at length about what Walsh was doing with his offense. Similarly, from time to time, I would call Sid Gillman, the guru of the modern passing game, to seek further insights about Walsh's approach; Sid spent many of his retirement hours watching films of 49er games because he thoroughly enjoyed Walsh's approach.

For twelve years, I watched Walsh's teams, Stanford and the 49ers, and I talked frequently with him . But even after all that, and my conversations with Stram and Gillman, I confess that working with Walsh on this book taught me how little I knew, because his strategy and system are so complex. It would be necessary to go back half a century, to Clark Shaughnessy's work with the Chicago Bears and Stanford, to see a coach whose designs were so far ahead of his competitors.

Now, Walsh tells readers how he did it, how he put together a system that continually baffled opponents, how he masterminded his drafts, and how he put together an organization that continues to thrive even after he has left for the television booth.

—GLENN DICKEY

1

Scripting the Game

The excitement, the intensity is unbelievable. The Dome seems to compress everything. We're in Pontiac, Michigan. It's hard to believe, but this is for the world championship. Eighty thousand people roaring in anticipation. The pressure is so intense. You're caught up in the moment. You're not sure you can think straight. You have to resort to instinct and nerve.

After all our preparation, in spite of our concentration, we fumble the opening kickoff. The Bengals recover on our twenty-six-yard line. Ken Anderson immediately drives his team inside the ten. Then Jim Stuckey gets a big sack. Dwight Hicks steps in front of Isaac Curtis at the goal line and makes a great interception. Dwight gets great blocks from Bobby Leopold and Carlton Williamson and returns the ball to the thirty-two-yard line. What a defense! Tough, poised, focused. Now we're in business. Our first offensive series. We don't have great firepower but we've got precision. We have our plan; we'll now put it to work.

A "quick screen" to Ricky Patton for 6 yards; fine blocks by John Ayers and Dan Audick. A "shallow cross" pass pattern to Dwight Clark—man, is he tough—for 6 yards and a first down. A "weakside toss" to Earl Cooper; the Bengals consume it. Joe Montana hits Freddie Solomon for 9 yards—thrown and caught before they could react. It's third and one. Cincinnati will be in its short yardage defense. This is the one defense we can predict. We have a surprise ready: the "triple reverse pass." We go with it. Montana hands off to Patton, who hands off to Solomon, who tosses it back to Montana who . . . throws to tight end Charle Young for 14 yards—a pro catch! Joe is really hit as he releases the ball. I hold my breath, but he gets up okay.

First down on the thirty-three-yard line. Joe is rushed hard, incomplete pass. Second and ten. We call "96 Basic"—Earl Cooper splits the defense for eleven yards. Great blocks by Keith Fahnhorst and Randy Cross. Another first down. We go with Bill Ring and Johnny Davis in the backfield. The call is "14 Lead" with an unbalanced line; Ring gets seven yards. Beautifully executed! Davis knocks their linebacker five yards off the ball.

We're now at the fifteen-yard line. Cooper on another toss play; they stuff it again. No way; that's the end of the tosses. It's third and three. They'll be in man-to-man coverage.

"Red right open, F left, short, twenty-four double square out." Solomon goes in motion, bursts upfield on the snap of the ball, breaks to the outside, wide open. Joe hits him for fourteen yards! There's now incredible crowd noise. Freddie had come in motion inside tight end Charle Young. The Bengal defense was confused and responded too late.

First and goal on the one-yard line. Here comes the Cincinnati goal-line defensive group. There will be a soft spot over our right side. Joe takes the snap, steps to the right, and dives through it on a quarterback sneak. Touchdown!

"Scripting" twenty-five plays before each game became identified with me and, as with so much of my offense, it started when I was quarterback coach and directed the passing game for the Cincinnati Bengals.

Head coach Paul Brown would say, "What do we have for openers?" So, on game day, offensive-line coach Bill Johnson and I would agree on 4 plays we could call at the start of the game. Paul was comfortable with that. Then it went to 6 plays. In 1976, while an assistant coach for the Chargers, I planned a 15-play sequence.

As time passed, that format was extended to 25 plays. After I left the Chargers to coach Stanford, the strategy was so successful that we scored on our first possession eight times in eleven games in 1978. But during the 1980s, the "scripted" offense was the hallmark of the 49ers.

Some people thought we called 25 plays, come hell or high water, which assumes that if we were on the one-yard line after our eighth play, we'd call a long pass. Obviously, the system had to be much more flexible than that to be successful.

We had special categories for each situation, everything from goal-line plays to extreme-long–yardage situations. We would construct a "ready list" with the opening plays but also have plays listed for specific categories.

For instance, with the Bengals in the '70s, if we got inside the twenty-five-yard line, teams would have a strong tendency to blitz in an effort to upset our rhythm. So, we had specific plays designed for the blitz, and when we got inside the twenty-five; we'd go to those plays.

Or, if we were near the goal line, we would use the sequence of plays we had prepared for that category during the week. It wouldn't be a long pass, for sure.

So, in all these categories, we had priorities. We didn't always go directly to them because as the game went on, we would analyze our opponent's strategy and make adjustments. But with all those considerations isolated, we could put together 25 plays that would enable us to smoothly begin the game, proceeding with our best chance of success.

In the great years with the 49ers, writers and television commentators like John Madden often would refer to our success in the first quarter, which was a direct result of specifically planning in advance what we were going to do. Scoring first certainly doesn't guarantee winning, but it did make it possible for us to continue to run our game plan and, in a sense, dictate to the other team.

With the 49ers, there were games when we'd go through all 25 plays, click, click, click. In the worst case, we might have used only 10 or 12. That happened when we would run up against a defense that simply surprised us, and even then, we tried to come back to work something against it.

Each year under Paul Brown, the playcalling became more and more refined, because we had a philosophy and a particular approach to the game. But even with the Bengals, there were gaps in the system that had to be eliminated. It was, finally, a critical loss that brought us to the realization that we should define every possible situation.

In 1975, the Bengals played the Oakland Raiders in a playoff game in Oakland; the winner would go to the AFC championship game against Pittsburgh. The Raiders were a great team and almost impossible to defeat in Oakland, but we played extremely well and, in the closing minutes, recovered a fumble on their forty-yard line. We trailed by only three points, 31–28, so we had a chance to at least tie the game with a long field goal if we could reach their twenty-five.

But at that point, I made some playcalling errors that really trouble me, even now. The noise was intense in the Oakland Coliseum, a stadium where fans seemed to be right on top of the field, and without everything on our play sheet that I needed, it became too chaotic to make the best calls. The pressure was incredible.

My first mistake came on first down. We had a special play that we had practiced, an option run with quarterback Ken Anderson keeping the ball or pitching out to running back Essex Johnson. It would have been a perfect call for that situation, but it just didn't come to mind. I didn't have it on my ready list, as I would have had in later years, because that category wasn't included in the game plan. Instead, I called a pass that fell incomplete.

After the game, that quarterback option occurred to me. Too late.

On the next play, Raider outside linebacker Ted Hendricks was blitzing off the weak side. Fullback Boobie Clark was assigned to block him. Boobie had handled Hendricks earlier in the game, but Ted was a great player and he knew how to adjust. By that time, he had learned how to beat Clark, and he made a big sack on Anderson.

That play demonstrated that we needed a more flexible pass-protection plan to deal with a great blitzing linebacker like Hendricks. Remembering that sack years later, when we played the New York Giants in a playoff game after the 1981 season, we had guard John Ayers pull out to block the Giants' great linebacker, Lawrence Taylor. Taylor had terrorized teams that year with his blitzing, because everybody was trying to stop him with a back. But Ayers neutralized Taylor, and we won the game.

Largely because those first two plays failed against the Raiders, we had to give up the ball. We got it back one more time, but with only fifteen seconds left on the clock. We simply had not prepared very well for that situation: just go deep and hope for the best. Of course, we didn't come close.

That game really had an impact on me. By the time I joined the 49ers, I made certain that we would account for those critical, almost desperate situations at the end of a game. We practiced plays for that and for every other conceivable situation. If we had one last chance to pull out a victory, we at least had a play prepared and rehearsed.

In my first two years with the 49ers, we failed to score in those situations because we were basically outmanned and were unable to execute. But in later years, our successful years, when we found ourselves in a situation that looked impossible, we at least had a chance to pull it out.

Ironically, the best example probably came against Cincinnati, in the second game of the 1987 season. That was a pivotal contest for us. We had already lost to the Steelers in Pittsburgh, 30–17, we were trailing the Bengals, 26–20, with only six seconds remaining—and they had possession. Instead of risking a punt on fourth down from the Cincinnati thirty, Sam Wyche, my long-time friend and former colleague, called a running play, thinking he could run out the clock. But we stopped it for a loss and took over on the twenty-five with two seconds to play.

Against the Raiders in that 1975 game, the Bengals had nothing to call at game's end. This time, the 49ers did, and Joe Montana threw a touchdown pass to Jerry Rice that, after Ray Wersching's PAT, won the game for us.

So, that win was directly related to that crucial last game of the '75 season, when we weren't fully prepared. I took great satisfaction in the touchdown and how we handled the end of that game, compared to the Raiders game in a time when football was less complex and sophisticated. I was reminded later that I actually skipped off the field with Roger Craig. I still get teased about that.

This was an example of the flexibility of our game plan. Even in the last seconds of the game, there was a plan from which we could draw. Whatever the situation, whatever the time, we had something ready. The first time it was third down and one, we knew what to call. If we reached the twenty-yard line, we had specific plays to call. If we found ourselves in a long-yardage situation, we referred to the long-yardage segment of our game plan.

On the last and winning drive of the game against Cincinnati in the

1989 Super Bowl, there were plays called by Joe Montana at the line of scrimmage and there were plays called on the sidelines—but they were all plays we had prepared and had rehearsed for that particular situation.

Beyond that, we had an audible package of plays that the quarterback would be rehearsed on extensively during the week. When he saw a specific defense, he knew he would have to change the play. For instance, on the last play of the drive in the '89 Super Bowl, if Montana saw a safety sliding over to help cover John Taylor, he was prepared to go to another receiver. The safety didn't come over, and Joe stayed with his primary receiver, throwing to Taylor for the touchdown.

There was another category: special plays, such as reverses. Those were designed to be used early in the game. Again, that was Paul Brown's formula. He complained so many times, "They ran their special plays before we did." I scoffed at that originally, but I later saw the wisdom of it. The first team to run a reverse, the first team to run a special play, was most likely to be successful, because once it had been run, everybody was aware of it, so both teams would be alert.

There's another reason to use special plays early: If you wait on these plays, you might find yourself well ahead late in the game and therefore you don't need to use them, or you are behind and unable to waste a play because the opposition is alert to gimmicks.

The whole thought behind "scripting" was that we could make our decisions much more thoroughly and with more definition on Thursday or Friday than during a game, when all the tension, stress, and emotion can make it extremely difficult to think clearly. The elements seriously affect a coach's ability to concentrate; severe wind, cold, or heat can damage it. Try going outside when it's five degrees and reach an objective decision that calls for problem-solving.

It's like planning for a sales meeting or organizing an advertising campaign: You preplan as much as you can with the information you have in a more clinical setting. It's easier than trying to make quick, spontaneous calls in ten or twelve seconds during the pressure and intensity of a game.

Preplanning means that you don't have to depend entirely on your spontaneous judgment during the game. Weather can be a real factor. I've been dizzy from the heat on the sidelines in Los Angeles and

Anaheim, for instance, and so cold in Chicago and New York that I could hardly talk. Having a ready list of plays helps counteract that.

Now, no system is perfect, because there's always the human element. There were times when I would become affected by the noise and emotion on the sidelines and get away from my prepared list. There were also times when I had to improvise, because for some reason, the plays we had listed just didn't develop.

For instance, there was a game against New Orleans in '86. The Saints were a strong, physical team; they were just stuffing our runs, and I soon lost confidence in our ground attack. Paul Hackett, who was then our quarterback coach, called down from the press box in the second quarter and said, "Damn it, Bill, the last five plays you've called aren't even in our game plan, let alone our starting twenty-five."

I shot back at Paul that we'd had to change because the Saints were set up to stop the plays we had ready. In this case I was right, so we changed formations and got the Saints off balance. By the third quarter, we could go back to our original list because the Saints were no longer concentrating on those plays, and we went on to win. In retrospect, I appreciated Paul's reaction, because I may have been starting to panic.

That kind of instance was rare, because the more planning you can implement, the more confidence and assurance you have going into the game.

It also makes a difference with the players. With the Bengals, we would tell players just before the game, "Here are our openers," and they would feel more secure about getting started.

Then, when I joined the Chargers, we'd go over the starting plays the night before the game. The players came to expect this information and became comfortable with it. The plays would be put up on a viewing screen with key points explained, and they'd study them later that night. Consequently, the players were confident the moment they stepped on the field, because they were in control.

By the time I joined the 49ers, the system had been further refined, so coaches and players could begin working with these "scripted" plays for a few days before the upcoming game.

When we could isolate and establish what our starting plays would be against a defense, we had the time to say, Now what did we do last week, what have we done in recent weeks, and what have we previously employed against this specific defense? NFL teams exchanged films for the three games preceding each new game, so we could go back further in the schedule and feel rather confident that plays we'd used previously would be ones on which our opponents weren't concentrating.

We had members of our staff, such as Sherm Lewis in recent years, who would be examining each week what we'd done before, what our success ratio was, and what we could do to make it more difficult for the other team to prepare for us. If the week before we'd run effectively with Roger Craig, for instance, we had the capacity in our next game to fake a Craig run and throw downfield to Jerry Rice.

This concept was most effective because staff members did the tedious research that was then directly applied to our plan. As one example, in my later years with the 49ers, I would constantly exchange with offensive-line coach Bobb McKittrick about how he appraised our early running game, and with Denny Green, who was responsible for our passing game, about how he saw our pass plays. If they had concerns the list could be expanded or revised.

It prepared the players and gave us something specific to practice, as well as confidence that in any circumstance that could develop, we had a way to deal with it.

The system also kept our opponents off balance. If we executed well, teams would have to adjust to our early tactics but because we knew what we were going to do, we could anticipate what the other team's adjustments would be, so we knew how to deal with them.

We sometimes used more than one formation with a specific play, an element of disguise that allowed us to repeat those which were more successful. We'd start a game using one formation with a play, and then Joe Montana would shift to another the next time we used that play, a formation we'd practiced, and that simple alteration gave us a lot more dimension.

We would also use one play early in the game, to set up another later. For instance, we might use a simple handoff to Tom Rathman. If we saw the defense overreacting, as the game progressed, we would look for an opportunity to fake that handoff and have Joe Montana throwing.

All this time, we were basically a step ahead, because the defense would have to react to what we had planned. We could observe how they responded to different plays and different formations, and then we could make our own adjustments, always going to something we had prepared during the practice week.

We were quite willing to go against the accepted strategy formula, to call a pass when other teams expected a run, or vice versa. That made it more difficult for teams to use special defenses against us, because there was no such thing as an automatic passing down or an automatic running down.

As an example, we might have a series set up in which we planned to fake a run and pass on first down, utilize a basic running play on second down, and then use a ball-control pass on third down. Because the first-down pass wasn't expected, the defense would probably go for the run fake. And even if the pass was incomplete, we would run on second down—again, going against what the defense expected—and then come back with a ball-control pass for 5 to 6 yards on third down to gain the first down.

That's the theory. No, it didn't work every time; we were competing with very capable coaches and players. But it worked often enough for the 49ers to have sustained success.

We had found a formula that was different from other clubs'. Some coaches are somewhat relieved to rely on a simplistic plan. If it doesn't work, they might then say the players didn't block hard enough, they didn't run hard enough, they weren't tough enough, they didn't want it badly enough.

We had taken it beyond that pattern of failure and finger-pointing, so that the responsibility for the success of an offense started with the coach, and the offense was then executed by players who were extremely well prepared. We were able to avoid the trap of getting in a desperate situation and just trying to wing it because we were not prepared—and then blaming players when it didn't succeed.

In some form, many coaches are implementing this form of offense now, and our offense, once referred to as "nickel-and-dime," is considered by many to be on the cutting edge of offensive football.

2

The Care and Feeding of Quarterbacks

Probably more drafting mistakes are made on quarterbacks than on any other position. In 1971, for instance, the top three choices in the draft were quarterbacks—Jim Plunkett, Dan Pastorini, and Archie Manning. Meanwhile, we got Ken Anderson for the Cincinnati Bengals on the third round. Plunkett, Pastorini, and Manning were undeniably good quarterbacks, but Anderson had the most consistent career.

Why do teams make mistakes on quarterbacks? Sometimes it's a matter of being sold by the media on the quarterback's performance in college, without realizing that he doesn't have the potential to become a solid professional performer. Or, it's being oversold on a quarterback's arm. You'll hear coaches and scouts saying, "He can throw the ball fifty yards on a line," or "Did you see that rope?" They won't account for other factors.

Alternatively, a quarterback might be first-rate, but doesn't have the supporting cast he needs to succeed. Manning played most of his career with a very poor team, the New Orleans Saints. Steve Young was downrated by many NFL organizations because he was with a weak team in Tampa.

Then again, a lot of the failures are due to poor coaching. College quarterbacks just aren't being prepared for the pros. They're put in the starting lineup too early; Plunkett was almost destroyed that way. They're played before they've developed fundamentals and then left to their own devices. As a first-year player, Plunkett came up with some big plays and the New England Patriots looked to him to make the same kinds of plays every week. He began taking a terrific beating and just couldn't continue his heroics.

Changing coaches frequently, as so many teams do, sets back a quarterback's progress, because he is never able to develop any continuity by building on what he has already learned. Changing quarterback coaches, or having a quarterback coach who coaches not just the quarterbacks, but the whole offense, can hurt, too.

I look for more in a quarterback than just a strong arm.

Natural competitive instincts are a prerequisite in quarterbacking. There have been quarterbacks who have been programmed through intensive practice repetition; Ken Anderson began in this manner. But the better the instincts, the more readily a man will become an effective performer.

He has to have some spontaneity, to be able to exercise his creativity, to go beyond the system. That's one factor that continued to impress me about Greg Cook with the Bengals.

Then, you look for a quick delivery. Some quarterbacks just naturally throw the ball quickly, rather than winding up—as boxers have a quick right hand. That makes them much more efficient players. The quicker the delivery, the less time defenders have to react to the throw.

Agility and movement are very important. A quarterback who can pick up his feet quickly, who can get away from center quickly, can set up more quickly to throw. Obviously, with the great pass rushers in the game today, it's a big advantage to be able to avoid the pressure. Joe Montana was effective early in his 49ers career, before we had really consistent pass protection, because he was able to avoid the pressure and make the play.

Functional, instinctive mental process—the ability to think on your feet—is more important than just basic intelligence. Some of my quarterbacks were very bright away from the field as well as on it—Anderson, Dan Fouts, Steve Dils. But a high IQ isn't as important as the ability to realize almost instinctively what is occurring on the field. Montana, for instance, is certainly bright enough; but more important, he has *athletic* intelligence and outstanding spontaneous instincts, which help him identify opportunities and solve problems the instant they occur in a game.

That quality can be observed in all the great quarterbacks.

You want a person who can thrive on the task itself and relate quickly, as Steve DeBerg did for the 49ers, as Guy Benjamin did for me at Stanford. You don't want to outsmart yourself; a quarterback has to be able to function within the coach's system. A mentally limited person is going to have trouble functioning on that level.

Once you've selected your quarterback, the first factor for success is his credibility. Do his teammates seriously believe he can perform? That credibility may take time to establish. For one reason or another, the rest of the squad may not take him seriously at first. Whether it's Ken Anderson coming out of tiny Augustana College, or Greg Cook entering as a number-one pick, the quarterback must sell himself through performance to his teammates.

Another major factor is establishing confidence in a quarterback. When he has proven himself over a period of time, players know what to expect. When a quarterback begins to play error-free football, players then believe the team can function smoothly, without devastating mistakes.

Then, there's the quarterback's resourcefulness. Players come to believe a quarterback will make the right play. They know that he's going to function in the most difficult situations without unraveling. He's able to make the critical plays as well as the routine ones. If it's a ten-yard pass that means the season, as in Super Bowl XXII, he'll make it as easily as he does in practice. That's the advantage the 49ers have had with Montana.

Finally, there is the intangible quality of leadership, when players are inspired by a quarterback, as they were by Fouts and are still by Montana. These quarterbacks lifted their teammates' level of performance. With these two under the center, everyone in the offensive unit realized his fullest potential.

It's all done by performance—not by halftime talks. It's not the dialogue in the huddle. It's the spontaneous move, the ability to make the critical play that wins the game. Montana can do that, Steve Young can do that—and each of these men I've referred to did this exceptionally well at some point in his career.

What players most look for is a quarterback with poise, a calming effect, so they know they can converse with him in the most frenzied moments, rather than a quarterback who is constantly screaming at them. Leadership in a quarterback does not mean overt posturing. It's *communicating* under the most difficult circumstances.

The quarterback can develop these qualities only in an atmosphere that promotes communication and open exchange.

Mechanical efficiency is the common denominator in developing consistency and continuity. Any unnecessary steps or movements directly affect timing, and the timing of the throw is vital. You don't want the defender to see the ball thrown before the receiver does. A quarterback cannot stare down his receiver and then throw the ball. And, you don't want the receiver breaking off his pattern before the quarterback is ready to throw, because the receiver's movement will take the defender right to where the ball is thrown.

Every movement of the quarterback has to be as efficient as he can make it, so he is prepared to throw early or late. If he throws early, he must time the pass perfectly so that it reaches the spot as the receiver does. If he must throw late, he must be able to avoid the pass rush and find a throwing lane between defenders.

We spent hours on everything a quarterback does: every step he takes, the number of steps he takes, how he moves between pass rushers or to the outside, when he goes to alternate receivers. It's similar to a basketball player practicing different situational shots.

With the 49ers, we treated every pass play as a separate entity. We would practice one pass, say a 12-yard out, just as a shortstop would practice throwing to the first baseman, over and over.

We worked on the quarterback throwing the ball when he's supposed to throw it, and on throwing a ball that's catchable. The quarterback knew how hard to throw on each specific play. I've seen too many instances of the strong-armed quarterback who throws everything as hard as he can and then blames receivers for dropping the pass. In some cases that mentality can go on for years and cost numerous coaches and receivers their jobs.

Then, we considered how our receivers would read a coverage, and the simultaneous read our quarterback would get. All these factors were isolated and practiced with endless repetition.

Each play has someone on defense who is the key. It might be the free safety, it might be the cornerback on the side you throw to, it might be a linebacker, it might be a strong safety. If the quarterback notes that this particular player is not in a position to stop the pass, he goes to the receiver in that area; if a defender is in close proximity, the quarterback looks immediately to another receiver. As this occurs, he looks for a throwing lane to throw the ball between passrushers. Without a throwing lane, he must hold the ball, and then go to an alternate receiver.

It's really not a mysterious thing, but the advantage we had was a complete system that had been developed and refined over a twenty-year period.

If we were to say, we're going to throw a "double-go" pattern—both wide receivers going deep down each side of the field—Joe would look to one side of the field for the wide receiver sprinting deep. He would look at the relationship of the receiver and the defending cornerback. If that coverage was too tight, he'd look immediately to his tight end hooking in the middle.

If his tight end was also covered, he'd expect to move quickly and find a running back serving as his outlet. Moving quickly is important because you have to assume that if the quarterback is forced to go to his third receiver, the pass rush will be right there. That would be an example of something we practiced continuously.

It takes years for even the great quarterbacks to develop these skills. We had at least thirty pass plays, each taking endless hours of practice.

I always felt, too, that it was important not to give the quarterback too much to handle. For example, the quarterback would basically use receivers only on one side of the field. This was designed to prevent those hurried throws to the other side that so often result in interceptions. We found it to be much more effective for the quarterback to concentrate on three of his receivers operating to one side of the field.

By about 1985, Montana was so proficient with the system that he was able to go to the opposite side of the field and find another receiver. And when we got Jerry Rice, we also developed plays where Joe would look late to Jerry for a deep pass down the middle, after checking the weak safety's field position.

We also took as much pressure as we could off the quarterbacks by calling plays from the sideline.

If quarterbacks were trained in high school and college to call plays, they would be much more prepared and informed as to how to do it. But for the last twenty-five years it has become a lost art.

Paul Brown demonstrated in the fifties that a quarterback, Otto Graham, could function beautifully without calling plays. Graham was certainly capable of calling them, and, in fact, wanted to, but with the plays being called from the press box or sideline off a previously prepared plan, Otto developed into a great quarterback.

Since then, the game has become so sophisticated that it's almost impossible for a quarterback to call plays and still function efficiently. One man just doesn't fly a jet liner; it takes a crew, and that's a prerequisite in orchestrating a football game. You've got the pilot, who's the quarterback, but it takes others in specific roles to complete the cycle.

The quarterback has a hard enough time absorbing physical punishment and then redirecting his thoughts back to the game without having to call plays, too. The modern style of defense, with multiple substitutions on virtually every down, makes it much more difficult than it used to be. The quarterback isn't going to be as able as a coach in the press box to see the substitutions and make corresponding calls.

When he quarterbacked the 49ers in the '60s and early '70s, John Brodie may have averaged 20 pass plays per game. Now, the 49ers may have 60 for a specific game. Perhaps only 30 will be used, but the coach calling plays has to have all 60 in readiness as different situations develop. That's an almost impossible task for a quarterback.

It's exhausting enough for a quarterback to do the job physically, especially in the 49er system, where passes have to be timed perfectly and each play is expected to be run with precision. It's too much to ask him to get involved in the strategy.

Now, I think Montana could call plays, because he's been in the system, he knows it so thoroughly, and he can see who's on the field. He's a master of his system. I'm sure there are other veteran quarterbacks, who have been with their coach for years, who could handle it.

But those quarterbacks are exceptions, and even then, it's best for a man in the almost clinical atmosphere of the press box, away from the noise and emotion of the field, to make the decision and call the appropriate play.

Even in the press box, you can't note everything, so we involved the players, too.

People like Jerry Rice or Dwight Clark would say, "Here's what I can do to this guy." Now, we might not do that right away because the down and distance might not be right. They were thinking of a specific situation, against a specific defense. I sometimes had players tell me something in the second quarter that I couldn't use until the fourth, when I expected that defense would show up.

We responded to what the players said. We needed their input. Often, it made a difference. For instance, in a game against New Orleans in 1987, I had told the team at halftime that we would call the pass off the slow draw when we got inside the thirty, but because of the stress and excitement of the moment, I simply didn't think of the play. On the sideline, Steve Young reminded me of it. He wasn't a bit hesitant. I called it immediately, and we scored.

In that situation, a coach can't let his ego get in the way. I couldn't worry about being embarrassed because I hadn't come up with the play. Results are all that matter.

There was another game against the Rams when we were trailing at halftime. Going into the locker room, I asked Guy Benjamin, our reserve quarterback, with a touch of humor, "Got any ideas?" Guy reminded me that, because the Rams defensive linemen were coming upfield so quickly, we could run a draw or quick trap. I jumped on his observation, and both plays worked well in the second half.

Of course, there was another time when we were near the goal line in a game against New Orleans when Guy suggested a third-down play that failed, and we had to kick a field goal. I noted that Guy was suddenly at the end of the bench, well out of reach of my headset cord. Of course his idea was a good one, or I wouldn't have considered it.

In getting information from players during the heat of the game, we had to realize that they were naturally consumed with their own personal battles and were not necessarily aware of what was going on elsewhere on the field.

For instance, offensive linemen much prefer run blocking, when they can fire out at an opponent, instead of pass blocking, when they have to give ground and fight people off. So, if we were running the ball effectively, they'd want to keep going, but I might see that, having set up the other team with the run, we could hit a play pass. If the pass didn't work, they'd come off the field saying, "Why the hell didn't we run?"

Or, tackle Steve Wallace might say, "I'm dominating my man," but he was doing that against a specific defense. If we called a play on Steve's side and the defense changed, the play wouldn't have a chance.

You also have to realize that players can be quite emotional in the heat of a game. You have to temper the input from players because they can overreact to what they see, because of emotion and competitive excitement. The coach has to use his instincts and wisdom to interpret what a player tells him.

We made every effort to keep a businesslike atmosphere on the sideline, with people thinking as clearly as they could, without becoming either distraught or so pleased that they were celebrating.

The most important man in sideline communication, naturally, was the quarterback.

When Joe Montana came out of the game, he would first check with me, then go to the phones with our quarterback coach in the booth. They would exchange about the pass defenses and coverages they'd seen. We also had Polaroid pictures taken of defenses, but those were primarily used at halftime.

It was an open forum, so I would always respond to whatever Joe said. I might help him by explaining the situation as I saw it, but if he persisted, we would often adjust or adapt to his desires.

There were some difficult times. He would be terribly upset at himself or another player, or disturbed by a call that hadn't succeeded. There were instances when I would say, "That was a bad call. It won't happen again."

As the years progressed, our communication became better and better, because Joe understood more of the system and I became more efficient in my role. In the early years, though he played extremely well because of his great instincts and spontaneity, he didn't fully comprehend our logic, so he would question certain play calls. But he was always striving to improve, and by our second Super Bowl year, 1984, he had full command of everything.

Of course, it was probably best that I didn't know what he said when he walked twenty feet away, out of my range of hearing.

There was another important element on the sideline: minimizing anxiety and a feeling of desperation. I did what I could, and Joe did what he could to ease the pressure and stress. There would be some teasing between us, even in the most difficult situations. I might make some irrelevant remark just to lighten things up. In the 1984 Cincinnati game, when Joe came to the sideline after throwing his third interception in the first half, I said, "How's it going out there?" He grinned, chuckled, and seemed to relax, and he played much better the rest of the way, as we pulled out a win.

There was still latitude for a quarterback to call specific plays. Each week, we practiced audibles and no-huddle plays that Montana would be expected to call at the right time. That in itself is enough for a given week, to know when and what to call at the appropriate time. Often, you get only one chance to attack just the defense you're looking for.

There are several factors to consider in calling such plays. We started with a category that we called "utility plays"—plays that could be run against virtually any defense. If the defense was changed into a radical blitz or an extreme form of zone defense, Montana then had audibles he could go to. Or, say it was a running play designed to work against the basic balanced four-three. If the defense overshifted, Montana would audible a basic utility play to avoid running into their strength.

The next category would be audibilizing to a play designed to attack a specific defense. No matter what the call is, if the quarterback comes to the line and sees this defense, he switches immediately. We are going for the big play. An example of that came in the playoff game against Minnesota after the '89 season. With the 49ers on the Minnesota five, Montana came to the line, and spotted that the Vikings were playing for the pass, with linebackers in blitzing positions between guard and tackle. As planned, he audibled to a quarterback draw, got great blocks from Jesse Sapolu and Guy McIntyre, and broke up the middle untouched for a touchdown.

Finally, you consider your down and distance. Say you've got third-and-ten. Well, a utility play won't help you, because it isn't going to get you enough yards. You have to have something better, and a coach in the press box with the game plan in front of him is better situated to select the right play than would be even the most knowledgeable quarterback.

So, you have situational plays for each category of defense. It takes years for a quarterback to experience enough different situations to respond quickly, almost instinctively, to everything. It can't be achieved by just a lecture at the chalk board. He has to be able to see what's happening almost instantly when he lines up behind the center.

That's why you'll see veterans calling so many more audibles than younger quarterbacks.

In Ken Anderson's case, he might have called five audibles his entire first year, maybe twenty his second. But by his fifth year, he was checking plays at the line of scrimmage frequently.

Montana's development has been much the same. By now, he's probably calling an audible every fifth or sixth play. He might go fifteen plays without calling one but then will call three in a row. Joe has become so proficient that he will almost instinctively call an audible based on what he senses the defense will show once the ball is snapped.

In his early years, though, there were many instances when audibles should have been called but Joe didn't spot the situation. It takes years to develop that skill. In contrast, the assertive but inexperienced quarterback will mistakenly call audibles. This drives the coach up the wall. Steve Young wanted to engage the system in his first year with the 49ers. The results were all kinds of erroneous calls. I'd find myself yelling, "Don't do it, Steve, don't do it!"

Joe Montana is certainly the most successful of the quarterbacks I coached, but he was somewhat of a gamble when we picked him in the first draft I had with the 49ers, before the 1979 season.

I had taken note of Joe because of his heroics at Notre Dame. The same day my Stanford team had come from behind to beat Georgia in the Bluebonnet Bowl, his Notre Dame team had rallied to defeat Houston in the Cotton Bowl. In miserable weather, Joe had brought his team back to win after they trailed by three touchdowns going into the final quarter.

As part of our preparation for the draft, I personally had seen all the quarterbacks who might be available to us. Because our first-round pick had been traded away to acquire O. J. Simpson the previous year, our initial pick in 1979 would be the first one in the second round, twenty-ninth overall.

We couldn't arrange to see Joe until a few days before the draft. He was in Los Angeles and I flew down to meet him and work him out with James Owens, a UCLA running back. The 49ers desperately needed speed, and Owens, whom we projected as a wide receiver, was a world-class high hurdler. That was a fateful day for all three of us. When I saw Joe's quick, nimble feet and agility, I was really excited about his potential as a quarterback in our system.

At the time, we thought Steve DeBerg just might be our quarterback for the future. I had not had time to evaluate Steve, but all reports were very positive. We were looking for somebody who would at least have the potential to be his backup. If the new quarterback was good enough to outperform Steve and replace him at some point, so much the better.

There were three prominent quarterbacks in the draft that year— Phil Simms, Jack Thompson, and Steve Fuller—but we correctly assumed they'd go in the first round, before we picked.

We felt Montana and Steve Dils, my quarterback at Stanford, would be available. Naturally, I gave Dils, who had performed so well for me, a lot of consideration, but Joe was taller, quicker, and smoother. Steve was later to play a number of years for the Vikings and Rams.

The argument against taking Joe was that he had been very inconsistent as a college player, that his concentration wasn't always there. He was also rather slight, only 185 pounds on a six-two frame, though he had broad shoulders and a lean, graceful physique. Scouts across the NFL questioned whether he could take the physical punishment of pro football.

Some questioned whether he had a strong enough arm. I thought it was quite adequate for our system. It was more important to me that he had quick feet and a quick delivery. I felt he could be disciplined to play well in our style of football.

John McVay, our personnel director at that time, John Ralston, Tony Razzano, and, above all, Sam Wyche, liked Joe very much, as did John Brodie, the former 49er quarterback who had recommended him highly to me before the draft.

On our first pick in that draft, we took Owens. James had explosive speed and was a tough, determined competitor who had performed extremely well as a running back at UCLA. I felt he could become a "big play" man at wide receiver. He had been a brilliant kickoff return man in college. I was reasonably sure Montana would be there for our third-round pick and, fortunately, he was. All published draft previews had Joe being selected in the later rounds. We had carefully and discreetly polled each team in the league to appraise their evaluation; none was contemplating even considering him until the sixth or seventh round.

After Joe was drafted, he spent endless hours on the practice field with Sam and me before he reported to our first training camp. Our evaluation had been accurate. He was quick and smooth, and he had a natural athletic rhythm. It remained to be seen whether he could effectively deal with the NFL pass rush.

It was a matter of developing his readiness by using him in situations where he had a good chance to be successful. To an extent, we also limited his plays, coaching him differently than we coached Steve DeBerg, who was the starter for most of Joe's first two seasons with the 49ers.

For instance, if we had plays designed specifically for the team we were playing, Steve would get all the work on them, because he had enough NFL experience to be able to change from week to week. Of course, anything that required moving to the outside, we gave to Joe, because he had the mobility to make those plays work.

In practice, we worked repeatedly on specific plays with Joe. When he was placed in a game, we called only those plays, because he could be confident that he could execute them. He thus began developing the credibility that gained him the unqualified respect of his team-mates.

As he proved in his third year, Joe became an effective performer much more quickly than the other quarterbacks drafted in 1979. We had to remind ourselves that neither DeBerg nor Montana had a complete supporting group with which to work. The other ten men in the offensive unit were in the process of developing just as our quarterbacks were.

When Joe became a starter, it was a shorter game plan at first, and we continued to emphasize plays he could run well. He immediately demonstrated quiet confidence and enthusiasm, and he really thrived on pressure.

By his second season, 1980, I felt that Joe was ready to take control of the team. In fact, he started seven of the last ten games that season. Even so, I thought he could never be the team leader while Steve DeBerg remained on the squad. Steve is a likable person and a tenacious competitor. He has a very strong personality. His charisma attracts people. I knew Joe would have a difficult time overcoming that. It was almost intimidating. At that point, Joe wasn't as outgoing and expressive as he was to become later.

So, we traded DeBerg to Denver for a fourth-round draft choice. We certainly needed the draft pick, but the main reason I traded him was to establish Joe as the uncontested starting quarterback. There were some in the organization who opposed that trade, because they weren't sure Montana would be a topflight NFL starter, but it was a risk we had to take. I was convinced he would not only do well but that he would become one of the best in football.

Once he had control of the team, Montana demonstrated the spontaneity that had been so apparent in his play at Notre Dame, and a resourcefulness that won games for us, particularly in our first Super Bowl year, the 1981 season. At first, some thought he was just lucky. When he threw the winning touchdown pass to Dwight Clark in the 1982 NFC championship game, some of the Cowboys said he'd been trying to throw the ball away. But that was a designed play and Joe knew what he was doing, as he's proved so many times since.

Joe is a coach's ideal quarterback because he will take directions. He will offer his own ideas but won't try to prove he's smarter than the coach or that he has some special gift.

He's been able to avoid becoming self-satisfied and selfish, qualities all too often inherent in stardom. He's always been very coachable and responsive to direction. Even after ten years with the 49ers, when I had a suggestion about improving his play or refining his skills, he would implement it immediately.

Years earlier, when I was with the Cincinnati Bengals, we drafted Greg Cook from the University of Cincinnati in the first round. He was the finest natural talent of any quarterback I have seen. He was a brilliant athlete—big, active, with a quick arm and great delivery—and he had the spontaneity of Joe Montana.

After we drafted him in 1969, he held out and almost signed with the Canadian Football League. I think Paul Brown had underestimated a Canadian team's offer. He was in Canada negotiating and we had to actually coax him back. I believe we gave him a $35,000 bonus, which was a lot of money at the time.

His ability was evident from the start. Cook had a high-strung, sensitive, erratic temperament, but he was a special kind of person with all the attributes you'd want in a quarterback. He had a flamboyant style, much like Joe Namath.

He had a great arm and instincts. As a second-year expansion team, with Cook as our quarterback, we first beat the San Diego Chargers and then decisively defeated the Oakland Raiders, who were then one of the great teams in pro football.

We had a 31–31 tie with the Houston Oilers when a penalty nullified a touchdown that would have won the game, and we defeated the Kansas City Chiefs, who would go on to win the Super Bowl that year. It was amazing, a rookie throwing the football with an expansion team, but he was an incredible performer and a natural leader.

But during that victorious game against Kansas City—and to this day, I feel bad about it—I called a rollout pass requiring our halfback to come across the formation and block outside linebacker Bobby Bell. Bell blitzed off the corner, overwhelming our halfback, Paul Robinson, and threw Cook on his shoulder. It wasn't until after the season that we learned he had torn his rotator cuff.

Cook kept playing. As I recall, our team doctors didn't realize the extent of his injury. He couldn't practice, he couldn't warm up, but with those great instincts, he kept playing, and he was the first rookie in history to lead the National Football League in passing. It was an amazing accomplishment, and it was a privilege to work with him.

He tried to come back over the next two years, after undergoing extensive rotator-cuff surgery, but failed to recover completely. In the meantime, I understand he further injured his shoulder in a pickup basketball game. The Bengals released him, but he tried another comeback in 1975, first with Kansas City and then with San Diego.

By that time, I was with the Chargers. I contacted Greg, he flew out and put on quite a show. He was very impressive in his workout, but he wanted a guaranteed contract, because at the time he had a solid, secure job in his hometown, Cincinnati. Tommy Prothro was impressed and willing to guarantee his contract, but to be honest, I didn't know if Greg would stay with it, so I suggested that we guarantee his contract for the equivalent of half the season.

I regret that now, because if we had met his terms, it would have been a real battle between him and Dan Fouts. As it was, he retired, having played only that one great season, when he led the NFL in passing and led the Bengals to unbelievable victories.

Today, with the great advances in sports medicine, the injury would be properly diagnosed and surgically repaired immediately. But in 1969, the rotator cuff injury wasn't diagnosed until after the season, when dye inserted into the shoulder showed the tear. By then calcium had formed around the scar tissue; ultimately a second operation was necessary.

At that time, doctors split the muscles when they operated on shoulders. Now, they would use arthroscopy and repair the damage very quickly and efficiently. If Greg had had the advantage of current sports medicine, he'd have gone on to a great career.

Those who saw Cook would have to say that, physically, he was the best ever to step on the field. He wasn't just a big Adonis who could throw the ball 100 yards. This was a quick, graceful athlete with a lightning-fast delivery and great instincts.

In contrast to Cook, very few had heard of Kenny Anderson when he was drafted by the Bengals in 1970. He'd played for a tiny school, Augustana College in Moline, Illinois, which competed at the third level of NCAA competition.

He had a good reputation, though his team had never won as many as it had lost. He was big and he had an arm. Pete Brown, Paul's son and our chief scout, saw him and took an interest, and he asked me to look at him. So, on a Saturday before our regular NFL home game I flew up to Chicago, then drove to the college. As I arrived in front of Augustana and parked, I noted it was Homecoming Day. There were about three thousand in the stands, a crowd somewhat smaller than I would see the next day.

As the game got underway, I could spot Kenny easily on the sideline because he was the biggest player. There wasn't another player on the Augustana team who was even close to his size.

Then he was injured, a hip pointer, but he continued to play. Ken was in pain and could hardly move around, yet he stayed in the ball game. This development proved to be one of the most important points of evaluation I was able to make. Yes, Kenny is tough enough and resourceful enough to make the transition from a very limited level of competition to the National Football League. His team lost, but he did throw the ball very well to squatty little receivers, who were really poor targets. No question he had an NFL arm. Paul's son, Mike, then the Bengals' general manager, also saw Ken and he was quite impressed.

I was heavily involved in another typically tough season, but traveled to Illinois to take a second, then a third look. At that point, I felt we had identified a real prospect. Before the draft, and after our season, with snow piled six feet high on the campus, I flew up, then drove to work with him privately. In a poorly lit, dank gym we played catch. I instructed Ken in the three-, five-, and seven-step drops. He picked up everything quickly. He was bright and intense and a powerful, agile athlete.

Though I was excited about him, it was difficult to convince the other Bengal coaches. Augustana's film was taken in the stands and every time anything good would happen, people would stand up in front of the camera. Or, as the game was going well, people would be stamping and pounding on the stands, so the camera would be jumping, and you'd get motion sickness just watching the game. Pete Brown and I gathered the staff, started the film, and sat back to demonstrate Kenny's ability, but one by one, the coaches found reason to leave the room "on business." Soon, Pete and I, joined by Mike, sat there convincing each other.

But Paul Brown gave true autonomy to his coaches during the draft, and he listened to me. It helped, too, that Mike and Pete Brown both wanted Kenny, so we drafted him in the third round. It was felt he was worthy of an earlier pick, but in polling other organizations and checking with various scouts, we found that others rated him in a fifth- or sixth-round category.

Around the league, other teams questioned the choice because they said Anderson couldn't throw long accurately. That had been true in college, but only because his receivers were so limited, he just didn't have any targets. I knew from working him out that he had the arm to throw any kind of pass.

It was clear that Ken was not a sophisticated world traveler. When we signed him to a contract, we celebrated by taking him to La Maisonette, the finest restaurant in Cincinnati. He had obviously never been in a restaurant like that in his life. Of course, I hadn't been there before, either.

We moved him to Cincinnati, and he and I worked day after day on the field, with Sam Wyche and our starting quarterback, Virgil Carter. It was evident that Kenny had the ability to play, but it was questionable whether he could meet the level of competition. He had such a limited background; he'd been a defensive back in high school. But he developed rapidly into a legitimate pro quarterback. Ken really had no bad habits to break. Everything was new. Consequently, his mechanics would be well grounded.

We brought him along much as we later would Montana, giving him part of the game plan and simple things, working on his mechanics by the day, by the week, by the month. We developed them to near-perfection before he ever saw much action, so he came in well prepared. Then, it was a matter of preparing him for the pass rush of teams like the Raiders and Browns. We played him in a controlled manner in his rookie year, emphasizing the short-to-medium–range timed passes.

In his second season, he started. We had a .500 year, but he led the AFC in passing. We began a string of very good years with Kenny, and he led the NFL in passing in his fourth and fifth seasons. His potential was limited originally because our outside receivers didn't possess great downfield speed. But when we drafted Isaac Curtis and traded for Charley Joiner, we had assembled an outstanding group, enabling us to develop an effective deep-passing game.

Kenny's rapid improvement was a credit to the system, and also to the players surrounding him. We had Essex Johnson at halfback, Boobie Clark at fullback, Bob Trumpy at tight end, with Chip Myers and Joiner alternating at one receiver and Curtis at the other. That combination of players was comparable to the 49ers of the late '80s.

Kenny possessed excellent running ability. We designed specialized running plays for him, much as I did later with Montana and Young. As his ballhandling improved, we developed the play-pass techniques that have been stylized since by Montana.

One of the great days of Kenny's early career was against the Steelers, when he completed 20 of 22 for an NFL record, with 16 straight completions. The pass that broke that chain was a "go" pattern down.the field. If we'd been concerned about continuing that streak, I could have called a shorter pattern. The only criterion that matters is winning. On this day we cut up the great Steeler defense and soundly defeated them. Paul Brown was never a man for statistics. That fact was to prove invaluable to me as a head coach in ensuing years. In our final two years together, Ken led the NFL in passing and our offense, along with Dallas, was considered the best in football.

When I became offensive coordinator at San Diego in 1976, Dan Fouts and Jesse Freitas had been sharing the quarterback spot with only average results. It was thought that Dan wasn't a good enough athlete to play quarterback in the NFL, that he was an average thrower and too slow on his feet. We went to work immediately on his mechanics and the very basic fundamentals of NFL-style passing. We spent endless hours on the field for three full months. Like Ken Anderson, Dan was an enthusiastic student of the game.

In training camp, unknown to me, the Chargers traded two second-round picks for Clint Longley. I guess they expected him to be their quarterback of the future. Longley's reputation really rested on one great play, a "Hail Mary" pass on Thanksgiving Day to beat the Washington Redskins in 1974. He had done virtually nothing else in his NFL career, and he was to be with the Chargers only briefly. He basically self-destructed.

Dan, meanwhile, continued to work hard, and it soon paid off. He had a great game against the St. Louis Cardinals, the best of his career to that point, and that game really made him. Don Coryell had come to town with his "Air Coryell" attack; it was a homecoming for Don because he had been so successful at San Diego State before going to the Cardinals. The game matched our newly developing offense against their established wide-open attack. On this occasion we destroyed them, 43–24.

Dan Fouts's career came of age at that point. Dan is an outgoing person, humorous but caustic, and he hadn't been well received by his teammates. The team would lose, and he would be critical and demanding of them, and they would say, in effect, "What have you done for us lately?" At that time, team morale was terrible. The losers' syndrome was well established. But as Dan improved, his leadership qualities took hold and the players began to respond. He was setting a standard for everyone. He was making things happen.

The key was to develop his mechanics and skills to afford him the opportunity to be as efficient as physically possible. Dan is well coordinated, but he doesn't look it. He's tall and at times appears awkward. He can be in sync and under control, but he's the only one who knows it.

He continued to improve all facets of his game. From attempting to function without any timing whatsoever, Dan became a sound, efficient, fully dimensional quarterback. As he began to perform more consistently and effectively, he could take advantage of his great courage and instincts. He couldn't scramble like Anderson, but he could stay in the pocket as well as anybody and could throw the ball with great accuracy with pass rushers and blockers within inches of him. He had a knack for feeling the pass rush and seeing downfield.

Call it an instinct, a second sense, a skill: The ability to peripherally feel the pass rush and see downfield is the very basis of professional quarterbacking. If a quarterback begins looking at pass rushers instead of receivers, he is doomed. The instant his concentration reverts from the receivers to the pass rushers, he becomes a running back.

Dan had real courage. He'd get flattened, but just keep going. And because he couldn't avoid the big hits, he took more punishment than anyone in the league. Dan was to become the greatest deep passer of our time. Later, Ernie Zampese would tutor Dan to a Hall of Fame career.

So often, quarterbacks are judged on their performance with little consideration given to the level of competition or their support system from both players and coaches. That kind of mistaken judgment damaged Steve Young's reputation when he first played professionally, both in the USFL and the NFL.

Young had a great career at Brigham Young University, but at the professional level, his lack of fundamentals betrayed him. He just didn't adjust to the quick, explosive players in the NFL.

The pass rush in college competition often isn't a factor. Steve could take his time and throw off his back foot from anywhere on the field, and if he didn't have a receiver open, he could run, as he possessed superb quickness and speed. But even in the USFL, pass rushers were getting closer to him, so consequently he flushed from the pocket and started scrambling and running before patterns developed downfield.

When he reported to Tampa, the style of football again forced him to run far too often. The patterns simply took too long to develop, and he didn't have alternate receivers. His team was continually behind, so the pass rush was on him every play.

His mobility and quick delivery are very comparable to Joe Montana's. While on a scouting trip, I discreetly found a way to be on the BYU campus when Steve just happened to be working out with members of the football team. I stood behind him and watched him throw just about every type of pass; I could see that he possessed a quick delivery and a fine arm.

We pursued him, but most coaches and general managers of other organizations thought he was too inconsistent to be a starting quarterback, not realizing that with hard work on the mechanics and techniques, you can measurably develop a man's consistency. I envisioned a great one-two punch with Steve occasionally alternating with Joe, thus forcing opponents to account for both a right-handed and a left-handed quarterback.

Our owner, Eddie DeBartolo, became actively involved in the trade negotiations. Tampa management had taken a stubborn stance, so to speed up the process, we decided that Eddie should contact Tampa owner Hugh Culverhouse directly. We immediately had a positive response, and after a series of telephone conversations, the trade was made. Traveling through Florida, Eddie was calling from phone booths to discuss our strategy. He trusted our judgment implicitly, so after we agreed on our next step, he would hang up and call Culverhouse, and we eventually acquired Young for a second- and fourth-round draft choice. Again, our flexibility as an organization made it possible to complete this most important personnel transaction. Egos were not a barrier in doing business.

Apparently, the trade gave Young credibility because immediately after it was made, two clubs who had also been negotiating with Tampa called us and improved their offers substantially. One club now thought he was worth a first- and second-round draft pick, and the other was willing to give up two seconds.

Our approach with Steve was the same as with our other quarterbacks, working with him for endless hours on the fundamentals of the game, and how they applied to the 49er offense. Our concepts were completely new to Steve, who had experienced only the most simplistic offenses. He was enthusiastic and excited about his career being revitalized. By this time, there was a 49er mystique, especially in regard to quarterbacking and pass offense.

He didn't necessarily master our offense the first year, still tending to run more often than he should have. Yet, he made enough transition to play well for us, and his running ability became a major factor. He won a game against Minnesota in 1988 with a great fourth quarter scramble and touchdown run.

There were times when I substituted Steve almost in desperation because we weren't protecting Joe well enough to function effectively; I hoped Steve's running ability could take advantage of a situation. That was tough on Joe, tough on Steve, and tough on me, but it was my obligation as coach to do whatever I could to win.

Each year, Steve has refined his skills. Though he's had limited playing time because he's behind a great quarterback, Montana, he would be a starter for as many as twenty other NFL clubs.

Aside from the quarterbacks I've coached, there are many others I've admired during my NFL career. This is not a complete list, but simply a brief description of some who have impressed me for specific reasons.

I've always had great admiration for Ken Stabler, who was a wonderful clutch performer with instincts. Other than Joe, he was the best come-from-behind quarterback I've ever seen.

Bart Starr and Bob Griese handled their teams beautifully. Jim Plunkett was as tough as they get. Jim Hart was the most underrated quarterback. If I needed a quarterback to throw 50 passes a game, it would be Sonny Jurgensen. I felt that Joe Theismann in his great years was comparable in many ways to Montana.

Roger Staubach was the consummate athlete for his position. Terry Bradshaw had a quick delivery and a super-accurate, deep-throwing arm. He could make spontaneous plays that would break a game wide open. I thought John Brodie was an all-round performer who could adapt to the game situation as well as any I've seen. With a complete team as support, he would have been a champion. Fran Tarkenton was certainly one of the most resourceful quarterbacks. Tarkenton could take full control of the game with his quickness and ability to keep the ball in play and buy time until he could make the right decision.

Len Dawson had superb downfield vision. He could beat you by throwing 10 passes just at the right time. Dan Marino has the quickest delivery in the history of the game.

One of the critical factors for quarterbacks is longevity, the ability to play at a top level for many years, as did Fouts, as did Tarkenton, and certainly as does Montana.

He wasn't able to sustain his greatness, but Joe Namath was the best pure passer I've ever seen. Unfortunately, his bad knees kept him from having as many productive years as he should have, and as years passed he didn't always have the best supporting cast. He had great receivers for a time, but the team couldn't replace them, or other impact players. The organization didn't stay abreast of its quarterback.

When he was in his prime, Namath was one of the most beautiful athletes to watch. He had the quickest feet. He got back from center so smoothly. He always had an excellent throwing position. That was why he was so accurate. He rarely threw off his back foot.

These quarterbacks, and the ones I coached, had unique styles and different levels of athletic ability, but they all played up to their fullest potential. They learned what it took to be successful. They sustained their excitement and enthusiasm for the game over many years, and they learned to thrive in the pocket with all that violence and physical combat exploding around them.

3

The Cutting Edge

Football is continually evolving. Creative innovations are being implemented, but, just as importantly, we continue to find ourselves reaching back into history. For example, take the wraparound draw play, or slow draw as we called it. In this instance, the quarterback drops back to pass beyond the blocking back, then hands off to him. This technique goes back at least thirty-five years, and possibly more.

I've taken a creative approach to the game, willing to develop elements that weren't well established, and to bring back plays from the past. I can't tell you when the wraparound draw was first used, but I remember Pop Ivy utilizing it with the St. Louis Cardinals in the '50s. I later used it myself as a high-school coach but hadn't employed it again until I was with the Bengals.

The first time I demonstrated the play for Paul Brown, along with the quarterback and fullback, he got a real kick out of it. I referred to it as the "slow draw." Woody Hayes was watching practice that day, and he and Brown were impressed. Other staff members thought it was just a gimmick.

We had excellent initial success with it, starting when Boobie Clark broke up the field for 20 yards against Cleveland (see Diagram A, page 269); but, still, no one else picked up on it around the NFL. It was

effective because we used it as a surprise element. The choice of when
to use a play is just as important as its design. We might not use it for
several weeks, but when pass rushers were recklessly coming up the
field, we'd go to our slow draw. Paul Brown thrived on the draw play,
which he had popularized with Marion Motley as early as the late
'40s. At one point, we developed a slow draw, a normal draw, and a
quick draw. All were designed to counteract the pass rush.

Around ten years later with the 49ers, I brought it back, and again,
it was successful because opponents weren't familiar with it. There
were defensive coaches who probably had never seen the play because
they hadn't coached against the Bengals when we revitalized it.

My offense, too, owes much to the past. There are elements, such
as the man-in-motion, that go back to Clark Shaughnessy's years at
Stanford, a half-century ago. The basic ballhandling techniques come
from Davey Nelson's Winged-T at Delaware, as relayed to me through
Rocky Carzo, a fellow assistant when I was at Cal in the early '60s.

The biggest influence on me was the Raider system I learned as an
assistant in 1966—and that system emanated from Sid Gillman, who
probably learned from Shaughnessy and . . . well, you get the picture.

With the Raiders, I learned the Gillman system of football, which
became the foundation of my philosophy of offense. I received help
from the quarterbacks, Cotton Davidson and Tom Flores, and from
John Rauch, who had an excellent football mind. John had learned
the offense through Al Davis, much as my assistant with the 49ers
later did through me. Sid Gillman brought refinement to the game.
Every technique, every skill was isolated. There were no philosophical
barriers to restrict Sid's creativity. The Raiders, under Al Davis, further
developed this system.

It was a fully dimensional approach. For instance, Gillman, with
Joe Madro, his offensive assistant, had developed a system of offensive-
line blocking—which Ollie Spencer used with the Raiders—that
employed virtually every conceivable blocking combination. It took a
year or two longer for Raider linemen to develop within that system,
but when they learned it, they were equipped to handle any situation.

The pass offense included an almost unlimited variety of pass
patterns as well as a system of calling them, and utilized the backs and
tight ends much more extensively than other offenses. A typical NFL
team might have three or four pass patterns for the halfback, but the
Raiders system had as many as twenty. To develop an understanding
of it took time, but once learned, it was invaluable.

When I accepted the offensive backfield position with the Raiders in 1966, I was an assistant at Stanford. Every night after Stanford spring practice, I'd drive to Oakland and spend the evening with John Rauch learning the Raider system. Then I'd return home late at night and be back on the Stanford job by 8 A.M.

When recruiting was over, I was finished at Stanford and joined the Raiders full-time at their spring minicamp in Santa Rosa. They were one of the first teams to utilize minicamps for teaching skills and techniques. We'd work for four to five days at a time. After practices were concluded, coaches worked into the early morning hours day after day, preparing in a much more complete way than other teams of that era. It was intense football, so intense that it was difficult for me to stay with the Raiders because it just consumed every minute of my time over a full twelve-month period. I learned more football in one year with the Raiders than in any ten years I spent elsewhere.

It became almost impossible to maintain a reasonable family life. By that time, I had been in coaching for ten years, and there had been little financial reward or career developments to objectively offset the sacrifices I had made. Possibly there was another vehicle in which to express myself.

I seriously considered a career change. I had applied for business school at Stanford and was waiting for acceptance the next year. In the meantime, I became an instructor at San Jose City College and coached San Jose's Continental League Football team, financed by the Raiders and the 49ers. It was to serve as a developmental squad for both organizations, as was the Continental League for the NFL. We finished with an 8–4 season, but it wasn't long before I realized that I wouldn't be happy unless I returned to coaching at the highest levels.

I had an opportunity to join Paul Brown in 1968 with his new franchise in Cincinnati. It was an honor and a privilege. Paul Brown, while with the Cleveland Browns, implemented a highly organized and structured format that transformed the game into the modern era. His teams were noted for their almost mechanical, error-free precision.

I was originally hired as receivers coach. I had been recommended by Bill Johnson and Tom Bass, who had already joined Brown's staff. By my second year, I was also coaching the quarterbacks. I became responsible for the passing game, and began to integrate many of the innovations that had been so successful with the Raiders.

We drafted Greg Cook and he had a tremendous rookie year. Cook would have made any system look good, but after he was injured in his rookie year, we picked up Virgil Carter, who had been a marginal NFL quarterback. Virgil had played with the Chicago Bears before being released. He was available and we needed a man immediately, so we signed him. We knew he was tough and competitive.

Virgil was a nifty athlete, but he was not considered to have a strong arm. We had to devise a system to fit his abilities. The timing of our passing game now became very important. Virgil would take three steps, throw, five steps, throw—short, quick throws within ten yards of the line of scrimmage. That took advantage of Virgil's instincts and quickness, without forcing stress on his arm to throw passes deep down the field. Or, we would have him sprint out, to take advantage of his mobility, and again throw the ball short.

With Carter at quarterback in 1970, we won our division with a "nickel-and-dime" offense. It was very effective, because we controlled the ball. We spent much practice time on the very specific pass patterns that would be run, throwing 5-to-10-yard passes, utilizing the backs and using the sprint-out patterns that were so popular on the collegiate level at that time.

Our specific objective was to make 25 first downs a game and control the ball with short passing and selective running. We couldn't dominate anyone with the run, so Virgil became our central performer. He finished third in the AFC in passing, and we won our division. Other people in the NFL couldn't believe Virgil could be that effective and that we could win that way.

We were always looking for ways to beat the blitz. I can recall one play we used when we played the Bears, Virgil's homecoming in Chicago. The Bears continually blitzed with everybody coming, including Dick Butkus. They assumed that when facing a total blitz, teams would naturally keep both backs in to protect the passer. They left only one man in the middle for coverage purposes, so we devised a play that put a back in motion, forcing that defender to follow him in pass coverage. We then hit halfback Essex Johnson releasing up the middle. There was nobody there to stop him. That touchdown beat the Bears 13–3 in terrible Chicago weather. I was to experience those conditions again, years later, in another big game.

When we drafted Ken Anderson in '71, we knew Kenny was a much superior passer, but we were also aware that he wouldn't have the necessary skills and expertise to throw the ball effectively downfield against sophisticated NFL defenses. We continued to use our ball-control passing game so he could play effectively as a rookie.

Many coaches didn't understand that style of 5-to-6-yard completions. They continued to play their basic form of defense, which made them vulnerable to our style. We'd have games when we'd accumulate 25, 27, even 30 first downs. Maybe we'd only score 14 or 17 points, but meanwhile, we'd control the ball and keep their offense off the field. It was a case of partially neutralizing an opponent's superiority with a little nickel-and-dime offense.

As we added talent to the team, we broadened our passing game. When Isaac Curtis was drafted, we emphasized passes down the field to take advantage of his great speed. By the time I left the Bengals, we had receivers like Curtis, Bob Trumpy, Charlie Joiner, and Chip Myers, all of whom became Pro Bowl players, so our offense had become much more potent and diversified.

But the basis of our passing game remained the same: timed passes and precise patterns, which we practiced extensively. Each year I was with the Bengals, we isolated the skills that we needed and the timing that was necessary until we were very proficient in all phases of offense. Whether the passes were deep downfield or five-yarders designed to control the ball, it was a system that early on made the most of limited personnel and, when we acquired talented men at the skill positions, made full use of their potential.

Originally, our style of offense was called "nickel-and-dime." Now, it's considered to be in the forefront of offensive football. And it originated from necessity, because we had young quarterbacks with a young expansion team.

The system proved to be extremely successful with quarterbacks at Stanford. Guy Benjamin had been only a part-time starter, but in his senior year, he was the NCAA's leading passer. The following year, Steve Dils also led the NCAA in passing, after having started only one previous game. In each of those years we defeated superior opponents in bowl games. Both LSU and Georgia failed in efforts to stop us.

As the system was refined, we developed distinct methods of dealing with both man-to-man and zone defenses. Against a zone, for example, we would have pass patterns that developed ten yards from the line of scrimmage in front of a defense that had dropped men down the field. Against a man-to-man defense, we would cross receivers close to the line of scrimmage, so defenders could not stay with them through traffic, similar to a screen in basketball.

On every pass pattern, as the receiver releases, he assumes he's playing against man-to-man until he recognizes zone. It's not difficult to spot the difference: If you're running across the field and somebody is chasing you, it's man-to-man. If defenders are dropping back, it's a zone. When the receiver recognizes a zone defense, he has a specific spot that he sprints to and pivots to a stop, between the defenders in their zones. Meanwhile, the quarterback has also read the defense, so he and the receiver are coordinated.

This is the key to the 49er pass offense. That's why you'll see Joe Montana looking and throwing the ball very quickly, seemingly without finding a receiver, knowing he'll be there against a zone.

If you have receivers continuously drilled to run and stop at a specific spot, in conjunction with a quarterback like Montana who instinctively knows when to throw to that spot, the ball can be thrown and caught before defenders react. That's why so many times a 49er receiver appears to be wide open.

Confusion can develop if the quarterback and receiver aren't synchronized as to whether the defense is man-to-man or zone. The quarterback almost always recognizes the defense, because he can see it in front of him, but the receiver might be mistaken. He is running at near-full speed, and must decide instantly. That's why in many NFL games, you'll observe the quarterback throwing to one area when the receiver is moving to another.

You seldom see that with the 49ers. The key is the receiver. He does not look at the quarterback until he's identified the defense, so the quarterback doesn't throw until he knows what the receiver is going to do. That cuts down dramatically on error, but I still see many teams that have not developed this tactic.

To that concept, we added the play pass, which involves faking a running play, hiding the ball, and then throwing downfield. This maneuver is designed to attract defenders, get them out of position, and throw the ball before they can recover. There are two distinctive objectives: (1) to fake the run, fool defensive backs, and throw deep behind them; or (2) to fake the run, draw the linebackers forward, and throw the ball between them. Throughout the years, our quarterbacks have been known for their deceptive ballhandling. Joe Montana is recognized as an absolute artist.

The next development was a back faking a run and then becoming a receiver, which really opened up the passing game. In this instance, linebackers, on finally recognizing a pass, would turn to run to their zones, only to have the ball thrown to the back who had just drawn them in. We utilized Roger Craig and Tom Rathman in this manner very effectively.

Finally, when Jerry Rice joined the 49ers, we were able to take the passing game yet to another level, using plays I'd first developed many years earlier for Isaac Curtis with the Bengals.

With Jerry and John Taylor, who are great athletes, Montana could be confident that they could beat virtually any defender covering them. But somebody else could be assigned to double-team them and disrupt the pass pattern, so we devised plays to eliminate everybody but the man covering Rice. That matchup we'd virtually always win.

For instance, if there was a linebacker who could help in pass coverage, we'd fake a run right at him, to tie him up. Or if a safety was supposed to look for Rice, we'd fake a run—he'd be distracted for a moment and couldn't recover in time.

We could also force miscoverages through varying alignments with our backs and receivers. Defenses have basic rules on coverage. A cornerback is most often assigned to take the receiver closest to the sideline, and a linebacker is assigned a man in the backfield. If we shifted Jerry Rice into the backfield and Roger Craig to the line, the cornerback could be forced to cover Craig, leaving the unfortunate linebacker to cover Rice. The linebacker would be completely mismatched. If the linebacker and cornerback shifted coverage, we could run at the cornerback, forcing him to play against big blockers from an unfamiliar position. Or, we could employ Craig on pass patterns from the wide receiver position against the linebacker forced into a disadvantageous coverage. As we began to employ these devices, opponents resorted to a pure zone defense. This was made to order for our timed, precise, short passing game.

The next factor in an effective offense is the quarterback knowing when—and when not—to throw a pass, to reduce the number of forced passes resulting in interceptions. Whether it was Guy Benjamin or Steve Dils at Stanford, Gary Huff, Matt Cavanaugh, or Jeff Kemp with the 49ers, we drilled them continually on going to their alternate receivers. One drill proved extremely valuable: The quarterback would be told to go to his third receiver, but not until he'd gone through the mechanics of looking for his first and second. That gets the quarter-back in the habit of spontaneously going to an alternate target.

Inexperienced quarterbacks tend to look too early for their alternate receivers without waiting for patterns to develop downfield. That is the natural reaction of a man who's not totally familiar with the system. Early on, for instance, Montana would often throw short, underneath passes when he conceivably could have gone downfield. It was just a matter of time before Joe mastered the system and acquired the patience to allow things to develop downfield before going to an alternate receiver. Now he's the master of finding alternate people.

So much of our practice was situational. This goes back to my coach at San Jose State, Bob Bronzan. He organized every practice almost to the play. When I became a head coach, I isolated every different situation that might occur in a game.

We might have, for instance, six short-yardage plays in a game, eight plays where we'd be backed up against our end zone, six plays with third down and twenty yards to go. In training camp, we'd regularly practice all these contingencies. Over a period of years, we became very proficient at dealing with each particular situation.

To repeat, it is important to remember that so much can be learned from the past.

When I was at Stanford, I searched for and finally found, in a warehouse, film of Clark Shaughnessy's 1940 Rose Bowl team. Watch-ing that reinforced my feeling about the use of the man-in-motion. Shaughnessy was using plays and formations very similar to those we were running at Stanford nearly forty years later.

The man-in-motion can be used to force the defense to change its pass coverage and run support. As an example, in a game against Houston when I was at Cincinnati, we began to use our flanker in motion with two tight ends, the simplest of tactics. When our flanker crossed the formation, Houston failed to adjust by bringing up a man to stop the sweep. So, when we put the flanker in motion, we'd run the sweep to the side where the flanker had gone, because he gave us an extra blocker.

Other teams would adjust by sliding their strong safety back, and their weak safety would come up when you put your man in motion. Usually, the weak safety is the faster of the two. So, each week we'd identify and analyze the strong safety. If the strong safety lacked speed we'd employ a flanker in motion, forcing the strong safety into the middle and the weak safety up to stop the sweep as the flanker moved to his side of the formation. Then we would send Isaac Curtis down the middle, because the strong safety wouldn't be able to stay with him.

We also used motion to force the defense to react and leave a particular area of the field open or vulnerable. When we put a back in motion, often it was to see if the weak safety would come out of the secondary to cover him. A typical play would be the fullback going in motion and the weak safety coming over to cover him, which left the middle wide open for a post pattern by a wide receiver.

That also indicated the defense was blitzing, because the safety had to come up to cover. If the safety stayed back, we knew the blitz was unlikely.

Utilizing the man-in-motion can be extremely valuable to the quarterback in identifying the form of pass coverage to expect. If a back goes in motion and linebackers begin to loosen, the quarterback can expect a zone. If a linebacker immediately moves with the back in motion, the quarterback can see man-to-man coverage.

We also used motion to flood a zone defense with additional receivers. Generally, when the linebackers drop back to cover a pass, they are drilled to defend against a traditional formation with a split end on one side of the field and a flanker on the other. If you put a man in motion, there's another potential receiver in that area, so we could stretch the zone wide open, outnumbering the defenders. Either the defense would overadjust, so you could hit a hooking receiver, or they wouldn't cover the man in motion, so you could throw to him.

We used the tight end in motion first by mistake. Cincinnati was playing the Raiders in Oakland. In the third quarter, Bob Trumpy lined up on the wrong side by mistake. He had to shift over quickly to the other side, and all hell broke loose. At that time, the Raiders had very specialized people. They had a weak-side linebacker, they had a strong-side linebacker, they had a defensive end who only played on the tight-end side, and they would shift their two inside linebackers. So, when Bob shifted, they all ran into each other in the middle of the field, trying to adjust.

Upon returning home and studying the films, Bill Johnson said, "What would happen if we purposely did that?" We looked at each other and doubled over laughing. At that moment, the "tight end in motion" was created. Initially it caused all sorts of havoc. But when he came to the line of scrimmage on the other side, he had to be stationary for a second before the ball could be snapped. Soon, some teams adjusted their defense as we shifted. The next thing we did was to put the flanker up on the line and the tight end off the line. We then put the tight end in motion, so he wouldn't have to stop and set himself.

That created all kinds of problems for defenses. First, we could force a major adjustment if teams were playing weak-side and strong-side linebackers. (The strong side is considered where the tight end locates himself to add a blocker for running plays.) If a weak-side linebacker was fast but had trouble handling a big, blocking tight end, we could force him to defend on the strong side any time we wanted, simply by moving the tight end to his side.

Also, the tight end in motion might be split out five yards and be moving to the outside when the ball was snapped, so he could become a more dangerous receiver and a different type of blocker.

By the time I got to the 49ers, I was using several combinations of a back in motion, the tight end in motion, the flanker in motion. We were able to keep defenses off balance, so with receivers like Mike Schumann and Freddie Solomon, Steve DeBerg set NFL records for passes attempted and completed.

Our style of play was often characterized as "finesse" football—intended by many as a put-down. The point was that we weren't really a tough, physical team.

Well, if you consider finesse to be skill and technique, yes, there was a lot of skill and technique in everything we did. There was much more attention to detail. If that's finesse, so be it.

Combining creative tactics and strategy with skill and technique has been a very successful formula for the 49ers. We were willing to complete a 5-yard pass instead of running for 3 yards. There's a remarkable difference between the more skilled "technique" approach and the simplistic style of football, where a coach might criticize players for not performing instead of concluding the fault lies with a limited style of play.

Finesse can bring success with less than great players. With tactics, skill, and techniques, we found a way to win, as in 1981, with a few outstanding individuals surrounded by less gifted players. As the talent improved, the techniques continued to develop and we became among the very best. So, ultimately, we combined our finesse with power and strength to become the team of the '80s.

You can call it finesse when John Ayers drops out of the line to block Lawrence Taylor and rides him out of the play time after time, but you can also call it great technique. It's finesse when Dwight Clark catches the ball time after time in a 5-yard area and knows where to run so he can get 8 or 10 yards, but it also took toughness because Dwight was punished by hard tackles.

The essence of our defensive philosophy has always been the proper use and application of personnel. For instance, we used Fred Dean, Jack Reynolds, Milt McColl, and Ron Ferrari in specific tactical situations. We didn't have dominating defensive players during those early years, but we had top-notch individuals, and we created ways of taking advantage of their specific talents. We didn't have a Howie Long, who played outstanding football on every defensive down, but we had players like Dean who could be devastating if used properly.

We also developed a team-wide mentality that emphasized moving more quickly than our opponents, whether it was the first step a center would take in blocking a nose guard or a receiver exploding off the line and getting an advantage on the defensive back. That quickness became the 49er trademark.

We continually talked about "beating the opposition to the punch." I used the parallel of the champion boxer who's beating the challenger to the punch by a split-second in the early rounds. Though the bout appears to be very close, the challenger is taking more punishment, and the bout is eventually stopped.

Throughout the game, our players would be saying, "Beat 'em to the punch, beat 'em to the punch." The results would begin to demonstrate themselves in the third quarter. We might even be behind early in the game, but our intensity and explosiveness would gradually wear down our opponents and bring them down late in the game. That's the boxing parallel.

That was clearly demonstrated against the Dallas Cowboys, the leading NFC franchise in the '70s. The Cowboys were a physically dominating team, with great defensive linemen and linebackers, but they weren't especially quick. When we coaches remarked to the team before a game against Dallas, we emphasized that our quickness should be the difference. Playing with quickness and explosiveness, we defeated the Cowboys all five times we played them after 1980. We simply "beat them to the punch."

We told players to strike their opponents just before they were prepared to absorb the blow. We would say, "Get there an inch before he does." As a guard fired out to block Jack Reynolds, Jack would attack him just as he was about to initiate his block. Or Russ Francis at tight end would strike the linebacker across the line of scrimmage a split-second before the opponent was ready.

Defensively, we had smaller teams than most; consequently we depended heavily on our quickness and explosiveness, shattering the blocker before he could get his job done. And even though we were relatively small, we were physical. We stressed that tacklers should put their bodies across the front of the ballcarrier, so he couldn't make an extra yard. That style was best typified by Ronnie Lott, Carlton Williamson, and Riki Ellison.

Everything in practice emphasized quickness, explosiveness, and movement, whether it was hitting the sled, or a lineman working on pulling, or a defensive back working on his backpedaling. Then, we talked about quickly recovering, if a player found himself going in the wrong direction, or out of position.

As one example, we emphasized that linebackers be decisive and explode into the hole. Well, if you move that quickly, there will be times when you miscalculate and find yourself out of position. So, we dealt with that by working on recovering just as quickly to get back into position. "Commit yourself, explode, recover if you're wrong."

Another key to our offensive system was our blocking style. Historically, pro players have tended to play the game standing up. So much of the game is protecting the passer, and they have gotten so massive that football today is played high off the ground, at chest level. Our approach was to take people low, to cut their legs out from under them and put them on the ground. That often provoked our opponent. Opposing coaches objected to this technique and defensive linemen often became enraged at our blockers. We utilized the reverse shoulder block originally developed and commonly used in the 1930s. Instead of driving the opponent off the line of scrimmage, the blocker drives his head for the far leg and hooks his opposite leg behind his opponent's leg. The defender is now tied up, unable to extract himself. Our opponents had a difficult time with it because they were unfamiliar with blockers who hooked with their legs. Bobb McKittrick, our offensive line coach, did a masterful job of teaching this technique. It has antagonized everyone but has been a major contributor to our success.

Strategically, we emphasized field position but in a new way. The traditional idea of field position is defensive; it is thought of almost as a war of attrition. We thought of it in offensive terms, because if we got the ball near midfield, we could open up our offense and strike quickly for a touchdown.

Our approach often ran counter to conventional wisdom. For instance, if a team has third-and-twenty, a television analyst will say, "They have to use a pass play that can get twenty-one yards." Some teams in that situation will try to pass for the first down, but it usually fails.

Our argument was that the chance of a completion drops dramatically over 12 yards. So, we would throw a 10-yard pass. Our formula was that we should get at least half our passing yardage from the run *after* the catch, so we might yet get the 20 yards we needed for the first down. But even if our receiver was tackled immediately, we had at least gained 10 yards of field position.

Our second Super Bowl, against Miami, demonstrated the importance of field position. We continually backed the Dolphins up against their goal line, and when their great punter, Reggie Roby, did not deliver, we got the ball at midfield three straight times and subsequently scored, gaining a 28–16 halftime advantage, and going on to dominate, 38–16.

I had predicated offense on controlling the ball through an opportunistic running game and timed, high percentage short passing. As this was established and the opponents geared themselves to stop it, we would have opportunities for the "big strike" downfield.

Nickel-and-dime offense? It works.

4

Disappointment in Cincinnati

Being an assistant coach, even one who has as much responsibility as I had with the Bengals, is quite different from being a head coach. Some assistants become accustomed to that role and thrive on it for an entire career. But I had the overriding ambition to become a head coach and was determined to reach that goal. On reflection, I was too anxious and it actually damaged my opportunities as years passed.

When John Rauch left the Raiders to go to Buffalo after the 1968 season, I impetuously called Al Davis and told him I was interested in the head coaching job. Al wasn't going to hire me. He was respectful, but he believed in promoting from within and even chided me a little for having left the Raiders after only one year. He then hired John Madden, and I remained in Cincinnati.

When I was with the Bengals, there were some frustrating years. I learned a tremendous amount from Paul Brown, at that time one of the most commanding persons in the NFL, and I gained a lot of confidence directing the pass offense and calling plays from the press box. But when I needed assistance in inquiring about head coaching opportunities, it wasn't forthcoming. Paul Brown was interested only in the development of the Cincinnati Bengals, not in the careers of his coaches. He felt that team harmony and productivity were more important than personal ambitions. The feeling of family was everything to Paul. If you were important to the Cincinnati Bengals, he wanted you to remain in the organization.

After about four years, I became confident I could be a successful head coach in the NFL, assuming there was a capable person in the administrative position. At that time, there weren't many who were doing both; typically there was a coach and a general manager.

I certainly had major responsibilities with the Bengals, which ultimately helped me develop an offensive system and related coaching techniques. Bill Johnson handled the running game, while I ran the passing game and called plays from the press box. As time passed, I began to assert myself more and more with the system of football we played, to the point where I became extremely involved in the orchestration of the game.

In 1971, Paul game me a $6,500 raise, monumental in those days, to equate me with Bill Johnson as the highest-paid men on his staff. This upped my salary to $26,500. I thanked him for the raise and he said, "You know what I had in mind." I appreciated that remark because I thought he was referring to me as his successor. I heard later that Paul had made a similar remark to Bill Johnson when he was hired.

Paul Brown did an outstanding job of directing the organization and putting it on the map. But as time went on, my presence asserted itself more and more. Meanwhile, Paul remained loyal to Johnson, who had been a player, then a coach in the league for many years. Bill was a tie to the old NFL.

As years passed, our offense won more and more notoriety, and it proved a distraction to Paul. I was very ambitious and overtly interested in becoming a head coach, but when I'd inquire Paul would say, "I haven't got any calls on you."

There were a couple of other occasions when Paul distinctly intimated to me that I'd be his replacement, which was probably in appreciation for the job I was doing. But he was also making the same kinds of remarks to Bill Johnson.

I sensed a problem in 1975. We had an excellent year, winning our division before losing to the Raiders in the playoff game I described earlier. I was now being directly credited for the offense by the media, and a subtle difference crept into the way Paul treated me.

A lot of people thought Paul was extending his coaching career longer than he should. He was almost seventy, and he'd be standing out on the practice field in the bitter cold. He was a very strong and determined man who wouldn't compromise on anything. Near the end of the season, he became quite mysterious. There were hints that he'd be retiring, but he said nothing publicly during the season.

The day after returning home from our last game—that frustrating loss to the Raiders—I received a call from Dick Forbes, a close friend of Paul and the area's most prominent sportswriter, who told me that Bill Johnson was going to be named the Bengals' head coach. The announcement was due the next day. Paul was out of town and out of reach, as was Bill Johnson. Paul's sons, Mike and Pete Brown, were scouting at the Senior Bowl.

Dick wanted my reaction. That was the first I had heard of it, so you can imagine how crushing the news was. Paul had said nothing to me, or to any of the other staff. Paul was out of touch, purposely, and he had Bill out of touch, purposely. He had put out a press release and wanted people to digest the news, and then he'd return to Cincinnati in a few days. Meanwhile, I was inundated by calls from the media because I was the only person available to speak for the Bengals.

Though I was devastated, I wasn't going to show it. My response was, "Bill is a fine coach," which was true, "and he's a good friend and I'm sure he'll do an outstanding job." Then, here came a TV truck up my driveway. I told the TV interviewer what I'd told Dick Forbes, that it was an excellent move by Paul Brown and that the organization wouldn't skip a beat.

It was bizarre. I was the one most damaged by Paul's decision, but I was also, for about a forty-eight-hour period, the only one available to speak for the Bengals. I couldn't refuse interviews, nor could I speak frankly about my disappointment, because I certainly didn't want to burden Bill Johnson, who had been a friend for many years.

So, I was on TV, I was there with the writers, and I think I handled it well. But as soon as I heard about it, I told my wife, Geri, "We've got to get out of here. We're going to have to leave." We had grown to love Cincinnati. It would be difficult but it had to be done.

Meanwhile, the Seattle Seahawks and the New York Jets were

looking for head coaches, and I was one of three top candidates. But both teams seemed to lose interest in me.

I was really excited about the Jets job because I wanted to coach Joe Namath. He was right at the end of his career, and I thought to have Namath directing my offense would be terrific. Some people thought I was the logical choice, but Lou Holtz was hired. Then, Jack Patera was named as coach of the expansion Seattle team.

In both cases, I learned, Paul Brown did not extend himself for me.

George Dickson of Tommy Prothro's staff at San Diego told me offensive coordinator John David Crow was leaving the Chargers and asked if I'd be interested. Well, I certainly was, and I talked to Tommy at the Senior Bowl. Meanwhile, I read in the paper that Paul had made me offensive coordinator. He had never talked to me about it, but his thinking was that you couldn't leave unless you were promoted in your new job, so by making me offensive coordinator, I would have to remain.

Paul got word that I'd talked to Prothro, so when I got back from the Senior Bowl, I had a meeting with Paul, Bill Johnson, and Mike Brown, and he told me I couldn't leave. I said, "Paul, my contract is up next Monday." He told me he would give me a substantial raise but that I was obligated to stay with the Bengals.

At that point, I broke down. They completely misunderstood me. They thought I was crushed because I'd been passed over for the head coaching job, but in fact, I was distraught because I knew I would be leaving, not because I was bitter. I'd been there eight years, Geri and I had made a lot of friends, and I'd be leaving Paul, for whom I had a lot of admiration, Mike, and Bill, a longtime friend, and Jack Donaldson, the Bengals' offensive backfield coach.

So Paul responded, "I want you to understand that you're going to remain here. San Diego has tampered by talking to you." I said, "No, I'm leaving and I'm going to explore all my options."

Paul felt sure I was going out to San Diego. When I arrived there to discuss the job, Tommy Prothro told me Brown had called concerning me. His remarks were not complimentary. Both Tommy and Gene Klein, the Chargers owner, understood the situation and were sympathetic to me.

I believe Paul wanted to have Bill Johnson on the field, where he'd been for many years, and me in the press box to retain the same system of playcalling. That formula would work out fine for Bill, an excellent coach who was to win ten games his first season, but Paul didn't take into account how I would feel about my future in football. Later, during a conversation with Al Davis, Al said, "You know, you're getting only cool recommendations out of Cincinnati. That may be the reason you're not getting those other jobs."

Paul felt I had been disloyal to him because I had talked to Tommy Prothro; it was unfortunate that he would draw that conclusion and not have any compassion for me and my circumstances.

It was difficult for us to leave because we had good friends in Cincinnati and our sons were doing very well in school there, but I knew that I could no longer feel as close to the Bengals. I felt I had become a good friend of Paul Brown, but after a legendary career in football, he must have been struggling emotionally with the thought of retirement. I can certainly understand that now, having gone through it myself. Naturally, his retirement took precedence over the way he named a new coach or how he handled those around him.

Tommy Prothro is a true gentleman. After I'd been with the Chargers a couple of weeks, he told me that San Jose State, my old school, had inquired about me as a head coach. He said, "Bill, I really don't recommend that," and I agreed. But when Stanford called after the year was over, he told me, "Bill, being a head coach in the Pac-Ten is a major position, and Stanford in particular. You know it will hurt me to lose you here, but I have to say that I told them you're the best coach they could possibly have and one of the two best coaches I've ever been associated with." Tommy was not only a great football man but his personal ethics and principles set a standard for me in future years.

At that point, I needed a shot in the arm, and I really appreciated it. My leaving definitely put his job in jeopardy, but he had demonstrated a fraternal feeling that I still remember with gratitude.

I had been frustrated seeing the pro jobs go by and thinking that I never had a chance, and it's difficult for a pro coach to get a college job because coaches are hired before the NFL season ends. So, it was really a gracious gesture for Tommy to allow me to interview while our season was in progress.

Stanford was the opportunity of a lifetime and it more than compensated for the Cincinnati disappointment. My original goal when I entered coaching was to become a head coach at a major university. In one quick stroke, I had achieved my highest expectation. Stanford's interest in me had developed through contacts that originated during my three years as an assistant there in the mid-'60s. It was a most positive and reassuring feeling to have someone seeking me out as a head coach. Athletic director Joe Reutz and alumnus Frank Lodato were instrumental in my being selected.

I had only been at Stanford about four weeks when I received a phone call from Al Davis. Al secretly had been asked to be the intermediary between Joe Thomas and me, to see whether I would be interested in being the 49ers coach. I told him I wouldn't even consider it, because I had just come to Stanford and I was very excited about the opportunity. Al understood completely.

The next contact of this type came after my first year at Stanford. Jim Finks of the Chicago Bears called, the St. Louis Cardinals called, there were other teams that had an interest. Most importantly, the Los Angeles Rams, through Don Klosterman, who had been a good friend for many years, told me they'd be very interested in my joining them if Chuck Knox left.

The Rams were going through a typical owner-coach upheaval. Knox had a very good win-loss record, but he hadn't been able to get his team to the Super Bowl, so Carroll Rosenbloom was considering replacing him out of frustration. I thought Chuck was one of the best coaches in football, but he was being undermined by the Rosenbloom family. Klosterman had dinner with Geri and me, during which he asked if I'd be interested. I said I would be only if the decision had already been made to replace Chuck.

I met with Rosenbloom in Malibu, and then the story that I was negotiating to coach the Rams was leaked to the newspapers. Meanwhile, at Stanford, I'd been given a one-year extension on my contract and a raise. I told Don I could go only a short period of time like this. There were headlines in the *Los Angeles Times* and *San Francisco Chronicle*, so I set a deadline; I would tell Stanford in five days whether I'd be leaving or staying. When the five days were up, I told Stanford I was staying. I never felt completely comfortable with the Rams because if Chuck Knox, among the best in the business, was going to be replaced, where would I be in a few years?

During this process, a campaign was started to hire George Allen. Stories were planted in the media, among them that I'd replace Rams quarterback Pat Haden with Guy Benjamin, who had been my quarterback at Stanford. I had an excellent relationship with Pat, and I called him to assure him that I had no such plans. But these rumors were meant to discredit me; one of the most prominent L.A. writers was really a George Allen advocate.

This development reminded me of how volatile the world of professional football can be. In contrast, life at Stanford in Palo Alto was serene, even with the pressures of recruiting.

Then, the Chicago Bears came into the picture. While recruiting, I stopped in Chicago and met privately with Jim Finks, one of the most respected men in the National Football League. I told him that I just couldn't tamper with my situation at Stanford. Though flattered by his interest, I would have been completely satisfied and felt very fortunate to remain at Stanford for the rest of my coaching career. As I look back, my two years at Stanford may have been the happiest and most rewarding of my career, because of the academic environment, the sense of participating in the educational process. Affording an opportunity for a young man to succeed not only in the classroom but also on the athletic field offers great satisfaction for the coach. In addition, living on campus proved to be a very rich and rewarding experience for Geri and the children.

As I approached the end of my second season at Stanford, the 49ers were in turmoil. They'd had 5–9 and 2–14 seasons and had gone through three coaches. Owner Ed DeBartolo, Jr., had lost patience with general manager Joe Thomas, and through Ron Barr, our Stanford play-by-play announcer, he contacted me to say he wanted to talk. And Eddie was now being publicly ridiculed. The entire San Francisco community had come down on the 49ers. They had traded or released all of their standout players of the seventies, had acquired a frightful public image that portrayed Thomas as a hatchet man, tearing apart their beloved team. Every vestige of 49er history had been destroyed or removed from their Redwood City offices. Even old film clips were discarded. It would be a new era with Joe Thomas; the 49ers would be born in his image. Above and beyond this, they were losing.

I discreetly met with Eddie and Carmen Policy, DeBartolo's attorney, in a San Francisco hotel to discuss the 49er situation. I told them I just couldn't work with Joe Thomas; my friend, Monte Clark, had resigned as 49er coach because of Thomas, and that was enough for me. An informal offer was made and I tentatively agreed, but Stanford still had to play Georgia in the Bluebonnet Bowl. Our agreement wasn't binding, and I would not sign a formal agreement until a couple of days after that game.

Meanwhile, Ed had a New Year's party in Youngstown as the Bluebonnet Bowl was being played. He told people I was going to be his new coach, so they started the party by watching the game. He envisioned it as a celebration, a sign that the 49ers would go in an exciting new direction with a new coach. But it was anything but a celebration. We were destroyed in the first half, getting knocked all over the field, and were behind, 16–0, at halftime.

Ed's friends gave us up for dead, so the party began to drift upstairs. One person briefly stayed behind to watch the game. He soon went upstairs to report that now we were behind in the third quarter 22–0. Needless to say, that put a real damper on Ed's party. His friends teased him, and I'm sure Eddie wondered at that moment why he ever took over such a frustrating, impossible franchise.

Meanwhile, I had my head up, but just barely. I remember reflecting on the sidelines, "What can DeBartolo be thinking now?" I was wondering if we'd even score one touchdown. We were supposed to have this high-powered, NFL-type offense, and we couldn't do anything.

The Georgia players began making effeminate gestures at us from the sideline, taunting as the score increased. They had proven that "students" from Stanford couldn't match up against a real football team.

But Georgia made the mistake of staying with a heavy blitzing defense, and of not accounting for adjustments in our offense. We had been throwing deep "out" patterns, which Steve Dils was missing, partly because we had trouble pass protecting. To give Steve a better chance, we changed our emphasis and threw quickly to "hot" receivers, like Darrin Nelson coming out of the backfield, and we just took Georgia apart. Gordy Ceresino, our middle linebacker, made two big hits behind the line of scrimmage, causing fumbles, and we scored right away each time. We won, 25–22, and, in fact, we could have scored again. We had the ball and were driving at the end of the game.

So, when I got back, it was almost to a hero's welcome because of the way we won. I got a call from Ed, who said he was firing Joe Thomas, and we quickly worked out the details of my contract. I went right to work, at $160,000 compared to $48,000 at Stanford. Had it not been the 49ers, my choice would have been to remain at Stanford.

Eddie was to become the best owner in the NFL. As time passed, we grew into our roles together; there is no question that we had the best relationship between owner and coach throughout the 1980s. Our chemistry sustained us through the most difficult situations.

It was agreed that if I was going to be the coach, I would be in charge of all football operations. At that time, the 49er reputation was not good. I thought it would be impossible to win unless the organization was completely restructured. It took some courage for Eddie to give me that responsibility.

Asking for that role was a major decision because I'd just been an NFL assistant and then a college head coach for two years. It was a real challenge, but my eight years with Paul Brown had enabled me to observe a genius at work, and they also convinced me that I should have control of personnel.

It still wasn't as much of an adjustment as when I became head coach at Stanford. After dealing with a limited group of players for years, I had, in a matter of fifteen minutes, the awesome responsibility of an entire football program. I was fortunate to have a good man like Joe Ruetz as athletic director; he gave me a lot of autonomy.

That experience of recruiting, of directing the Stanford program—all the things that go into being a college head coach—was important to me when I took the 49ers job. I had been in the trenches just long enough to give me confidence and minimize my natural anxiety.

I had gone from working with the Chargers directly into recruiting for Stanford. Sitting in a high-school gym in Tucson, Arizona, with students dribbling popcorn down the back of my shirt, I often wondered, "What am I doing here?"

With the 49ers, I had a little more time because we didn't have anything on the immediate horizon except the draft. But before draft day, we did need to hire a management team.

I visited first with George Young, then the personnel man for the Miami Dolphins. I offered him $50,000, slightly more than he was making with the Dolphins, but George lost interest very quickly. As it turned out, his was a smart decision, because a year later, he went to the New York Giants as general manager, that organization's chief executive officer. I talked to Dick Mansberger of Seattle, at that time regarded as one of the top personnel men in the NFL. But after a meeting, he said it just didn't sound right to him. I talked to Ernie

Accorsi, who was at Baltimore. He was knowledgeable and bright, but he wanted to have more authority.

It soon became obvious that most people were reluctant to align themselves with the 49ers. Things had gotten so woeful in San Francisco, organizationally as well as on the field, that good people just didn't want to take on such an overwhelming task.

I remember having breakfast with Eddie and Carmen, and remarking that the kind of guy we were looking for might not be out there, so Eddie said, "Why don't you be the general manager?" Initially I was unsure; "Me a general manager like Jim Finks or Tex Schramm?" But then it began to make sense. At that point, it had to be me. I would have to find top talent to fill specific roles, while retaining the ultimate responsibility and authority.

I'd be making the draft and trade decisions, but we still needed somebody who could manage the front office—somebody I respected and trusted. John Ralston, who had hired me as an assistant when he was head coach at Stanford, called me. John was then offensive coordinator for Dick Vermeil in Philadelphia. We discussed what his role would be and he enthusiastically agreed to join us.

I methodically set about putting together an organization by using all the contacts I'd made in coaching. I was fortunate to have Norb Hecker join me from Stanford as my administrative assistant and defensive backfield coach; Norb had coached for Vince Lombardi in the Packers' glory years and later had been head coach of the Alanta Falcons. I was also pleased to have Denny Green, who had been with me at Stanford, as my special teams coach. Since both Norb and Denny were already in the area, they could start work immediately. I had full confidence in their ability to represent me in the early stages.

But there were some immediate confrontations. The head of scouting, Howard White, wanted to be GM. I hadn't interviewed him because he hadn't been recommended by Monte Clark or Eddie. White came in and told me he was resigning immediately and that all the scouts were resigning. The scouts were in town as part of their yearly predraft meeting.

If the scouts have resigned, I said, so be it. John Ralston called and told them we accepted their resignation.

Subsequently, a group of shaken scouts came over to the 49ers facility and emphatically assured me that White didn't represent them. They knew nothing about it, they wanted to stay, and they were glad he was leaving. That meeting allowed me to keep, among others, Neil Schmidt, who turned out to be one of the NFL's best scouts and has continued to be a vital factor in our draft. Ernie Plank was another who has remained with us all these years.

I'd known John McVay since he was coaching at Dayton and I was with the Bengals, and I'd later lectured his New York Giants staff on offensive football. John had resigned as Giants coach, so I quickly contacted him, and he agreed to become our director of player personnel.

Former coach Monte Clark reminded me as often as he could, and in as many ways as he could, that some employees weren't up to standard, and I quickly learned what he meant.

The 49ers business manager, assigned from Youngstown, was reporting directly to people at DeBartolo corporate headquarters. His reports often were distorted out of proportion, so Eddie was being misled and really didn't have a true picture. He was a disruptive element because, initially, I assumed his policies were directed from the corporate headquarters. Instead, they were being initiated by him.

When I hired Sam Wyche as my quarterback coach, I told Sam to rent a car for househunting and transportation to and from his motel. This business manager immediately called Eddie DeBartolo and told him that $120 had already been wasted toward this rental, and he thought Eddie should know that. Eddie flew out to find out what the hell was going on with his new coach. Later that week, at the Eclipse thoroughbred racing dinner in San Francisco, Eddie, Ed Sr., and I discussed the situation. Soon thereafter, we were assigned Keith Simon as business manager. Keith worked out extremely well. Everything was direct, businesslike, and with excellent communication between Youngstown and San Francisco. He was and continues to be both sound and creative in financial dealings, especially valuable player contract negotiations.

Before this, my authority hadn't been totally spelled out to everybody, so I'd been walking on egg shells. What Eddie did was impress on me and everybody else that he would give me real autonomy in directing his organization.

I needed that authority, because I had to try to put together a respectable team from the ruins. Because of my experience instituting an effective offense at Cincinnati, San Diego, and Stanford, I felt we could win six games the first year.

I'd soon learn how wrong I was.

5

Planning the Season

Before my first 49er training camp, I went with my family to Lake Tahoe for a brief vacation, but I hardly left the condo. In a seven-day period, I set up the schedule and planned the agenda for the entire camp, accounting for every hour of every day. When I returned, I laid that out for the entire staff. They were surprised because they'd never seen anything like that. I owe the utilization of a meticulous, thorough, long-range plan to Bob Bronzan, my former coach at San Jose State. He had adopted that approach from coaching associates Frank Leahy and Bud Wilkinson.

Each year after that, I met with my assistants and revised and refined that schedule, to fit the needs of our team.

Our first step in developing a plan for the upcoming year would be to hold a series of meetings with our coaching staff, collectively and individually, to discuss the four basic categories of team development: (1) the teaching of individual fundamentals and skills; (2) choreographing the action of groups, such as defensive backs or offensive linemen; (3) the development of team execution, such as the offensive unit; and (4) the implementation of situational football, as related to specific game circumstances.

I would request each coach to isolate those fundamentals and skills for his position and prioritize them, and then explain and justify the drills required to develop them. I determined that each drill must have a direct relationship to a specific action the player would experience in a game. A defined amount of time would be allocated for this category. The coach would then determine the amount of time necessary for each particular drill. Bobb McKittrick, our offensive-line coach, eventually isolated up to thirty skills he felt were necessary.

That time then would be allocated over the four-week training-camp period. As just one example, defensive backfield coach Ray Rhodes would know exactly how much time he would have in practice for tackling drills, or for teaching individual coverage techniques, and which days it would be scheduled.

Football requires coordinated movement between groups of players. As examples, the offensive guard and tackle often work in combination, as do linebackers and defensive linemen. Consequently, drills are established in which these groups work together. This is the toughest category to plan and then implement in practice. It takes continual monitoring to minimize any wasted effort and duplication. Endless hours are spent in tedious preparation for this segment of our training-camp schedule. Specific blocks of time are set aside and scheduled on a daily or weekly basis.

If there's an enjoyable part of practice, it is bringing players together and working in units, offensive or defensive. This is the basis of the game and the basic reason players participate. This category, too, must be specifically planned. Coaches can get lost in this phase of practice and waste time in unproductive routine.

Each day, a specific number of team plays were scheduled. They would be preplanned so we wouldn't waste time. Certain categories of plays were emphasized in each session. For example, if our offense was stressing the outside running game, twenty of the thirty-five plays might be sweeps, and we might also call five play passes, five traps, and five deep downfield passes. We monitored our practices throughout the training-camp period to make certain every segment of the offense got the necessary attention.

Every logical situation that might occur in a game was isolated, and strategy and tactics were accordingly devised. These situations were given practice priorities with a specified number of minutes.

We practiced specific plays against the defense we expected to see in a game, simulating a game situation by using the clock and officials.

We would practice such things as our "goal-line offense," which normally comes into effect at the four-yard line; our short-yardage offense, which would be used when we had third down and less than two; our two-minute offense; and even plays we ran when there were only a few seconds remaining in the game.

Players learned to appreciate this regimen because they could be confident that what they learned on the practice field, they could apply in a game. The 49ers have continued this system since I've left. I take pride in that, as well as in the fact that those of my coaches who have moved on to other teams are organizing their practices with the same format.

There were additional considerations for setting up our training-camp schedule. These included prescribing a level of intensity for each drill and each session and providing the best possible atmosphere for individual learning and team development.

We would start first with a calendar and decide how many days we would have available to practice, and then note the days when we played preseason games. We'd establish four different practice formats, from a very hard, grueling two-and-a-half-hour practice to a light, thirty-minute practice the day before a game.

We never scheduled more than two hard workouts in a row, because I wanted to make sure players did not become so weary that they were unduly vulnerable to muscle pulls, or that their only concern in practice was to simply survive.

It's vitally important that players take the field to learn something each session rather than to have only their courage tested. This approach should be reflected all the way down to the Pop Warner level. There are only so many times when a coach should test a player's courage or willingness to totally sacrifice. The player should be taking the field to learn, and usually to practice something specific that has been discussed with him beforehand.

There were at least four major benefits from precisely scheduling training camp and practice during the regular season:

1. **No time was wasted on the practice field.** Historically, coaches have unwittingly wasted precious minutes on the practice field. They've spent time on drills that weren't relevant to actually playing the game. Or, they've run meaningless "filler drills" on one part of the field while other players at other positions worked on specific techniques, because the schedule has not been organized to incorporate all players working on important techniques concurrently. Typi-

cally, then, that coach would come to the realization, with just a week remaining before the first game, that he still had eight or ten things left to address.

2. **The learning process was accelerated.** Players would see the practice schedule the night before, so they knew those areas they were going to emphasize. We would specifically review each category, whether it was a particular pass pattern or a certain segment of defense.

When you take the field, you want the best possible learning environment. Most often, when that learning is taking place, the player is also getting the needed physical work. We didn't spend as much time on conditioning drills in training camps as some teams do. We felt that we would be in excellent condition when the season started and we didn't want to fatigue the players so much that they would lose their concentration and be more susceptible to injury. Teams hold practice for two reasons: to improve their skills and techniques, and to prepare for their next opponent.

During these sessions, it is vital that players communicate with each other. We made a concerted effort to establish an atmosphere in which players communicated in the huddle, at the line of scrimmage, and between plays. Visual and verbal communication can be an extremely important reinforcement during a game. We wanted players to exchange information on the situation, to know what to expect, and, more importantly, to make those absolutely necessary "calls" or signals relevant to the play or defense itself. For instance, as certain formations are identified, the entire defense may be changed through audible calls by a linebacker or safety. Or, something like a simple man-in-motion can change the defense just an instant before the ball is snapped, so we needed clear, concise, instant communication.

3. **We could approach the game on a broad base, rather than piece-meal.** We worked on every phase concurrently. We did that in 1979 and '80, so, by 1981, a solid foundation was being established in all phases of the game. Rather than utilizing a limited system geared to the abilities of the players we had in '79 and '80, we implemented one that enabled us to take full advantage of talented players when they joined us in '81. Through our style of football and teaching, I believe we developed our squad to its fullest potential. Then, as exceptional individuals joined us, they were the catalysts that brought almost overnight success.

It wasn't a matter of saying that as soon as we develop a running game, we'll develop a passing game, or as soon as we develop a basic defense, we'll develop a blitz. We emphasized all facets of football necessary to ultimately compete with the best. Perhaps we might have had more wins in 1979 if we had concentrated on a more limited game, but we were laying down a foundation for the future.

4. **Initially, I coached the coaches.** We developed the skills of players who wouldn't be with us in the future. In effect, we were coaching a phantom team, because many of the players on the '79 team would no longer be with us two years later.

But as the coaches taught skills to those players, they were becoming more proficient themselves, and they were able to do a great job with the more talented athletes we acquired in ensuing years.

We coached all the players, not just the best ones. We had a distinct philosophy: As long as a man is on the field, he's a 49er. All players, regardless of stature, would get the same consideration. Every player was told, if you're a 49er in training camp, you're a team member. Because of numbers, we may eventually have to release you, but as long as you're here, you're a viable member of the squad.

This approach was also consistent with a "hands-on" style of coaching.

There are different categories of coaches. One extreme is the "administrative" coach, who makes sure that everything is in place so his staff can coach the team. John Ralston was that kind of coach when I was on his staff at Stanford. John gave his assistants considerable autonomy, and five eventually became NFL head coaches.

Another type concentrates on a specific aspect of the team and then surrounds himself with staff who coach the other areas. George Allen was an example. He concentrated on special teams and defense while his offensive staff did its job without input from Allen. But he was shrewd. He knew his defensive brilliance often was the difference between his team and others.

The coaches who have been the most successful are usually the ones actively involved in the on-the-field, day-to-day coaching. Players will sacrifice for a hands-on coach, because they identify with him as an integral part of the team.

A head coach who sees his role only as motivating the team and organizing the staff is at the mercy of other people. Having spent so many years as an assistant coach, I became more and more aware that someone had to be the source of game strategy and tactics. I felt my offensive skills could be the difference between our team and many of our opponents.

I seemed to demonstrate that at Stanford, where we developed a style of play that led the conference in offense. Our brand of football was so different that we became a competitive team, without having comparable depth and team speed.

On the professional level, it is important that the coach work with individual players and be actively involved in practice, rather than standing remotely away from everyone. Exchanging on a first-name basis is very appropriate. There really isn't much room for protocol in an atmosphere where so many sacrifices are made. Insecure men may need the continual reinforcement of being referred to by title—"Coach Smith" for example—but players will be much more willing to openly exchange, to express themselves if formalities are set aside.

Unfortunately, the term "coach" can be used in a condescending or contemptuous manner. When I was at Cincinnati, Pat McInally, an extremely bright, Harvard-educated punter, would call me "Coach." I became very uncomfortable. He seemed to say it in a superior way.

So, when I arrived at Stanford, I immediately told the team that everybody was on a first-name basis, that it was a two-way street, that I considered them mature men:

"Set aside the student-professor relationship. You are in an arena that calls for bonding among everyone involved. Sacrifices will have to be made, there just isn't time or need to distinguish between roles and responsibilities. From this point forward we're a group of men who collectively have one common objective, to compete and to win."

This freed them to totally express themselves on the football field and challenged them to demonstrate their maturity.

There isn't any reason a coach can't become more effective each year, if he can retain enthusiasm for his work. When a coach starts becoming more of a symbolic leader, instead of being directly involved with coaching, he'd better start looking for career alternatives because his lack of input will begin to negatively affect the team. This erosion may be gradual and may not be demonstrated immediately. Eventually, the result will appear on the scoreboard.

Because the game is so severe and intense, people under such extreme conditions can mistreat each other. In order to survive, the athlete conditions himself for this kind of treatment. This often can result in demeaning and even humiliating experiences. In most severe situations, coaches might demonstrate disdain or indifference to a player. As an example, a player may be benched with no explanation, or a player who has continued playing while injured may be critically judged for his sub-par performance, or in the process of releasing a player the explanation to that player may be given little priority, as the coaches are distracted with other duties. This also occurs among coaches. Tough, sharp language is used which can really hammer another person's ego. There are some that don't survive.

It's a battle of attrition for the coaching staff. So much sacrifice in time and energy is given, that as the season wears on, you wonder if you can sustain your efforts. In my job as TV analyst, I for the first time had an opportunity to note the telling fatigue on the faces of my coaching contemporaries as they completed their fourteen-hour-a-day training camps. Then as the season wore on those emotions would come closer and closer to the surface. It could be often noted by rage directed at officials. Yet throughout this, it is vital to overtly demonstrate complete composure and control to the squad.

6

Worse than Expansion

When I took over the 49ers, we were acknowledged as the least-talented, least-experienced franchise in the NFL, and with less chance to improve than an expansion team because we didn't have many of our draft picks in future years.

We didn't even own our first-round pick because it had been traded away by Joe Thomas for O. J. Simpson. That one deal cost the 49ers five draft picks in two seasons.

Thomas earned the reputation of being a draft whiz because of his success at Miami and Baltimore, but he had made few good choices in his two years in San Francisco.

Dan Bunz, one of Thomas's draft choices, played well as a strong-side linebacker late in his career. Fred Quillan later became a Pro Bowl center. Archie Reese became a starter at nose guard. But those players and reserve lineman Walt Downing were the only players Thomas drafted in his two years, 1977 and '78, who were still with the team by 1981.

Ken McAfee, an early first-round draft choice out of Notre Dame, typified Thomas's judgment. McAfee was not quick enough to play tight end, so we eventually decided to move him to tackle. That had worked for Keith Fahnhorst, a tight end in college at Minnesota, but it didn't work for McAfee. He became very bitter, having been a great player at Notre Dame and joining the 49ers with much acclaim. But his physical abilities weren't suited to what was expected of a tight end in the NFL.

Meanwhile, many veteran players—players who could have contributed—had been released. Thomas even cut quarterback Jim Plunkett, who had been the subject of another earlier "blockbuster" trade. Jim had been an All American at Stanford, the Heisman Trophy winner, and then was totally mishandled at New England. Returning to the Bay Area and the 49ers was a natural move for him. But the ultimate in reckless arrogance occurred when Jim, after a couple of disappointing games and absolutely no coaching support, was waived. Plunkett went to the Raiders and eventually was the MVP in the Raiders' 1981 Super Bowl win over Philadelphia.

One defensive back got cut after one bad game because Joe was venting his wrath. He made the decision on the airplane as the team was returning from an away game. As I remember, he was the only legitimate NFL corner on the squad. But if Joe suffered, the players would suffer. Of course, people simply do not respond to that kind of tension and vindictiveness.

Joe Thomas had his shot at rebuilding the 49ers and now we would get ours.

I also didn't appreciate the atmosphere in the locker room. Veteran players like Cedrick Hardman seemed to dominate and intimidate the others. Players were bewildered because of how quickly teammates were coming and going. They felt totally insecure just being there.

I hadn't been with an organization with such poor talent. Even the Chargers, who had been considered one of the NFL's weakest teams, possessed superior talent, in quality and quantity, to the 49ers.

The worst area was the secondary, which was outmanned and inadequate. Linebacking was especially weak. Off their reputation, I had thought the defensive line could give us a good pass rush. But they were well past their prime, except for Jimmy Webb, an undersized but bright and tough tackle. Cedrick Hardman looked good physically, but he had only one move left, a pass rush straight up the field. Time after time he would make that move, and the opposing team would run the ball inside him. On the sideline, we coaches just had to grit our teeth. Later, we were to trade Cedrick to the Oakland Raiders, and he helped them win the Super Bowl in 1980, as a situational pass rusher.

The offensive line was young and not big. Fahnhorst was solid at tackle and Randy Cross at guard. Quillan had potential at center. John Ayers would later become an excellent guard, but he had yet to play in the NFL. Eventually, these four would be the nucleus of a strong offensive line that would lead us to the Super Bowl, but in 1979, they were too small and inexperienced to be considered much more than barely adequate.

Steve DeBerg could throw the ball with accuracy and feel. He wasn't mobile, but he gave us a way to move the ball, with his touch passing and our system of football. Mike Shumann was a sure-handed receiver, though he lacked breakaway speed. Freddie Solomon as a receiver had remarkable quickness and speed but had been totally inconsistent.

We also had an effective runner in Paul Hofer, who was a better player than most people realized. Paul was called an "overachiever," a term I've never understood. Either you're an achiever or you're not. Paul rushed for 615 yards that year, with an excellent average gain of 5 yards. He was a good back, with fine cutting ability, whose career was unfortunately curtailed by injury the next year. Though Paul played in 1981, his injured knee kept him from appearing in the Super Bowl.

I had miscalculated on O. J. Simpson. O. J. was one of the greatest runners in NFL history, the holder of the single-season rushing record, but he'd suffered a knee injury and developed arthritis before being traded to the 49ers. I thought we could still get some productivity out of O. J., but his knee was so bad there were times he couldn't even trot. He often couldn't practice, and he couldn't cut on it in a game. He gained just 460 yards, a 3.8 average, his final year in football.

We had the good fortune of drafting Joe Montana in the third round, with Dallas's pick, and later drafting Dwight Clark. Those two have been outstanding for the 49ers, and became the basis for our later success.

Our first pick, James Owens, had won the NCAA hurdles in 13.3. He obviously had great speed and was extremely tough as a college player. He was only 185 pounds, probably not big enough for a running back in the NFL, so we'd have to use him as a wide receiver.

I traveled to Los Angeles just before the draft, after reviewing all the quarterbacks that might be available, to work out Owens and Montana. Owens displayed explosive quickness and speed and showed reasonable ability to catch the ball. Unfortunately, I didn't realize at the time that James had a history of muscle pulls. That tendency would recur in his career with us. Sometimes he couldn't even practice for weeks, so his playing time was extremely limited.

The play that probably most typified his career came against Detroit in his second season. After the Lions had scored the game's first touchdown, James took the kickoff and broke into the open, but pulled a muscle running downfield. He limped across the goal line for a 101-yard touchdown, but we didn't see him again for several weeks.

After working out Montana and Owens, I felt they would be good choices if we could get them with our first two picks—on the second and third rounds, remember. Other teams considered Owens before we drafted but decided, perhaps reluctantly, to pass on him. When our turn came in the second round, we took James, a terrific guy who, as I said, just couldn't make it for us as a receiver because of his injuries.

We tried him very briefly as defensive back, but it was a disaster. In the Bears game, we were leading going into the final five minutes of the game. He was playing free safety. That was my idea. I had forced James on our defensive coordinator, Chuck Studley, because we had no speed in the secondary. If the Bears broke any of their wide receivers, it would be a touchdown. I felt James, with his great speed, could run down an open receiver if necessary. So, I requested that Chuck put James in. Unfortunately, we called a man-to-man defense instead of a zone, and on the first play, a receiver ran right by James for the winning touchdown. James eventually was traded for Johnny Davis, who helped us in the 1981 season.

Before the draft, I had also traveled to Clemson to see their quarterback, Steve Fuller. I was also looking for a big receiver to play split end—much like Chip Myers had been with the Bengals—who could go against linebackers and catch the short- and medium-range passes underneath the coverage, and take punishment from bigger men. We wanted somebody who was over six-two and could run in the 4.6 category, fast but not possessing the blazing speed that so many teams expect from their wide receivers.

Dwight Clark was one of many on my list. He was a delightful human being, outgoing with a great sense of humor and very natural with me. The first time I met him, I took an immediate liking to him. He was impressive on the field, too. Dwight demonstrated good speed, a loose stride that would be excellent in the open field. He was big and had good hands, and I thought he would be an excellent candidate for what I wanted.

Dwight wasn't listed in the scouting reports. He wasn't even the top receiver on his Clemson team. He had caught only 12 passes, but on the film I saw, he ran effectively after a catch, important because our style of offense has always depended on receivers running with the ball.

And though he was not supposed to have good speed, on that film he caught a pass and ran away from defensive backs for about a 50-yard touchdown. That was one of the reasons I wanted him. Dwight's times for the forty, the traditional way of evaluating players, were not impressive, but in full stride he had good speed. I can't recall him ever being caught from behind when he played for us.

I came back to San Francisco and said I wanted Clark. The scouts told me he'd be available as a free agent, that he wouldn't be drafted, but I insisted and selected him in the tenth round. I wasn't about to lose him as a free agent.

Initially Dwight played special teams well for us, and also played some at wide receiver, catching short and medium-range passes. He kept improving and became a brilliant receiver, leading the NFL in receiving one year and setting club career records. We were very, very fortunate to have Dwight, and even more fortunate to be able to work out Joe just before the draft.

Players who have the instincts, are effective, and have one or two strengths or qualities, but have a deficiency—lack of a rifle arm in Joe's case, lack of blazing speed in Dwight's—often are overlooked in the draft. The draft itself has become so computerized and structured that scouts concentrate on raw statistics, rather than on functional performance.

Montana and Clark were choices for the future more than the present, but I didn't have the luxury of doing that with other draft picks. We had to get players who could help us immediately, even if we knew their potential was limited.

As one example, we drafted Tom Seabron as a linebacker in the fifth round, a great guy who played his heart out and even started some games for us, but lacked the overall strength to have a long career.

Years later, when we had a solid team, I also could draft Michael Carter in the fifth round, projecting him as a great player for the future we didn't need to start immediately. That's the difference between building from a poor team and building from a good one.

Knowing how poor a team we had, we thoroughly checked the waiver wire daily during training camp. Several people in our organization had known other people in the league well and could get reliable information on players being released, so we claimed any we thought had a chance. Our staff would evaluate them on the field during our lunch period. If I felt a player could remotely improve us, we'd sign him, and he'd be on the practice field that afternoon. If we didn't think he could help, we'd send him on his way, so he wouldn't disrupt the others. Tough business, very impersonal: It's no fun shipping people in and out. This was not something I could take for very long.

Most of the players we claimed couldn't help, but we did garner some good talent through waivers. One was Dwaine Board, who was cut by the Pittsburgh Steelers because they wanted to stay with their veteran lineman. He was small for a defensive lineman, only about 235 pounds, but he was quick and explosive, a great athlete. We were fortunate to claim and sign him, and he was outstanding for us through three Super Bowls.

Dwight Hicks came to us as a free agent, and he later became a Pro Bowl player, the free safety on our first two Super Bowl teams. Mike Wilson, who didn't get a good look in Dallas because the Cowboys wanted to stay with their veteran receivers, became a solid receiver for us, one of only five players (with Montana, Cross, Keena Turner, and Ronnie Lott) who later played on all three of my Super Bowl teams.

There were other players we claimed through waivers who helped us get from ground zero to champions. In some cases, they weren't there in the championship years but they were there in our rebuilding phase, which was just as important.

Many times, scouts will remark of a player, "He's just good enough to get you beat," or "This player is one you'll always want to replace." That might be true, but in the meantime, you have to field a competitive team.

If a player was just good enough to get us beat, well, that was all right because without him, we might have been beaten by a larger margin. If he was somebody we wanted to replace, I'd do it when we signed a measurably better player, but meanwhile, he was playing as well as he could and he was better than anybody else we had. We signed players of lesser caliber even if they'd been released by other teams because we were improving by degrees. We knew these players weren't capable of winning a championship for us, but it was important to keep improving.

We had a network of scouts and coaches, and we also had less orthodox methods of searching for talent. For instance, we had a workout camp in Youngstown, Ohio. Men came from miles around. Truckdrivers would stop in on their lunch break, put on a jersey, and work out. We had more than two hundred work out there. We had tryouts in Redwood City, too. We found a player, Billy Ring, who played six years for us, in our tryout at Redwood City. So, if we got just the one player out of perhaps 500 who participated, well, it was worth it.

In 1979, our squad turned over continuously. It improved and became competitive, though not able to win more than two games that first season. We probably went through fifty defensive backs in two years. I remember Ray Rhodes suffering through that process. Ray had been an excellent wide receiver and then a defensive back with the Giants. He joined us and played well but was at the end of his career. Because of his enthusiasm for the game and his ability to communicate we asked if he would join our coaching staff. Ray served in our intern program for one year but then was offered a fulltime defensive backfield position. Our intern program has included men like Tommy Hart, Cas Banaszek, Bruce Coslet, and Chip Myers. Ray has directed the most effective defensive backfield in football since becoming a coach.

We worked with the media, trying to break through their apathy toward the organization. A lot of rhetoric had been forthcoming from the 49ers in previous years, with no results, so we tried to be as honest and straightforward with the press as possible and still sell tickets.

We attempted to make it as upbeat as we could. There was a lot of humor in our team meetings because we wanted everybody at least to be able to laugh together.

Some players, though, couldn't do that. For instance, Ron Singleton, our left tackle. Singleton had been a tight end in college; I had tried him out with the Chargers, and he didn't make it. He caught on with the 49ers as a left tackle, the key position in the offensive line because if a pass rusher gets by the left tackle, he comes in on the blind side of a righthanded quarterback.

Singleton was tough, but a very difficult guy to get along with. After starting one year, he decided to hold out for $90,000—a $40,000 pay raise. His agent came in and demanded the money, saying Ron was one of the top tackles in football. In the locker room, Singleton became belligerent, threatening those who didn't get along with him, including our equipment man, Chico Norton.

Though he may have been as good an offensive lineman as we had, I directed executive assistant R. C. Owens to clean out his locker and leave his belongings on his front steps. We released him. He went from believing he was one of the best tackles in football to being a free agent. Other teams weren't interested in him, and that was the end of his football career.

We set about teaching fundamentals and skills, establishing a system of football on offense and defense, and establishing a positive atmosphere and attitude.

We were enthusiastically involved in developing the players we had, trying to improve their consistency and effectiveness. I think our staff did an admirable job the first two years, working in most cases with men who could not compete in the NFL, developing them to their fullest potential.

We were unable to stop opponents with any consistency. If we blitzed, our defensive backs couldn't cover. If we didn't blitz, the other team would run right through us. Offensively, though, we moved from twenty-eighth in the league to sixth.

There were so many frustrations, times when our team would play well but have individual breakdowns because of lack of ability, which made it impossible to win.

Against the Chicago Bears, for instance, we moved the ball methodically down into field-goal range near the game's end, but I called one pass too many, and Steve DeBerg threw an interception. We lost, 28–27.

We had several games like that. There were times when I made playcalling errors in the fourth quarter, putting it on the shoulders of a quarterback known for throwing critical interceptions. In retrospect, I can see that I probably should have called more runs with Paul Hofer. He conceivably could have won that Chicago game for us.

More than once I wondered, how could we ever become competitive in the NFL? It was like raising the *Titanic*. I thought it might be impossible. The team was down so far, I wondered how we could ever acquire the number of people needed to get even to 8–8. I feared that by the time the team got to .500 there would be another coach in charge. But Eddie DeBartolo treated me extremely well through all this. He was appreciative of the team's improvement. Everybody could see we were much more competitive, and much more interesting to watch.

In the early years, when it was most difficult, Eddie DeBartolo, Jr.'s enthusiastic support, his sincere camaraderie, and his accessibility were a source of confidence and inspiration. To this day there is a popular notion that it was his spending that brought our success. Although spending did allow us to function freely, we won Super Bowl XVI when we were at the bottom of the NFL salary ranking. Spending became necessary as the team developed established stars. As of this writing, NFL structuring negates "buying a winner." Only through true free agency will financial resources afford franchises an opportunity to dominate the fortunes of football.

I remember another game against St. Louis. The Cardinals had just fired Bud Wilkinson and were in disarray. We came into St. Louis thinking this would be a game we could win, but we lost it, 13–10. On one play late in the game, DeBerg used a head bob to pull the Cardinals offside. The strategy worked, and Steve threw a touchdown on the play—but the winning touchdown was called back because we were penalized for the head bob.

Then, we were driving again for what could have been the winning touchdown, and Steve threw an interception.

That's the kind of year it was. We lost five games by less than a touchdown.

*   *   *

There were some players who played well. Archie Reese, at nose guard, played very physically in the early years and was a major contributor as a starter in our first Super Bowl. Bobby Ferrell gave 100 percent as a special-teams player.

Joe Montana was showing signs of becoming a topflight NFL quarterback, although some in our organization doubted his potential.

There were also games that were encouraging even though we lost. For instance, we moved the ball consistently on Dallas against their great Flex defense, so well that we took field position away from them. The Cowboys would have to go the length of the field to score, because on each possession we would make a series of first downs before giving up the ball.

We were in the game until late in the fourth quarter. In fact, we were leading at halftime, 10–6, and Dallas didn't go ahead until just three minutes before the end of the third quarter. With ten minutes left in the game, the Cowboys intercepted a DeBerg pass at the twenty and scored. We kicked a field goal to close to 19–13, but then Steve got sacked in the end zone, for the 21–13 final. We came right back, driving to the Dallas five as the game ended.

When a wildebeest or zebra is finally entrapped by the lion, it submits to the inevitable—its head drops, its eyes glaze over, and it stands motionless and accepts its fate. The posture of defeat is also demonstrated by man—chin down, head dropped, shoulders slumped, arms hung limply. This posture is often visible as players leave the field in the later stages of the game when things are going against them. I often brought this to our players' attention using that example from nature, and we became very sensitive to it. I would remind them never to allow this to occur. I would assert, "Even in the most impossible situations, stand tall, keep our heads up, shoulders back, keep moving, running, looking up, demonstrating our pride, dignity and defiance."

After the game, I commented that we couldn't say we'd arrived because we'd made some woeful errors, but we had demonstrated that our offense was legitimate. If we could move the ball that well against the best defense in the conference, we should be able to do it against anybody.

Because of performances such as this I assumed our press corps would enthusiastically endorse our progress. Unfortunately they were conditioned to failure. The previous regime had entered the scene with bravado and high-sounding promises—and look what happened.

Even in our final game in Atlanta, when O. J. Simpson was given the ball for the last time, Steve DeBerg completed 29 passes for 345 yards. I can recall their coaches saying we were the best passing team in football, or at least that we had the best scheme. Leeman Bennett remarked to me coming off the field, "God, you can really throw the football."

I was relieved when the season was over. I kept waiting each week for a win, but the continual losing numbed me. So, I was more relieved than disappointed when the final gun sounded.

By that time, I could even forget about Thomas Henderson, otherwise known as "Hollywood."

7

Hollywood Henderson and My Drug Education

Thomas "Hollywood" Henderson gave me my first hard lesson in drug addiction. It couldn't have come at a worse time, when I was already struggling to try to make a talent-starved team respectable.

Henderson had been regarded as one of the truly great performers in the NFL. I thought he was the best outside linebacker I had ever seen. He was so quick and had tremendous range over the field. But, after playing well in his early years with the Dallas Cowboys, his game had deteriorated and he was making wild charges about Tom Landry, the coaching staff, and his teammates to the media. Thomas was demanding a new contract, but more importantly did not believe he should have to abide with Cowboy dress and behavior codes. He had become more vocal and more quotable than Tom Landry himself. The Cowboys realized that drug use was a big part of his problem. They had to move Henderson, and we were among the teams interested.

Most clubs weren't interested, rightfully so in retrospect. But I felt that I could deal with him. I'd had a good history of working with athletes who had problems, but I didn't realize how far down cocaine could bring a person.

And, of course, I was very eager to get a player of his stature for a team with no stars and few players who even met minimum NFL standards. Thomas could have made a big difference to us, because he was capable of being the big-play type of player we so badly needed on defense.

My naivete was understandable. That was a very difficult time for coaches, because we had had no experience with hard drugs. Alcohol was the drug of choice for our generation.

We could spot a player suffering from a hangover, and we could be reasonably sure that that player wouldn't be stupid enough to go out and get drunk again that night, after sweating through a workout.

Coaches usually knew, too, which players were heavy drinkers, because they would generally do it in public, at bars. So, we could talk to them about that, because we were familiar with alcohol's effects. But we really didn't know anything about the effect of cocaine, or even how to spot players who were using it.

We weren't alone. At that time, even some doctors were quoted as saying that cocaine was a recreational drug with no aftereffects and that it was not addictive. There seemed to be those who considered it a recreational drug similar to alcohol that would not harm persons, and those who were much more cautious and realized how addictive and destructive cocaine can be.

Tom Landry, a man I held in the highest esteem, wanted to do the honorable thing, so he gave me a choice in making the deal. He said first that he would take a fourth-round pick for Henderson. If Henderson had been in normal condition, he would have been worth at least a first-round pick, but in his current state, a fourth-round pick was all Landry felt he could get.

Then Tom told me he would take a third-round pick but give me the option of releasing Thomas before the trading deadline, well into the season; if I released Henderson before that, the 49ers wouldn't have to give up anything.

I felt Henderson would work out, and I didn't want to give up a higher draft pick if I didn't have to, so I chose to trade a fourth-round pick for Henderson. As it turned out, if I had taken the other option we wouldn't have lost anything, because Henderson had to be released before the trading deadline, six games into the season.

I visited with Thomas immediately after the trade. He was very positive. He has a charming way of expressing himself; he's quite intelligent. He and his wife, Wyetta, a beautiful woman, flew to San Francisco, and Geri and I entertained them in our home on the Stanford campus. Wyetta played the piano for us, beautifully, giving our daughter Elizabeth a quick lesson. Thomas was gregarious and open, and he entertained us all. But later I learned that when he excused himself during dinner to go to the bathroom, he'd used cocaine.

After dinner, Thomas said he wanted to take a walk, and we strolled around the campus. He told me I was the greatest coach in the league, a minor overstatement. Then he said he wanted to revise his contract, and he persisted, using every device he could think of to squeeze more money out of me. He told me he was the greatest special teams player who ever lived, that he would be our special teams captain and wanted $40,000 more for that role. I politely refused, but I began to sense something was wrong. Suddenly he seemed more irrational than I'd expected and was acting unstable. I sensed that either he had serious personality problems, or he was on drugs. Of course, he was high on cocaine.

We moved him to San Francisco, but we had problems almost immediately. For instance, we couldn't seem to agree on a time or a place for his spring workouts. He always had some kind of business commitment, but in the meantime he would remind me of his grueling physical fitness regimen that he followed in strict privacy. Still, he made a good impression on everybody with his personality. He's a handsome man, bright and able to express himself beautifully.

The problems became more serious when we reported to training camp in Santa Clara. One day he was outstanding, as fine an athlete as I've ever seen. He actually covered our best wide receivers man-to-man and shut them out, a remarkable performance for an outside linebacker. But then the next day he said he had a toothache, and he had to go to the dentist. He came onto the field with a towel wrapped around his head like a bandage, as people did in times past. Later, I learned that he was using drugs in his room and trying to entice others to join him, sometimes successfully. Every effort made to address the problem through counseling went nowhere. Thomas would completely defuse the matter with impenetrable charm.

During the exhibition season, he couldn't play very often, for one reason or another. When he did play, he appeared to be confused about everything. By that time, I knew there was no longer any hope that he would help us, and I tried to trade him. We came close to making deals with Houston and Miami, but nothing materialized.

About this time, too, his wife came to me, terrified over Thomas's irrational behavior at home. I was really beginning to understand what a human tragedy this was.

To cap it all off, there were all-night parties that included members of our secretarial staff. Then, of course, there was the physical altercation between two of our secretaries in the parking lot over who would have Henderson's charms. Both were asked to resign. Good God, what next?

Then began a cat-and-mouse game, as we tried to release him and he tried to stay until he was paid at least part of his salary. Thomas had twisted his neck in an exhibition game and we gave him several weeks to recover, though we questioned how serious the injury was. Our doctors gave him a clean bill of health, but he kept saying he couldn't play.

I realized that despite all this great talent, he was not going to be able to play football, but we couldn't release him if he claimed to be injured, because of NFL regulations. Rules or not, we wouldn't have released him if we thought he was truly injured. This entire matter had become a distraction to everyone. I would spend half of my press conferences countering Hollywood's remarks and at the same time defending his privacy. It seemed to be the main topic in the *San Francisco Chronicle* each day.

We had to have him on the field to practice, but getting him there was most difficult. I named him to the starting team, thinking that might help motivate him to come out to practice. But when that day arrived, I found Thomas flat on his back in the locker room, with players stepping around him on their way out to the field.

Somehow, we got him up on his feet and dressed, and out onto the field. He worked for about fifteen minutes as we filmed him. He left the field, feigning dizziness, but we had enough proof that he was healthy, so we released him. Houston claimed him, and he played for the Oilers on special teams the rest of the season. He then went briefly to Miami but was soon out of football.

It was a great waste of talent, but to this day, I recall Hollywood as a charming, gregarious, thoroughly likable human being. As a matter of fact, we still see each other on occasion and are good friends.

From that time, I was much more sensitive to the problem of

cocaine abuse, although even then I didn't realize the extent to which it was being used in sports, from the college level to the professional.

All too often, college coaches were as naive as I had been about the use of drugs. Coaches also would conveniently overlook drug use by their players. That was misguided; they'd have served the player better by getting treatment for him.

In 1981, we heard that a player in whom we were interested had a history of both cocaine and alcohol use. When that rumor was vehemently denied by his coaches and trainers, we drafted him. Unfortunately, when he arrived, it was soon evident that the innuendos were true; though he started in the Super Bowl and played well, he soon self-destructed. Later this player got off drugs and turned his life around after leaving football.

I was never able to completely stop drug use on the 49ers. After our first Super Bowl year in 1981, I heard that several of our players had been using cocaine during the season. I later learned that one substitute, who did not play in the game, was snorting cocaine in the john at halftime of the Super Bowl. The next year, he was working in a warehouse. Drug abuse may have curtailed the careers of as many as eleven players on that team. Some are still suffering the negative effects.

The use of cocaine was very common in the NFL at that time. My guess would be that despite our problems, fewer 49er players used drugs than did players on other teams. Stories emanating from other cities about drug abuse were rattling the game. My conversations with others in NFL management corroborated these startling, unfortunate revelations.

Any number of times players would report in with the flu or a cold or some kind of malady they could use to explain their inability to practice. We coaches suspected something, but we couldn't be sure. We were obligated to give players the benefit of the doubt, especially since you just couldn't believe a player could be doing that to himself.

Regular users would not sleep for hours or days and wouldn't bother to eat, so consequently, they would lose weight and were constantly fatigued. They'd become paranoid, feeling that everybody was taking advantage of them and not supporting them.

There's no question that drug abuse affected the performance of the team, especially in 1982 and 1985, the years after our first two Super Bowl wins. Some surprise losses—some frustrating, disappointing losses—could indirectly be attributed to drug use by players who eventually left the team.

At the league level, executives were as naive as coaches and, though well intentioned, made miscalculations about drug involvement. The early NFL policy was inadequate, and as the league attempted to deal more seriously with drugs, new policies were just as unrealistic because they were too stringent. Players were identified as users by minimal traces of drugs in the blood that may have resulted from being around others using drugs, such as marijuana, in a social setting. As soon as one innocent person is unfairly accused, a program loses credibility. The tolerance limits set by other institutions such as the railroads and airlines were not as stringent.

Players on drugs are not aware of the resulting impairment of judgment and performance. After an athlete has taken cocaine regularly for a period of time, he becomes a shell of himself. His reflexes are gone, so he becomes susceptible to injury. One of the telltale indicators is a series of minor injuries, attributable to a loss of reflexes and the punishment a user's body absorbs. He suffers from a form of malnutrition because he doesn't eat regularly. And the lack of sleep, as I reminded coaches and players, is critical. Drug effects aside, just losing sleep can significantly affect performance.

It has taken time for us coaches to educate ourselves. Players have also had to learn about the terrible effects of cocaine.

In lecturing the team on drugs, I know there might have been some players who were laughing behind my back, but most understood there was a support system within the 49ers. Most importantly, our team program had strict confidentiality, which cannot always be said for the NFL program. Over the years, there was virtually no public awareness of players who were in counseling or treatment.

We had organized a complete program for those in need of assistance, ranging from initial interviews to in-patient treatment in specialized centers. Those with abuse problems were treated individually and a plan was implemented to speed their return to a drug-free life. Because our program was totally confidential, there were several players able to return to a productive life. Unfortunately, there were also those who stepped forward only when our program was the last resort. It made others aware of their problem and it became very difficult to keep those cases confidential.

Whether it's alcohol or drugs, a person with an addiction will do everything he can to mislead you. He'll deny ever using it, remind you that he's a good Christian person, and become outraged that you could even suspect him of something like that. That is a trait common to all addicts. They deny their addiction so convincingly because they need to use the drug so much: they feel their very existence depends on it. So, they'll do everything to throw you off, and that has fooled a lot of coaches.

Finally, they get to the point where everyone is aware of it. Then they will finally admit to use and ask for help. But on occasion, even that's been a ploy. Once caught, they plead mercy, get help, and then, on their release, go right back to drugs.

So many of these players abused drugs in college. They became users because drugs were often acceptable in collegiate social settings. Then as professionals, they had the money to afford anything they wanted. Through years of exposure and experience dealing with these problems, I found a major contributor often was a close friend, usually a girl friend, who would continue using while the athlete was attempting to quit. In that circumstance, it was almost impossible for the player to get away from his problem.

Unfortunately, drugs can be a way of being accepted in a new environment. A young man, sometimes black, joins his first professional team, buys himself a new condominium, nice furniture, and the car he's always dreamed of, only to find that he is out of the social mainstream and very lonely. He's broken with his campus ties, and his support system of family and friends.

Unfortunately, veteran teammates usually are not sensitive to this and fail to include him in their social activities. He can feel like an outcast on his own football team. The problems can seem overwhelming in a matter of weeks. The player's agent has failed to keep contact with him and may not have been interested in anything but his initial contract.

The easiest places to make social contacts are bars and nightclubs, where drugs are common. These impressionable young men are immediately accepted because of their stature as NFL players and their financial status. They meet a lot of new "friends" and find themselves in the middle of a drug scene that demands their money and prestige.

Everything goes wrong. The coaches ultimately become aware of it and wade in to help but sometimes it's too late. Not only is it a personal disaster for the player, but a financial disaster as well.

Unfortunately, we saw players lose everything, including a career in the National Football League.

Not surprisingly, as talk of drugs became public, all sorts of rumors surfaced. Our policy was not to discuss drug use; I never referred to it when a player was released, even if it had been a factor.

Drug rumors can touch everyone. When they involved our star quarterback, Joe Montana, we finally had to confront them publicly.

There had been stories circulating about Joe for months. Nobody who had any connection with the team could avoid them.

As I recall, there were several different stories involving Joe. Each rumor would be basically the same, but with some different twist. For instance, there was one in which he'd been pulled over by a policeman and cocaine had been found in his car. But each time I heard the story, it featured a different town, a different police force.

There was also a story that he'd been caught using, that he was seen in public—but it would always have a different setting.

The rumors were so persistent. Virtually everywhere I went, there was another version. One story even had him in the hospital. Another insisted that I had bailed him out of jail. It was all absolutely ridiculous. These always surfaced after Joe had had an average game.

I visited with Joe at length, and he said he would even be willing to take a lie-detector test. I recommended that he have a press conference and bring it out in the open. It had to be dealt with directly.

So Joe had his press conference and denied everything. He challenged anybody to produce evidence that he had been using cocaine. Of course, there were no takers, and I think by confronting the issue head-on, he defused most of the rumors.

But Joe still can't avoid the rumors. Before the 1990 Super Bowl, a Washington, D.C., television station reported that at least three white quarterbacks had failed NFL drug tests but had been allowed to play. Joe had to deny several times that he was one of those quarterbacks. That story proved to be absolute bunk.

The use of anabolic steroids among athletes has become widely known—and publicized—in recent years. Coaches were often passively aware of their existence, not realizing the extent of their use, of their damaging physical effects, and of the grave risk taken by those athletes who, over a period of years, took steroids.

Had coaches been aware of steroids' positive effects, they might have actually endorsed them. Extended planned programs of steroid use can result in as much as a 20 percent gain in strength and explosion, a marked increase in speed and quickness—and a significant negative personality change. Typically, a 240-pound man who runs a forty-yard dash in 5.0 will reach a weight of 265 pounds and can bring his sprint speed to 4.8.

But the side effects can be insidious. The continued use of anabolic steroids will result in an athlete becoming prone to muscle pulls because the muscle attachments cannot support the dramatic increase in muscle size. Consequently, you have an athlete who performs better but is often on the bench.

The athlete becomes much more aggressive and much more intense, almost out of control on the field. At certain positions this results in a more effective football player, but the personality changes all too often result in severe problems off the field. Any number of times, wives have complained about no longer knowing the man they're living with. He's become an absolute brute and has been emotionally and physically abusive.

Most importantly, studies have determined that continuous users of anabolic steroids have severe and chronic health problems and a shortened life expectancy.

Once alert to the steroid problem, it was not difficult to identify those on our squad who were users. Our problem in weaning players away from steroids was that over the years they had developed a psychological dependency. They no longer felt they could compete without them. Much like the cocaine user, they had to be convinced that they could function normally and perform effectively without that crutch.

8

The First Breakthrough

Our first major breakthrough as a competitive NFL franchise was our 1980 opener in New Orleans.

The Saints were big favorites, and deservedly so. They'd never had a winning season, but that lack of success had given them high draft picks for several years, and they'd stockpiled some talented players, especially on offense—quarterback Archie Manning, running backs Chuck Muncie and Tony Galbreath, wide receiver Wes Chandler, tight end Henry Childs. Defensively, they had Derland Moore in the line, Joe Federspiel at linebacker, and Tom Myers at free safety, all of whom became Pro Bowl players during their careers.

The previous season, the Saints had reached .500, at 8–8, their best record ever, missing the playoffs by only one game. This year, they expected to make the playoffs, and they figured to get going with a win over the 49ers.

That the game was in New Orleans gave the Saints a big advantage. The 49ers had had a miserable road record, and were simply unable to win away from Candlestick.

During the '79 season, each time we played on the road, I lectured the team on playing well, but didn't emphasize winning. Realistically, I knew we had very little chance to win, but I thought it was important to play well, to prepare for the future. If I'd emphasized winning, our continual losses on the road would have been disastrous. Consequently, we played reasonably well on the road in '79, better than 49er teams had in the past. But we lost every game.

A squad doesn't become a quality team until it can win on the road against strong opposition before a hostile crowd. Playing in New Orleans was particularly difficult because of the noise level in the Superdome, due to the dome and the Saints' fanatical following. The game, of course, was a sellout. At practice the day before the game, we played rock music over the loudspeaker so players would become accustomed to such a high noise level and be able to block out the crowd. That worked well, and I later used the same practice technique before we played in our first Super Bowl in the Silverdome, another domed stadium in Pontiac, Michigan.

In our coaches meeting, we discussed how we could best motivate the team and deal with playing before such a loud, unfriendly crowd. As Paul Brown had said so many times, one of the most satisfying things in sports is to go into another city and see fans leaving early. When we could look up in the stands and see people filing out in the third quarter, we knew we had the game in hand.

The 49ers had been humiliated on the road for years. I told the team, now we had to stand and fight.

Well, that's exactly what happened that day. We stunned the Saints, 26–23. We were ahead all the way, but never by more than 3 points. The Saints tied the game with a field goal in the fourth quarter, but we came back with a field goal of our own to win it. It was a great feeling, to open the 1980 season by beating a good team on the road. It was a critical break. The next game was important because we beat the Cardinals in overtime in San Francisco, 24–21. Paul Hofer made the big play of the game, going 26 yards on a sweep to score the tying touchdown in the fourth quarter. Ray Wersching kicked the field goal to win it in overtime.

Next, we traveled to New York to play the Jets, and I told the team that if we were ever going to arrive, we had to win in New York, because it was the media capital of the country. We had to prove ourselves to the New York press. Just as in the '40s and '50s, when fighters weren't appreciated fully until they won in Madison Square Garden, a football team needed to win in New York for people to respect them.

Steve DeBerg, our quarterback, had laryngitis and lost his voice. We had experimented that week with several amplifier systems and finally found one that he could use, strapped to his back under his uniform. He spoke into a microphone and it came out of the speaker on his back. Naturally, the Jets were trying to destroy the amplifier the whole game. Fortunately, we had two of them, so when one was eventually damaged, we were able to replace it.

It was an incredible game. We led, 24–0, at one point in the first half, but we had so many injuries on defense, we barely had eleven men left to field a defensive unit. In fact, we had only three healthy defensive linemen. Trying to come from behind, Jets quarterback Richard Todd had to throw, and with our diminished defense, he had a great day statistically, completing 42 of 60 passes for 447 yards. Running back Clark Gaines caught 17 of those passes. The Jets scored three touchdowns in the final quarter. Todd's 42 completions are still a Jets' record, as are Gaines's 17 receptions. So, we allowed the Jets to set records, but we won the game, 37–27. After winning just two games in the 1979 season, we had started the season 3–0, and two of those wins had come on the road.

That day I also inserted Joe Montana into the game in specific situations near the goal line where he would have a good chance for success, with specially designed plays. The point was to give Joe a positive feeling and to enable him to take some pride in his progress as a quarterback. The strategy worked perfectly. Joe ran 5 yards for one touchdown, on a rollout where he had the option of running or throwing, and he threw for two more touchdowns, completing 4 of 6 passes.

Our marketing slogan that year was "Roaring Back!" and it looked great after three games. But we had suffered some critical blows, with a knee injury to Dwaine Board probably the most damaging to the team, and we didn't have the depth to overcome them. We went from a three-game winning streak to an eight-game losing streak that I thought would never end.

Our low point came against Dallas, the sixth game in the season. The Cowboys just poured it on, beating us up physically and mentally, 59–14, using trick plays and throwing the ball even when the game was long since over. The Cowboys were like that in those days, very contemptuous, and with fans who were just as cocky, taunting the visiting team when the Cowboys were on a roll.

Ironically, we had felt going into the game that we could play with the Cowboys, though they were the class of the NFC at the time. We had played them close the year before, and even after losing two games, we were 3–2. But they showed us just how far we still were from the upper strata of the league.

Those were most difficult days. When you're devastated like that, how can the public feel its team is ever going to be anything more than an embarrassment? How could we ever accumulate enough talent to be competitive? It seemed impossible, because everybody seemed so far ahead of us. I didn't see how I could last through four or five years of losing. Already fans and the media were losing faith. Our first three wins had given them some moments of hope and optimism, but now, the season had collapsed.

Throughout all this, Ed DeBartolo was very supportive of us. I think Eddie had almost conditioned himself to losing. Since he'd taken over the team, there had been one disaster after another, so he had to wonder if this was just NFL football.

That loss to Dallas was even more bitter because we also lost Paul Hofer to a serious knee injury. I feel bad about that because I may have made an error in judgment, bringing Paul back too fast from a knee sprain. When he reinjured his knee the next season, his career ended, far too early.

The game also virtually ended DeBerg's career with the 49ers, too, but for a much different reason. Steve had a terrible day against the Cowboys, the team that had originally drafted him, completing only 12 of 35 passes and throwing 5 interceptions. That game convinced me that I should start seriously considering the switch to Joe Montana. Joe started the next game against the Rams and, though we lost, played well, completing 21 of 37 for 252 yards. Joe started seven of the last ten games of the '80 season, including the three we won.

We made the decision to make Joe our starting quarterback, knowing that we might be limiting our chance of winning immediately. Steve had won some games and played well, but we had to find out if Joe, with his mobility, could make things happen for us. He proved that he could, so that was very important.

Joe had a spontaneity and excitement that invigorated everybody. Still, he didn't really gain a lot of self-confidence because he didn't have the talent around him to take advantage of the system. How was he to know that it wouldn't always be that way?

Joe's heart was really tested. Week after week, we would be on the short end of the score. Even if we put together a good drive, so often the other team would immediately come back to drive the length of the field, because we didn't have the defense to stop them.

Still, Joe was having some success, and he was learning the system. His statistics were solid, comparable to the better quarterbacks in the league. Playing in our ball-control passing offense, he completed 65 percent of his passes that year and threw for 15 touchdowns.

After the Dallas debacle, we recovered and were playing better football, coming close week after week—but still losing. Later in the season, we went down to Miami and played well. We were behind, 17–13, and had a good sustained drive. We kicked a field goal, but we were called for holding. We kicked another field goal but got penalized again. Then, we threw a pass that I thought would have given us a first down, but the placement of the ball left us inches short, so the Dolphins took over.

What I remember most of that game is that every time the officials made a call, Miami coach Don Shula would be on the sideline, yelling at the referee, and the officials would come over to explain the call to him. I couldn't get an audience before, after, or during the game. That was at a time when everybody thought that Shula had great influence with the officials. I could see that the officials figured the Dolphins were a power in the league and that the 49ers were just another team on the schedule.

That game reminded me of how little respect the league had for the 49ers. As if I needed the reminder.

On the long flight home, I sat alone, reflecting not only on this loss but on the fact that we had taken eight straight losses. After a 2–14 season with its frustrations, we now in our second year had lost eight in a row. In my solitude I started to break down. I felt that I had done an excellent job but questioned whether we could ever become competitive; maybe it would take someone else to get it done. It didn't work. I had no regrets.

Dealing with the press during that losing streak became very difficult. The same carping atmosphere that had characterized the Joe Thomas era surfaced again. I could understand that. For so many years, there had been frustration and disappointment, and now we were losing again. The writers had to write something. You can't keep telling the press that all is going well when you're losing every game.

Finally, we broke the drought, shutting out the Giants 12–0, at Candlestick. It was incredible. We had been one of the worst defensive teams in the NFL, but in this game we were able to effectively pressure the quarterback for the first time. We allowed the Giants only 51 net passing yards.

We followed that with an excellent game against New England, again at Candlestick. There was talk in New England that the Patriots would go to the Super Bowl, but we went head-to-head with them and defeated them, 21–17. That was proof we could beat a very good team, and one that had much more incentive to win than we did at that point. That loss by the Patriots actually kept them out of the playoffs because they finished a game behind Buffalo in the AFC East and, with a 10–6 record, didn't qualify as a wild card team.

Playing New Orleans for the second time that season was another really significant breakthrough because we finally managed to come back in a game. We had been unable to overcome a lead. If we trailed at halftime, that was it. That's typical of a team that not only doesn't have physical ability but lacks the necessary on-field character. We were being blown out, 35–7, at halftime of the game against the Saints at Candlestick. Our lone touchdown was a punt return by Fred Solomon. We had gained just 21 yards in the entire half. Joe Montana was 8–for–12, but only for 7 net yards, because he'd been sacked three times.

I felt terrible for our fans, because we had seemed to be playing well again, and then to see something like this was heartbreaking. We were emptying out the parking lots; there would be no postgame traffic jam at Candlestick that day. And those who left weren't listening to the game on the radio, either. Those who did stay were now calling for Steve DeBerg, which was a switch. Montana had been the fans' favorite, and it wasn't necessarily his fault that we were stumbling so badly. We just couldn't get anything going. I had gotten beyond the frustration stage; I was totally depressed when we left the field at halftime.

Of course, it wasn't just that we were playing poorly but that the Saints were playing so well; they'd accumulated 324 yards of total offense in the first half. Archie Manning was throwing beautifully, and Chuck Muncie was running well. Emotionally, they were at a peak because Dick Stanfel had just been named head coach, after Dick Nolan was fired. Stanfel, who was very popular with the players, had been an All-American in 1951 at the University of San Francisco, and now he was home. His family was in the stands, rooting for Dick and the Saints. I can imagine how his family must have felt with his team ahead, 35–7.

At halftime, as they passed by our locker room, the Saints players were pounding on the walls shouting, "Seventy points! Seventy points!," threatening to score as many points in the second half as they had in the first. At that point they weren't going to get any argument from our fans.

It's critical under stress to maintain your normal procedures and not disrupt the players further by desperate changes. We coaches concentrated on what we could do that would work, and analyzed the Saints' defense. It was a workmanlike and businesslike atmosphere, exchanging information and setting our plan.

There was no Knute Rockne type of inspirational pep talk. That's never been my style, and I'm not sure it was Rockne's, either. From what I know of Rockne, he was a taskmaster who depended on great players and execution, not speech making, for success. He probably didn't make more than three or four of those inspirational halftime speeches in his career, but that's part of his legend.

When we got the team together, I remarked that we would probably lose this game, but how were we going to lose it? Were we going to be tough or just cave in? Were we going to come back and play well and get back in sync and execute and get something out of the game, or were we going to lose by a huge score?

I told the players, "In the next thirty minutes, you're going to learn a lot about yourself. You'll have a better understanding about how you stand up to absolute adversity. You may like yourself, or you may not."

It was important to be as specific as possible as to what had happened in the previous thirty minutes and what had to be done in the next thirty. There was no value in blaming and threatening.

Then I added, "There is a chance that we can win this game. They will be overconfident and lose concentration. Looking at the Saints' history, that's likely. They'll begin to make mistakes and get sloppy. At the same time, we'll have to take advantage of every mistake they make. We have to play intense football and execute, and count on them self-destructing. We can't let them score again, and we're going to have to get in the end zone with almost every possession."

The second half didn't start well, either, as James Owens fumbled the kickoff on the goal line and could only get out to the twelve. But on the first play from scrimmage, Montana hit Dwight Clark for a 48-yard gain, and we went on to drive 88 yards for a touchdown.

Still, it was only 35–14. We had to stop them, and we did. Then Montana connected again with Clark on a 71-yard touchdown. Dwight cut back across the field, outmaneuvering and outrunning supposedly faster defensive backs; Owens made a great block to give him running room.

At that point, you could see the Saints begin to lose confidence. Though they were still ahead by two touchdowns, they acted almost as if they were behind. You could almost hear them thinking, "Here we go, we're going to lose again." Their history was against them.

On their next three possessions, the Saints fumbled away the ball twice, and had to punt the other time, after Manning had been sacked.

We scored after both fumbles, driving 83 yards and then 78. That was amazing, to have three long touchdown drives in one half. It was also amazing that we gained 409 yards in the half. Modern 49er history started there. That was really the first true indication of the explosive offense that would earmark our championship years, and the beginning of the Montana–Clark combination that was the key to our early success.

But during all this, there was a constant fear that New Orleans would make a big play again. It was almost like waiting for the other shoe to drop. Would our luck continue? Every time we stopped them, there was a tremendous feeling of excitement and relief on the sideline.

We finally tied the score, 35–35, and sent the game into overtime. The Saints moved the ball well on their first possession, until they had a third-and-seven on their own forty-five. Manning had one receiver running a short pattern to get the first down, but he thought he would surprise us by throwing deep. He didn't surprise Dwight Hicks, who intercepted the ball on our seven. Two series later, Ray Wersching kicked a field goal to win the game.

That's still the greatest comeback in NFL history, and it's unfortunate that so few people actually saw it. By the time we finally won the game, there were far more empty seats than full ones.

In my 49er coaching career, there were only two games that produced absolute euphoria—this one and the 1987 game at Cincinnati, when we scored on the very last play. When we drove nearly the length of the field to win the 1989 Super Bowl, it was a matter of execution, and I almost expected it. But to go from being absolutely embarrassed at halftime to a win in overtime was unbelievable.

That game was an excellent example of the importance of keeping your poise.

It was also important that we allowed for mistakes by the Saints. So often, when athletes are in the heat of battle, they fail to appreciate that the other team is also feeling that heat, experiencing the same apprehension and doubt. You must not defeat yourself.

At that point, though we were well below the .500 mark, we had reached some important milestones. We had won on the road, we had won in New York and, in fact, had beaten both New York teams, and now we had proved we could come back to win.

All these accomplishments were significant because our goal going into the season hadn't been so much to win as to gain respect for the way we played, as we built for the future.

There were other positive signs that year. In 1979, we had won just two games and lost five others by less than a touchdown, so theoretically, we had a chance to win seven games. In 1980, we won six games and had five others in which we lost by less than a touchdown, so there were eleven games we had a chance to win. And, we had bounced back from that horrendous midseason slump when we had consecutive blowouts, 48–26 by the Rams, 59–14 by the Cowboys.

After the Saints victory, we lost our last two games, to Atlanta and Buffalo, but the loss to the Bills was encouraging because it was only 18–13, against a division champion. On a muddy, miserable day, we played them evenly most of the way. A fumble by Earl Cooper on the Buffalo seven cost us a chance to win it. Earl had otherwise played beautifully.

We finished the roller-coaster season at 6–10. I was disappointed by the falloff in our offensive stats. Part of that was losing Paul Hofer; part was the result of other teams taking us more seriously. But, though we couldn't always appreciate it because of our frustration over close losses and injuries, we were laying some of the cornerstones for our future success.

Joe Montana had gained valuable experience and had played well enough that I was willing to trade Steve DeBerg. Steve continues to be a good quarterback, but Joe had more of the physical attributes we needed for our system.

At the same time, our offensive line was getting experience playing as a unit and would be a big factor in our later success. Fred Solomon and Dwight Clark were developing as receivers.

With all our frustration, the coaches as a staff still had come together. We had a solid coaching unit. And our ability to function as an organization was important. An attitude and environment had been established that enabled everybody to work together.

I can't say, though, that we recognized this at the time. We were working so hard to establish a competitive team that we weren't stopping to take bows.

After that season, the Philadelphia Eagles lost to the Oakland Raiders in the Super Bowl. I was very close to Dick Vermeil, the Eagles coach. Dick was from northern California, the Napa Valley, and we had both been assistants on John Ralston's staff at Stanford in the '60s. We had visited during Super Bowl week in New Orleans.

I had such high regard for Dick. He had accomplished one of the greatest coaching jobs in NFL history, taking a losing team and building it into a champion. But when I went down to the dressing room after the game, Dick was crushed. I couldn't understand that. I thought, "My God, you made it to the Super Bowl, you won the conference championship, you have a great team, how can you be emotionally devastated?"

Later, after we became a championship team, I remembered that incident and I understood exactly how Dick felt. But at that point, we were so far from being a contender. I was concerned that we would never get to 8–8, let alone to a Super Bowl.

It seemed as if we were still at the bottom of a very deep pit.

9

Building an Organization

I can distinctly recall driving to the 49er training facility in Redwood City for the first time. I readied myself for the seemingly awesome responsibilities I had just taken on. I reflected on the years I waited in frustration for this opportunity. Fortunately, as it turned out, I had been gaining invaluable experience. I was self-assured and confident and, for the first time, appreciated those years. As I parked and headed for the entrance, I reminded myself to have patience, let others do much of the talking, make this a study of people, and that it was going to take time.

Running a football franchise is not unlike running any other business: You start first with a structural format and basic philosophy and then find the people who can implement it.

In my case, I felt it was important to have control of all the football operations. At that time in the NFL, it was common for organizations to have a hierarchy that included an owner, a general manager, a head coach, and a personnel director. But with the 49ers in such disarray, I felt it was important to avoid management by committee.

The advantage of having a coach and a general manager is obvious: You have two people with clearly defined responsibilities who can concentrate on their individual areas of expertise. There's certainly enough work for two men.

In some cases, that division of labor has worked very well. Perhaps the best example would be the Dallas Cowboys from the mid-'60s to the mid-'80s. Tex Schramm as general manager and Tom Landry as coach collaborated successfully for a long time, and the Cowboys were the dominant team in the NFC for that period.

The disadvantage is that often the general manager and coach aren't compatible, a real problem because the two have to work together in difficult circumstances, through long periods of stress and sometimes frustration. The most important aspect of building and sustaining a sports franchise is the acquisition and development of talent. In this critical area, the two men can evaluate players' abilities and potential differently.

If the two differ, there can be delays, confusion, stalemate, and even chaos. For instance, the coach may feel he is in desperate need of an experienced offensive guard but the general manager thinks that the rookie just drafted should be put in the starting lineup. Or, the coach believes that a quick trade can be made for a specific running back who could start and have a real impact on the team. The general manager is less than enthusiastic because the running back has a history of minor injuries. In both cases, the general manager does not aggressively pursue the trade, yet reports to the coach that he is doing everything he can to complete the transaction. The coach senses the situation and the trouble begins. Conversely, the general manager may acquire players he feels are important to the team's future, but they are not developed as he anticipated because the coach doesn't want them, or doesn't have the same opinion of their value. These situations are fairly common in the NFL.

Each man's priorities can be diametrically opposed because of their roles and basic responsibilities. The general manager's first consideration is the economic bottom line: How much will it cost? He thinks of the team's long-term future, perhaps five years down the road. For him, winning in the current season may be secondary. The coach, for his own security, must emphasize winning immediately. Then, he thinks of the short-term future, which is the next season. Financial ramifications are his last concern, if he even thinks of them at all.

Often, too, you have an owner who dabbles in the team, demanding to be involved in some decisions but not in others. A potential conflict exists between a general manager who wants a methodical, functional style of management and an owner who impulsively wings it. When the owner is present, he takes over, but when he's absent, he expects everyone to carry on with their normal duties. This can result in hesitancy in management. For example, an owner might involve himself directly in a specific type of decision. The next time this type of decision comes up, the owner can't be reached, so the general manager can't decide whether to act himself or wait until he can contact the owner.

In recent years, the role of the personnel director has changed dramatically. Historically, he had been the chief scout and, with his small staff usually consisting of a secretary and two other men, would go about quietly evaluating college players and make his recommendations during the annual draft.

Today, it has become a subindustry. The personnel director will have two full-time secretaries, a personal aide, an NFL player scout, and a college scouting staff of six or seven men. Also, the club will contract with a national scouting combine.

With this newfound authority and visibility, the personnel director begins to play a major role, not only in evaluating future choices but in deciding whether or not those choices are being properly utilized or developed by the coaches. With daily access to the owner and general manager, he can remind them that his selections were great and blame the coaching for any disappointments. If one of his selections is not playing well, he convinces the owner and general manager that (1) the coach isn't utilizing the player properly; (2) the style of play doesn't make use of the player's talents; (3) the coaching staff simply isn't improving the player; and finally (4) team morale is so poor, no player could do well. The tail is wagging the dog because the scouting staff should be serving the needs of the coach, rather than the reverse.

The prospect of all four working together compatibly and effectively can be further compromised if any one of them craves public attention and needs to either take credit for the team's success or shift the blame if the team is losing. When the general manager or personnel director becomes the team's primary spokesman on football matters, it's an ominous sign for the coach.

When the team is out of contention, the general manager will say he's given the coach everything he needs to win, from talented players to superior facilities and proper accommodations on the road. The personnel director will say he's had excellent drafts for years. The owner complains that the stadium isn't full; for the money he's spending, he should be getting better results. He's embarrassed and humiliated because his friends seem to know more about the game than his coach does. He can't show his face in public.

Meanwhile, the coach is sequestered in his office, working into the early-morning hours, looking at game tapes, examining scouting reports thoroughly, worrying about injuries, putting together the game plan for the next Sunday. He's totally unaware that his fate is being decided by the owner, general manager, and personnel director over a nice dinner with an expensive bottle of wine in a fine restaurant.

The owner and executives will agree that the coach has many fine qualities. He's loyal and hard working, a good family man with high moral standards and loves his players. Then the owner will say something like, "I just don't understand why he went for the field goal instead of the touchdown in our last game." The others will nod in agreement, and they'll reluctantly decide that the coach isn't what they need to win on the field and draw at the gate.

This scenario repeats itself every three or four years with many NFL franchises. The media has a field day with it. Everybody is excited about the new coach and celebrates, and then the process begins again.

Teams that have had sustained success have had either the same coach and general manager for years, or a coach who has been the titular head of the organization and responsible for personnel moves and, in some cases, virtually *all* of the organizational decisions. Don Shula in Miami would be an example of a coach having primary authority. With the Raiders, Al Davis—a successful "hands-on" owner—has always had control of personnel, but he had very little turnover within the organization or with his coaches when the team was a champion.

Though the organizational structure of the Dolphins and Raiders is different, in each case there is one very capable dominant personality, so decision making is much simpler.

When decisions are made by committee, any one person in the chain who balks or who has trouble accepting others' conclusions, can obstruct the decision-making process. Individual animosities may develop, which can turn an objective discussion into a personal one. An atmosphere of quiet frustration can develop and the organization can't get off dead center. When a mistake has been made, or a miscalculation has occurred, or a decision doesn't bring the proper results, ego prevents people from admitting error. One of the major factors in successful leadership is the willingness to concede a miscalculation or mistake and change course immediately. Much of the San Francisco 49ers success in the '80s can be directly attributed to our decisiveness. When we recognized an error or miscalculation, we immediately took action to correct it and move in a different direction.

The stylish, graceful, accommodating, easy-going, affable, "players' coach," "he understands us," "he lets us decide what we need": That approach will get you up to 80 percent of the job done. The final 20 percent can be directly attributed to making tough decisions, demanding a high standard of performance, meeting expectations, paying attention to details, and "grabbing and shaking" when necessary.

In building the organization, I also stressed the importance of not making enemies. We didn't want to expend energy on anything other than the project at hand. We couldn't afford an enemy, whether it was NFL coaches and management, league employees, players, the press, college coaches, and local citizens. One enemy could do more damage than the good done by a hundred friends.

I continually stressed this to everybody, from coaches to front-office staff. We were doing business in the community, and I didn't want anyone in our organization offending people. That went for all our employees, whether they were answering telephones, accepting deliveries, selling tickets, or whatever.

As a team, the 49ers made every effort not to antagonize others. You didn't see the 49ers pouring it on or ridiculing other teams, and we tried to be as gracious as possible in defeat. It might have been natural for players to lash out in disappointment or gloat in victory, but we tried to avoid both those extremes.

In the stress of a season, coaches can often get on each other's nerves or step on each other's egos. I emphasized that they couldn't afford to differ for long. Ongoing dialogue just couldn't stop because coaches were sulking and avoiding each other. They would have to find a way to reestablish communication. There is a formula: You find a way to acknowledge something the other person has done, whether it's a project or decision, outside the original dispute. Don't expect to resolve philosophical differences with one conversation. You have to work at it. Be sensitive to each man's personality and find a way to account for it in your day-to-day work.

Nor did I want a schism with the press. If, for instance, Lowell

Cohn of the *San Francisco Chronicle* wrote a very critical column, I made an effort to have a personal conversation with him at our next meeting on an unrelated subject of mutual interest, such as boxing. It was important to keep our lines of communication open and remind ourselves of our respect for each other.

The point is not whether you're right or wrong. Even if you feel you're right and the other person is wrong, you have to make the effort to resume communication. You can't afford to let the dispute fester because the longer you wait, the more entrenched it becomes.

When I came to the 49ers, I had known beforehand that we had to totally change the organization's public image. As general manager in 1977 and '78, Joe Thomas had antagonized absolutely everybody, which reflected poorly on owner Ed DeBartolo, Jr. We hired two men who were key in changing this image, Ken Flower and R. C. Owens.

Under Thomas, the 49ers had disenfranchised all former 49ers. He wanted nothing to do with them; he had contempt for them. He wanted the 49er history and those who symbolized it to be forgotten, as if he were administering a brand-new franchise. We had to bridge the gap with fans and former 49er players, and R. C., who had been a legend on the 49er teams of the '50s as a wide receiver, was perfect in that role. Everybody likes R. C., who is a warm, gracious person.

A former star collegiate basketball player at USC, Flower was ideal for working with the community because he comes from a San Francisco family and is very popular and well respected in the city. It was vital to have Ken undo the damage that had been done to the 49er relationship with the citizenry, business community, and city government in San Francisco.

The important point is not only that we had to mend fences, but that we had to do it with very competent people like Flower and Owens, who could succeed because they were so well respected.

Monsignor Peter Armstrong served as personal counsel for everyone in the organization. He proved invaluable to Eddie DeBartolo, to me, and above all to the families of our squad members.

In a sense, everyone in the organization had to be educated in the dynamics of doing business. I knew we would have a long process of rebuilding, so we needed the support of everybody. As a result, the 49ers have come to be known as a class organization, as well as a championship team.

Throughout my ten years with the 49ers, Ed DeBartolo, Sr., with his wisdom and intuition, was a continuing source of counsel. He had a blend of patience and tough-mindedness that served as a standard in making the kind of decisions necessary to get the franchise off the ground and then to sustain our success. Men like Bill Moses and Paul Martha actively participated in 49er operations as requested by Ed Jr.

Through years of experience in the NFL, with men like Paul Brown, Tommy Prothro, and others, I was able to bring to the 49ers a philosophy broad enough to meet the challenge of a complete rebuilding job. There were certain qualities I was seeking in those we brought into the organization:

• I needed to feel comfortable with them, because I knew there would be difficult times, stressful times, when people can misunderstand each other. At such times, any little idiosyncrasy is magnified. Differences can become monumental if people are unable to have an open exchange on an ongoing basis.

   In critical management positions, you prefer to work with somebody you've known well or known of for a long time, so you can gauge how he'll react to the pressures of an intense, highly competitive atmosphere.

• I wanted functional intelligence, because I knew that one person who is not very bright but very aggressive in pushing his ideas can destroy an organization. He can steamroll others, so you waste time undoing the damage he's done.

• We needed knowledge and experience in the business dynamics of the National Football League. It takes many years to understand the NFL's operational procedures.

• I wanted people who would be enthusiastic and inquisitive, and who would thrive on work.

The first two men I hired in the front office, John Ralston and John McVay, had all these qualities.

John Ralston is a great organizer and a person who has an almost nonstop approach to work. We really needed that kind of personality in starting and establishing our new operation.

I had been on John's coaching staff at Stanford for three years, but we were friends for several years before that. I was his administrative assistant as well as coach at Stanford. He seemed to be a logical choice, because he had pursued an administrative position.

When we decided that I'd be general manager, John's role as chief of staff, so to speak, seemed a natural. He is a diligent man, and very good at working with people.

John could share his experiences with the Denver Broncos with me. He left the 49ers after a year to pursue other interests, but for that time he played an important role.

John McVay had had a shocking experience while coaching the New York Giants. In a game against Philadelphia, the Giants were leading with just a few seconds to go, when quarterback Joe Pisarcik tried a pitchout that resulted in a fumble. The Eagles ran it in for a touchdown to win the game. John refused to divert the blame for calling the play on the assistant coach involved. Somebody had to be the scapegoat for the loss and it was John.

In light of that play, John wanted to remove himself from the limelight for a while. John originally had worked in administration for the Giants and had accepted the Giants coaching job when Bill Arnsparger was released during the '76 season, so he seemed a natural for a managerial position. The aptitude he had shown for evaluating personnel with the Giants would be important in our own search for talent, because we knew we had so many weaknesses to address. With his warm, easy manner and attractive personality, he always got a good response from his associates, and I thought he would be a good choice for the job of personnel director.

When Ralston left, McVay took over his responsibilities. Together we handled all the administrative duties. Meanwhile, Tony Razzano, who had been one of our scouts, became head of college scouting, essentially replacing McVay. Tony is an excellent organizer and a dedicated professional.

John McVay has been an oustanding executive; he was named NFL "Executive of the Year" by his peers in 1990. He continues to demonstrate remarkable patience, resolve, and the wherewithal to negotiate successfully with player agents. He has been extremely effective in all the low-profile operational matters that are vital to ongoing success. Over a ten-year period, we worked together beautifully and remain close friends.

I also had definite prerequisites for the assistant coaching positions:

• He must have a complete working knowledge of the game, because the players respect that above everything else. Athletes can be coached in almost any style if they're confident that the coach really knows what he's doing. The players must know that the coach is up-to-date and contemporary in his approach and able to adjust quickly to the tactics of different opponents.

• Coaches must be able to effectively implement a program for each player that best develops his individual skills. Taking a personal interest in each of his players, regardless of their roles, is absolutely essential. If you combine that with expertise, a coach will fully develop the skills and effectiveness of the athletes.

• You must have people who can communicate well under the stress of a season, so you need the kind of personality that can work with others. There's a broad range in that area. Not everybody is ideally suited to working well with just anyone.

• The ability to express oneself is vital, because a logical, articulate person is best suited for teaching. If he can both impart what he knows to the player and deal with others under stress, he's your man.

• The coaching ethic of commitment and personal sacrifice is the basis of the job. There are some who just can't bring themselves to work a coach's long hours. By and large, those men have eliminated themselves by the time you get to the NFL level. It takes a person who can enthusiastically accept the values and philosophy of a head coach.

• The chemistry of the staff is vital. Everyone has his own distinct personality, so you must bring together a group of men who will not only work smoothly with the head coach but also with other coaches and with the players.

You can't assume that every staff will immediately work well together. If a coach is unable to meet some of the criteria you've established, changes have to be made. Sometimes, a head coach realizes that a good friend or associate does not meet the needs of the organization and has to be released. That's probably the most difficult decision a head coach must make.

The life of the assistant coach must be a labor of love. These are the men who have totally committed themselves to the game. The sacrifices in time and effort, the lack of long-term security, the relatively modest compensation, and in a sense obscurity can be equated only with a sincere dedication. It's almost a "calling."

Families bear much of the sacrifice. The coach is away for sustained periods of time working extremely long hours, and then he brings home the stress and tension of his work.

In a sense, the obscurity is a requirement of the job and, speaking from experience, this can be frustrating and repressive. In such a competitive, even volatile arena, a singular voice or symbol of control or command is necessary. An outspoken, openly vocal staff member can be very disruptive. An organization just can't function effectively when sending out mixed signals.

Only those who can adapt to public scrutiny survive in coaching. Most find very soon that being judged by others is an inherent part of the job. Once players, writers, the public, even other coaches identify a coach as being too sensitive or prone to becoming very uncomfortable when caught off guard or when under pressure, his effectiveness is dramatically compromised.

Football coaching is only for certain people. It may appear to be an exciting, adventurous existence. As a career it is often attractive to young assertive men who have the need for continuous satisfaction and gratification, and who enjoy a competitive arena. Often the young coach will be a very impetuous, aggressive individual who wants results with his career almost before he gets results with his team.

Coaches have to remind themselves that the gratification they get from their work should come from their day-to-day involvement, the process itself, and not so much from reaching a titled position with high visibility. The means itself should be more important than the ends. When it isn't, we see examples such as the high-school coach who so desperately wants to become a college coach that, throughout his high-school career, he never fully enjoys the players, the game, and the wonderful environment of education. A coach should celebrate because his players *are*, not because he has just won another game.

Or we see the young assistant college coach who feels surely destined to become a head coach and so will disdain any conscience or ethics, walking over his fellow coaches if necessary and bending or even breaking recruiting rules in order to receive recognition from his head coach.

Or the head coach who, under the pressure to win, will compromise everything. Players become objects, and he will manipulate them and everybody around him to survive, to satisfy his own personal needs.

I've always felt coaches should always appreciate the athletes and remind themselves that the game was not designed for him to orchestrate but for the athletes to participate. All too often the coach prefers to feel that the athlete will do anything for him. He is willing to ridicule the athlete and embarrass him in front of others. In fact, though, the athlete only tolerates the callous, self-centered coach so he can play the game.

The athlete plays because he thoroughly enjoys the game. He will tolerate almost any kind of treatment in order to participate and enjoy the camaraderie of his teammates. He will tolerate an overambitious coach who is thinking more of his career than his players. The coach thus may think he is the most important factor, but when he is more concerned with his own ambitions than his players' needs, he becomes dangerously irrelevant. By doing this, he hurts himself. This type of coach will unfortunately not be at his best regarding improving the athletes, even though he may be a gifted, knowledgeable coach, because he is thinking of his own career, and that is given priority over the athletes and the day-to-day satisfaction that should be part of being a coach.

You'll see coaches who are quite prominent early in their careers, only to disappear when they should be at their best. These are the coaches who depended so much on rhetoric and dialogue and buzz words, or how many times they had been in the audience with certain people, and on what kind of impression they gave to people, instead of developing their knowledge and expertise and skills.

The coach who does develop his skills will become important to people, who will want to work with him to develop a winning program. The coach who fails to do so will hit a brick wall at age forty, when he'll be replaced by a man who is younger and knows all the new buzz words.

If after completing a season a coach can look back with pride on the progress made by individual players and on his team collectively playing to the full potential, he can justify the sacrifices he made. The game must have a redeeming value. It isn't simply a vehicle for enhancing the coach's image. Being titled "genius," becoming quotable, and indulging the public with zany antics take the coach and everyone with him to a dead end.

The assistant coach who tends to be impetuous, emotional, and involved can fail to appreciate the positive dynamics of the game. I was one. So were Sam Wyche and Paul Hackett. In all three of our cases, we were in the center of the action but not able to express ourselves in a significant way publicly, and we may have even resented it. All three of us broke the "code" on occasion and it was damaging. Paul Brown handled me okay and I think I tempered Sam and Paul. With experience and seasoning, all three of us have found peace within ourselves.

One man who handled this circumstance as well as anyone was Denny Green. He was always possessed of a serene maturity that transcended these pitfalls. Denny joined the 49ers after working with me for two years at Stanford. He returned to Stanford as offensive coordinator the next season—and I didn't take any more coaches from the staff because I didn't want to decimate it. George Seifert joined the 49ers as a defensive backfield coach in 1980, after staying one more year at Stanford.

Norb Hecker also joined me from Stanford and was invaluable. He had been both an assistant coach with the Packers and a head coach with Atlanta. His experience with Vince Lombardi and as a former head coach provided a source of wisdom.

My key selection, though, was defensive coordinator. As I saw it, there were three areas of responsibility I was confident I could handle with good support: head coach, offensive coordinator, and chief administrative officer. I was well aware that I had neither the time nor the working knowledge to direct the defense. Consequently, my number one priority in putting together the entire organization was hiring the right defensive coordinator, because if I made a mistake there, it could have been disastrous.

Chuck Studley and I had worked together and had become very close friends when we were with the Cincinnati Bengals. Over the years, as we drove to work together, we continually discussed football. During that time, I gained great appreciation for Chuck's knowledge of the game and his organizational abilities. I always had respect for Chuck as a teacher. He didn't take much convincing. Chuck was excited about being a defensive coordinator, and joining me in California would be a real adventure for him and his family.

He did a fine job for us under very difficult circumstances. He took the brunt of the criticism in the early years because, without quality NFL talent, he still had to put together a defense. It was destined to do poorly because he didn't have the personnel or the time to develop a competitive unit.

Chuck had to work with constant turnover, and he had to deal with some outstanding offensive teams, such as the Dallas Cowboys and Los Angeles Rams. We would often play well early and we'd be very excited, but inevitably, there would be breakdowns later in the game that would cost us. We didn't have team speed or dominating players, so we were at the mercy of other teams who would come up with a big play or a sustained drive that we just couldn't stop.

With excellent contributions by Bill McPherson, Norb Hecker, and Ray Rhodes, Chuck established a solid defensive system. When we acquired defensive backs Ronnie Lott, Eric Wright, and Carlton Williamson in the '81 draft, and also added veterans Jack Reynolds and Fred Dean (after picking up Dwight Hicks, Dwaine Board, and Keena Turner the previous year), we were able to play dynamic, inspired defense week after week in '81.

Chuck departed for Houston following the 1982 season, becoming head coach later that year. With our complete defensive system in place, it was crucial for me to replace him with somebody on the staff. Continuity at that time was extremely important.

I had to make a tough decision between two outstanding men, George Seifert, our defensive backfield coach, and Bill McPherson, our defensive-line coach. Both had all the qualifications and were well suited for the position.

I named George because of the absolute importance of the defensive backfield. The secondary play and pass defense and the development of pass coverage were critical. If any weakness in our defense existed under Chuck Studley, I felt it was in pass defense and the development of coverages related to the nickel defensive package. Chuck had concentrated more on stopping the run, because he had originally been a defensive-line coach.

So, it was decided that Bill would concentrate on the job of stopping the run and George would concentrate on pass defense. Ray Rhodes was given the important job of defensive backfield coach without a lot of experience, and he's done an outstanding job since.

Bill, being the man he is, adjusted very quickly despite his disappointment, and we developed one of the finest defensive staffs in the NFL.

George Seifert had had just two years of experience in the NFL before becoming defensive coordinator because his previous career was at the college level. He was an excellent technician and taskmaster. He had a gifted mind and was extremely well organized.

George had a unique aptitude for the technical aspects of the game. He was not a light, quick-witted, amusing type of coach but a very demanding, no-nonsense, business-oriented man who quickly got the respect of players because of his expertise and concentration, and his willingness to work long hours. That wore people out, but it proved to be very successful. There were endless meetings with George and the players, but he put together a style of defense that was fully dimensional with a flexibility that enabled it to deal effectively with new and varied offenses. George's defenses were often a step ahead of everybody.

One of the absolute keys to defense is personnel, and I was continually involved in acquiring players. If you look at our drafts, you'll find that we usually concentrated on defense. With my style of offense, I felt we could move the ball with less talented personnel, as we did in '79, but we needed defensive players.

I also was involved with defense approach and philosophy, and with player substitution and overall game strategy. During the game, I concentrated on our fourth-quarter strategy. During the week, it was very important that we coordinate defensive and offensive game plans. I would ask George how he wanted to plan the game. Then, I would tell him how many points we anticipated and how many first downs we would register in the process. As an example, if George was wary of an opponent's quick-strike ability, our offensive game plan would emphasize ball control. If the opponent was a ball-control team, George would design a higher-risk defense to get the ball back as quickly as possible.

Because of the emphasis on a highly sophisticated pass offense, our quarterback coach's role was much more prominent than with most teams. We had some good ones, starting with Sam Wyche.

I had coached Sam as a quarterback with the Bengals. He was a good athlete but not a gifted one. He was a tenacious competitor, extremely bright, and directed his team very well, though he possessed just a fair arm.

While I was coaching Sam, we found that our personalities were compatible. Although there was no question he'd be successful in any career, it seemed to me that coaching was a natural for him.

When he left football, he and some friends started up Sam Wyche Sports World, a profitable sporting-goods operation, with nine stores throughout the Southeast. I twice tried to get Sam into coaching, first when Mike White became head coach at Cal in 1972 and later when I became head coach at Stanford in 1977. Sam gave both offers a lot of thought. He decided that he was too involved with his business to make a change, but he told me that he eventually wanted to coach.

So, when I was hired by the 49ers, I called again, and this time Sam joined me enthusiastically. He had no coaching experience, but I didn't doubt that he could be successful if he put his mind to it. Sam adapted quickly and soon became extremely effective. He was important to the early success of our passing game.

If I could identify one person who played the biggest role in the development of Joe Montana, it was Sam; I think Joe would agree.

We agreed philosophically, and he absorbed my system of football well. Since I had coached Sam earlier, he naturally adopted much of my coaching style.

I knew Sam was intelligent and had a feel for the game, and I soon realized that he had the most creative and innovative football mind I'd ever seen in a coach at that stage of his career.

It didn't take Sam long to have his own ideas, or to express them. I don't remember arguments as such, but I can recall times when he was frustrated because I didn't agree with his thinking, and he'd share that frustration with the press. That was especially true in 1982 when he could see mistakes I'd made, which was not very hard to do that year.

But his biggest frustration as a 49ers coach was probably a tennis match he lost to me at training camp. It was a hundred degrees that day and we had just completed two practices. Our match went on and on. We were both exhausted, but neither of us would quit until I finally won the final set, 16–14. He didn't know it, but I was ready to quit if the match had gone another point because I had begun to hallucinate. He went storming off the court, and it wasn't an act. We stared straight ahead and didn't speak to each other the entire ride back to Sierra College.

Sam has always had an impetuous personality. In a sense, that's a strength, but people have to adjust to it. We've had a marvelous and lasting relationship. Sam has had to understand me, and I've had to understand Sam.

Being so creative and adventurous and motivated, Sam felt he was ready to be a head coach after only three years. I understood his ambition and I knew he wouldn't be able to last for many years as an assistant. When he got an opportunity to coach on the college level, at Indiana, I told him he wouldn't be happy for long as an assistant, that he'd flourish as a head coach.

So, he went to Indiana and after just one year there, he was hired by the Bengals as their head coach. Just six years after he left the 49ers, we coached against each other in the Super Bowl.

Paul Hackett was similar in many ways to Sam. He was extremely bright and well read. Paul had had a long tenure as an assistant coach at the major college level. Mike White hired him at Cal in 1972 when he was twenty-five, so he'd had quite a bit of experience when he came to us, even though he was still very young.

Like Sam, he was impetuous and aggressive, and very ambitious. He needed visibility and thrived on attention. Once you got past that, he was bright, knowledgeable, and totally dedicated. I've never met a man who thrived more on the game.

Paul, in a sense, had been a student of mine for many years. When he was a Cal assistant, he'd traveled all the way to Cincinnati to visit our training camp.

He was an unusual talent, with a real feel for our style of football, to which he adapted quickly.

Because he was eager to become a head coach, Paul could not stay anywhere long as an assistant. Before coming to the 49ers, he had gone successively from Cal to USC to Cleveland, and was with Dallas after leaving us. Paul seemed to think that an advancement by degree of responsibility meant he was moving toward getting his head coaching job.

Since then, he's achieved his goal by becoming head coach at the University of Pittsburgh. Through all of this, I think he's become one of the top coaches in the country and has a great career ahead of him.

He was enthusiastic and had a youthful, dynamic approach with our players, though he had some problems with staff members because he was so self-oriented. Some other coaches had questioned how long Paul would stay. He was so driven that he hadn't been able to stop and "smell the roses."

Paul also contributed on the technical end. He developed a close relationship with Joe Montana, and helped Joe's development. Of course, there are probably seven or eight people who will step forward and say, "I developed Joe Montana." We'll be hearing from them for some time.

When Paul left, Denny Green joined us from Northwestern. He had done a courageous job there. It was a hopeless situation. The school was obligated to remain in the Big Ten, because they could reap television and bowl income as long as they could field a football team. That enabled Northwestern to finance its athletic program, which was admirable, but the university never gave the football program the support it needed to be competitive.

Northwestern has high admission standards, but that wasn't the main problem. Stanford has even higher standards, but while Stanford has been able to field competitive football teams in the Pacific Ten, Northwestern has gone into the doldrums. That's the result of administrative priorities, not entrance requirements.

Denny was "Coach of the Year" in the conference one season because of some upset wins. But I could see that he was struggling to survive, while handling the added burden of being the only black coach of a major college football team. Each year when we visited I could see that he was becoming more and more exasperated. He thought that if he left, he would be giving up, but I convinced him it was an impossible situation and invited him to join our staff.

Denny was hired to coach the receivers and was given the responsibility for the passing game. Soon thereafter, I hired Mike Holmgren from BYU to coach the quarterbacks.

In a sense, Denny began to serve as offensive coordinator. He did a beautiful job. Denny is one of the brightest and most capable coaches in the game, extremely well organized and a fine motivator. Among all our coaches, he would rank right at the top. He did an excellent job of directing the offense.

In that period, Mike was quickly learning the offense and did a capable job of working with Joe Montana and the other quarterbacks. His style, in contrast to our previous quarterback coaches, was quiet and subdued.

The head coaching job at Stanford became available late in our 1988 season, and Denny Green was the ideal man for the job, which is why I recommended him. I realized that this could be a distraction for our team at such a critical point in the season, but this was a great career opportunity for Denny and he had my full support.

When Denny accepted the Stanford position, Mike was thrust into Denny's shoes for the last weeks of the season. He demonstrated his ability to take command, showing true executive leadership. The next year he was named offensive coordinator, and he did an outstanding job for the 49ers.

I take great pride that four of my offensive assistants—Wyche, Green, Hackett, and Rod Dowhower at Stanford—have become head coaches. They had a great impact on my career, and I like to think I had the same on theirs.

There were many who felt that the members of our coaching staff were the best in the game throughout the '80s. I felt our staff did the most effective job developing talent and skills and orchestrating players into a precisionlike football team. Among those who have made significant contributions were black coaches who I personally attracted to our organization. Over the years I have been sensitive to inequities and the difficulty they've had in being included in the established coaching fraternity.

We hadn't felt limited to only attract those with whom we were well-acquainted or with those who had the best contacts. We had simply sought the best coaches available. Men such as Milt Jackson, Billie Matthews, Ray Rhodes, Tommy Hart, Denny Green, Sherm Lewis, Al Lavan—these individuals had done a most notable job, and without any one of them we may not have been the team of the '80s.

To introduce more men with these considerable talents to the NFL, we initiated in 1987 a fellowship program for minority coaches. This program was directed at men who were coaching at the major college level. They spent three full weeks working with the 49ers at our Rocklin, California, training camp. They were involved with coaching first-year players and were included in all coaching-staff meetings and related activities. Thus, they became familiar with the NFL, were exposed to football as taught at the professional level, and further refined their own coaching skills. This program served to identify those coaches with the potential to become part of the NFL as an assistant and ultimately as a head coach.

There were some difficulties in establishing a program of this kind on a league-wide basis. I presented this concept to fellow members of the NFL competition committee during a spring meeting of 1987, and it was not readily accepted because there was another Black Coaches program in place. But I felt the 49er Fellowship Program directly addressed the issue of minority opportunity. Those men, best suited to ultimately become head coaches in the NFL would be former athletes who had received extensive educational preparation and who were now employed by such schools as UCLA, Ohio State, or Penn State. They would be the aggressive, talented, dynamic, ambitious young coaches looking at unlimited futures.

Since that time, a number of men have passed through our fellowship program and are now coaching in the NFL. This model program has since been adopted by the entire National Football League.

10

Drafting for Success

We went into the 1981 draft knowing exactly what we needed: defensive backs. Strictly speaking, we needed help everywhere on defense, but the defensive backfield was the most critical area. We had one legitimate NFL player, free safety Dwight Hicks.

So, our first five picks were: Ronnie Lott, John Harty, Eric Wright, Carlton Williamson, and Lynn Thomas. Except for Harty, a defensive tackle who never developed his full potential because of serious foot injuries, the picks were all defensive backs, as we had anticipated.

Concentrating on one area in the draft was unusual. Most teams would have taken a couple of defensive backs and then tried to plug some of their other holes as well. But we were desperate. Nothing is quite so discouraging to a team as knowing that no lead is safe because the other team can score so quickly through the air. We remembered that lesson well from our 1980 game against the Jets.

We had won a three-way coin flip with Cincinnati and Washington, who had matched our 6–10 record the previous year, so we were drafting eighth in the first round. At that spot, I thought I knew who we could get: Kenny Easley, the great safety from UCLA. He wanted us as much as we wanted him. He wanted to stay in California, and his agent, Leigh Steinberg, sent telegrams to the teams ahead of us warning them that Easley would not play for them, advising them not to waste a draft choice.

I spent considerable time studying film of Easley before the 1981 draft. He and Lott were clearly the class of the defensive backs, but I had discounted the possibility that Lott would be available by the time we drafted.

But, no matter how much you plan and how much you try to predict what other teams will do, there are surprises. Seattle called Steinberg's bluff and took Easley before our turn came, which meant that Lott would be available.

Though we hadn't given Ronnie much consideration because we were sure he would be gone, when he became available, there was no question who we would take. He was a truly great player. Easley became a Pro Bowl player for Seattle before a kidney injury prematurely ended his career, but Lott has played up to Hall of Fame standards for the 49ers, first as a cornerback and then as a free safety. Most people in football regard him as the best free safety in the game's history.

Our pick of Missouri's Eric Wright in the second round probably surprised some people. Eric had played safety in college and some teams thought he couldn't play corner, but our staff had the advantage of coaching him in the Senior Bowl, so we had a better chance to project how he would adapt to the change of position. George Seifert, then our defensive backfield coach, was very high on Eric.

In the third and fifth round, we took college teammates from Pitt, Williamson and Thomas. Carlton had a reputation as a really physical player, and we sorely needed somebody who could come up with the big hit. We had him listed behind Easley as the best strong safety in college football, in contrast with some other scouting reports. Thomas was to play well at cornerback in his first and only year in the league.

Most important to me was that all of these players had been in successful college programs. Lott came from USC, which is consistently a national power. Pittsburgh was a strong team, and Wright's Missouri team had been to a bowl game. Plus, Dwight Hicks, whom we had signed as a free agent to play safety, had played on Michigan's Rose Bowl team. They were all accustomed to playing pressure games before huge crowds, so they would have a better chance of adapting to NFL football than players from lesser programs.

That draft truly set the stage for our success, but there were others that were memorable, too:

• **1980.**   This was the first time I had had a first-round draft pick because the previous year's pick had been traded away for O. J. Simpson. Potentially this was the very first pick, because we had tied Detroit for the worst record, 2–14.

But the Lions won the coin flip and selected Billy Sims, the Heisman Trophy winner from Oklahoma. We would have done the same. It would have been impossible to pass up Sims. He was a great runner and probably would have been in the Hall of Fame if he hadn't injured his knee later in his career.

Since we had lost our chance to get Sims, I had to weigh getting an "impact" player with our pick or trading it for two other picks. The idea of trading appealed to me because a big gap existed between Sims and everybody else in the draft that year, so I traded with the New York Jets for their later first-round picks, thirteenth and twentieth overall.

This was our first experience in trading draft choices. It provided a procedure for later years, when it became a regular part of our draft philosophy. The Jets drafted Johnny "Lam" Jones, a very fast man who because of injuries never developed into a top receiver. Years later, after he'd bounced around the league, we actually traded for him, but he couldn't make it.

We drafted fullback Earl Cooper and defensive end Jim Stuckey with our two picks. Neither was to become a Hall of Fame candidate, but they immediately strengthened our squad and were starters on our 1981 World Championship team. Jim and Earl played the best games of their NFL careers in Super Bowl XVI. Both were simply outstanding. They were major contributors throughout the 1981 season. Without either one of them, we could not have made such strides, and I doubt we would have become world champions.

One of the most important picks we were to make was in 1980 with the selection of Keena Turner, a linebacker from Purdue. This man not only became one of the best linebackers of the eighties but he proved to be our single most dynamic leader on the team over a ten-year span. He set a standard on the field through performance and quietly and firmly influenced his teammates off the field. Keena possessed a serene maturity that epitomized the personality of the 49ers.

• **1985.**   We were drafting last in 1985 because we'd just won the Super Bowl. We were solid and strong at virtually every position. When you reach that point, your only chance for measurable improvement is to acquire a true impact player. When at the very top, you must be bold. It is not the time to be conservative. You have to act.

On occasion, teams get lucky—Miami drafted Dan Marino with the twenty-seventh pick in the first round in 1983—but realistically, our only chance to get an impact player that year would be through a major trade.

There was one position that concerned me: wide receiver. Fred Solomon had been a great player for us, but his hamstring injury was being continually aggravated, and maybe he had lost a step. There were three great college receivers in the draft that year—Eddie Brown, Al Toon, and Jerry Rice—but it was logical to assume they would be gone before our pick.

Intriguing stories had been coming out of Mississippi about a phenomenal young receiver who was becoming almost a legend. As a junior, he had caught over 100 passes and was shattering records again this season. I really hadn't paid much attention to his name or to the school until we arrived in Houston on October 21 to play the Oilers in our eighth game.

As usual on the night before a game, I was in my hotel room watching television to learn the college scores. It was near midnight and I was beginning to doze off when I heard the sportscaster say, "Following this break, we have some incredible highlights of Jerry Rice and the Mississippi Valley State game." That caught my attention and I sat up to take a look at this "living legend."

It was quite a show. I believe Jerry caught 4 or 5 touchdown passes, in each case, running more than 50 yards. His explosive movement, his fluid strides and great hands were spectacular. God, what a player! Having spent my life working with pass receivers, I had never seen anything like him.

When it was over, I turned off the lights and as my mind returned to the next day's game, I distinctly remember picturing what it would be like to have Joe Montana throwing to this kid. But then reality hit. I reminded myself there wasn't a chance. We were en route to having a great year so once again, we'd be drafting very late.

Not everybody in our organization believed Rice was a top-flight prospect. In fact, one of our most prominent scouts thought he was no better than a sixth-round pick. Some thought he lacked the really blazing speed we wanted, that he would be no better than 4.6 in the forty. What they overlooked—as scouts also did with Dwight Clark—was his "functional" speed, when running with the football.

Players have historically been timed for 40 yards, but what's really important for a receiver is his speed when he's in full stride, from 30 to 60 yards. Two of our greatest receivers, Rice and Clark, were not known for their speed before they came to the 49ers, but once they got open, they couldn't be caught. Dwight demonstrated good speed, and Jerry demonstrated outstanding speed.

When I saw Rice on television, I had thought, if we could ever get a man like that, we could do so much more. We could get him downfield and challenge the free safety, and that would give our offense another dimension.

But, how could we get him? At that point, I had some serious misgivings about the NFL draft system, because teams that continued to flounder had access to the best players year after year. In a sense, players as talented as Rice were wasted, because they never got a chance to play for the most successful teams.

I felt Jerry was worthy of being one of the first five picks, and it was extremely unlikely that we could trade up that high. But other teams seemed to be looking more at his forty times than his performance, and he was passed over early. I got excited again, because I thought, "Now, we might just have a chance at him."

In the days preceding the draft, as he did every year, John McVay called every team in the league that we felt might consider a draft-day trade. People listened, but nothing serious developed until the night before the draft. At that point, Dick Steinberg of New England said they might be interested in our offer of our first- and second-round picks for their first pick, sixteenth in the draft, and we agreed to discuss finalizing the trade the next day.

The next morning, as the draft proceeded, we reached agreement and found ourselves with New England's pick, with which we immediately drafted Rice. Of all the picks we've made, this was the one that truly excited me because I was so involved personally. I'd become so obsessed with Rice because he'd made such a striking impression on me. We'd completed the bold stroke to get the impact player we needed.

• **1986.** When people talk of great drafts, it's usually a team that drafted very high and was able to acquire great players early. We didn't have that advantage in 1986, drafting eighteenth on the first round. To make it worse, we had only eight choices, so I had to scramble to make the best use of our limited opportunities.

We had evaluated the players who would be available to us in our first-round pick and quickly concluded that there was little difference between them and players we could pick up later in the second round, or even further down. So, I decided I would trade that pick to get more selections in later rounds, and eventually, through trading we acquired fourteen picks.

Because of our history of draft trades, we naturally received calls each year from everyone considering a move of some kind. John McVay was on the phone continuously in the days preceding the draft, discussing possibilities and documenting them. We then knew what our options might be.

After meeting with scouts, we concluded that though there were few truly outstanding candidates in the draft, many were still capable of becoming viable NFL players. By the morning of the draft, our strategy was set: We were going to go for numbers.

Once it got underway, it really got quite frantic. The atmosphere was like the commodity market. Sometimes, John would have a phone at each ear.

On a special board, we listed and prioritized those players we felt would be good picks for San Francisco in each given round. As the draft progressed, the men on our list were not coming off the board. This didn't cause us to doubt our evaluations. It simply meant that we could continue trading backward to acquire that many more of our prospects.

Naturally, each of us had players we particularly liked. Fullback Tom Rathman, linebacker Charles Haley, defensive end Kevin Fagan, and offensive tackle Steve Wallace were at the top of my list. In our trading, I wanted to be assured that enough choices would be available to pick men like these.

If we had kept our first-round pick, Larry Roberts, a defensive end from Alabama, was one of those we might have selected. We felt that Larry could become an outstanding pass rusher. As the draft progressed, men on our list just weren't being chosen, so it appeared that Larry—or one of those we'd projected as a first-round pick—would still be on the board well into the second round. And, in fact, we picked Roberts then.

The same scenario kept unfolding throughout the day. With so many players in the same rating category, each team was working from its own evaluations. At one point, the trading process became more important than the talent. We knew good athletes would be there and so were working to acquire as many choices as possible. We were in such a trading frenzy for a time that I couldn't have said exactly how many choices we had.

Finally, I turned to the others in the draft room and said, "Now, it's time to get to work." John McVay nodded approval.

Overall, we made six trades and didn't start picking until late in the second round. But when we finally did start, we got, in order, Roberts, Rathman, cornerback Tim McKyer, wide receiver John Taylor, Haley, Wallace, Fagan, and cornerback Don Griffin. All have been topflight players since then and played important roles on two Super Bowl championships.

In addition, we traded reserve quarterback Matt Cavanaugh to the Philadelphia Eagles for a second-round pick in the next draft, in addition to a third-round choice in the '86 draft, used to acquire McKyer. With the 1987 second-round pick, we drafted offensive guard Jeff Bregel from USC, who started until a back injury required surgery in 1989. And I was also able to trade our second-round pick in '86 for Washington's first-round pick the next season, with which we got Terrence Flagler, a bright prospect as a running back later traded because he got restless in his role as Roger Craig's backup.

There was some risk in the Cavanaugh trade because we gave up a solid backup, but I had a man in mind to replace him, Jeff Kemp. We acquired Kemp in a trade with the Los Angeles Rams later on draft day.

We also traded a second-round choice for Washington's first-round choice in 1987, assuring us of future draft strength. Rarely are these kinds of trades made, because too often, people in professional sports think only of the short term.

Teams spend so much time and money to prepare for the draft, they want to see immediate results. All year, there's talk of how picks will come in and immediately improve the team. If it doesn't happen, everyone is disappointed.

We could make these decisions because we had developed a successful franchise and could look toward the future, and we had owner Ed DeBartolo's complete confidence.

Considering our draft position, that the draft was weak, and that we started with only eight picks, the '86 draft may have been the best of the '80s. Certainly, it was the best we had when I was with the 49ers.

There are often disappointments in the draft because people put too much emphasis on the jump-reach, bench press, and forty-yard sprint, using the simplest evaluations. In a sense, that protects scouts because they don't have to make subjective judgments. They can't be blamed if a player who rates high in these categories doesn't make it; it's the coach's fault for not developing the athlete.

We tried to evaluate players on how they functioned on the field, not on whether they matched some arbitrary standard. We had our own criteria and didn't worry about others'. Much of that philosophy could be traced back to my own experience. For years, Paul Brown never gave much credence to artificial tests.

Why are players timed for 40 yards? That's just the way it's done. It's the old school. The norms have been established through the years, and they're used to compare one player with another.

The Dallas Cowboys reinforced that philosophy, because they had rigid physical standards that players had to meet; if they didn't meet those standards, the Cowboys wouldn't draft them. And, of course, the Cowboys were very successful over a twenty-year period.

A lot of self-promotion emanated from the Cowboys' personnel department about their superior scouting system and draft decisions. Whenever a free agent made the team, it would be credited to scouting, not coaching.

I believe the major reason for their success was a great job of coaching by Tom Landry and his staff.

We tried to look beyond the obvious. For instance, Roger Craig and Tom Rathman both had the reputation of being unable to catch the ball when they were in college, but that was because Nebraska had a run-oriented offense and never threw to the backs. We worked them both out before the draft and satisfied ourselves that they could catch, and they both became dangerous receivers out of the backfield. Tom's 4.7 time in the forty would not have met the standards established by other NFL teams—further proof that the forty shouldn't be the only basis for evaluating a player.

We didn't consciously try to be different, to separate ourselves from other teams. We just did what, in our judgment, would best meet our needs.

My tactics on draft day varied, but the overall goal remained the same: to improve the team. The three constants in every draft were: (1) philosophy; (2) very, very thorough preparation; and (3) an atmosphere among coaches and scouts conducive to making the best decisions.

Philosophy first. Most teams eliminate prospects; if an athlete doesn't meet their physical specifications, which might be speed for a defensive back or size for an offensive tackle, they won't draft that man. Their first question in evaluating a player might be, "Could he ultimately start in the NFL?"

In contrast, our scouts and coaches were encouraged to ask themselves, "What can this man specifically do that can help the Forty-Niners?" It might be covering kicks, returning punts, or being able to substitute at more than one position, as, for instance, offensive center and guard, or defensive safety and corner. Our question was: "Is there one redeeming thing that this man can do that would improve the Forty-Niners?"

We wouldn't be necessarily thinking of this man as a standout, just as a player who could help us in some category. Consequently, we drafted prospects who might be marginal replacements for other players. They weren't expected to start or be Pro Bowl players, but they added to our depth.

Obviously, there are some players with the potential to become superstars, but they are rare. All too often, teams would look for potential superstars and overlook players they regarded as "journeymen." We never used that term. We just looked for players who could play, in whatever category.

Two cliches are universally repeated by scouts: "He's just good enough to get you beat," and "He's someone you'll always want to replace." We would say, "Is there anything he can do that would improve the Forty-Niners?"

It was important that our scouts realized what we needed at each position because our system of football often had different physical requirements from those of other teams. As examples, Dwight Clark or even Joe Montana could flourish in our system and not necessarily meet the requirements elsewhere. Dwaine Board wasn't as bulky as other defensive linemen but he performed extremely well in our system.

Though public attention is focused primarily on the days the draft is held, the process is an ongoing, evolving one that really lasts year-round, with area scouts visiting virtually every school in the nation.

To save on the monumental costs of scouting, clubs have joined together and contracted with scouting companies. The two groups that currently provide necessary information are Blesto and United. At this writing, there are only three teams who do not participate in this process.

In theory, the advantage of a combine is that more scouts can be employed and, thus, teams get more reports. I'm sure there are some very good scouts involved, but often the reports were too general and too vague. So we dispensed with combines and went to a specialized system with a larger scouting staff than other teams, and ones who had been with us for many years. They would be assigned different areas of the country, with cross-checks, so we'd get at least two opinions on every player going into the draft.

Tony Razzano attempted to see the top players nationwide, so we would have a further evaluation. We'd come into the draft with reports on each player from his junior and senior year, plus spring practice, and film documentation of at least four games, and more likely six.

During that time period in which they were evaluated, the criteria would obviously include height and weight, and results from specific physical tests such as the 40-yard speed and jump-reach. For linemen, strength tests such as the bench press would be emphasized. A physical history of the athlete would also be included, with considerable attention given to history of injury.

To assure a full measure of communication between all athletes, black and white, Dr. Harry Edwards, professor of sociology at the University of California at Berkeley, joined our organization to serve as a counselor and personal consultant. He and I formulated a test, a profile of athletes that told us how they'd respond to different methods of teaching, to the utilization of specific teaching tools. This test also indicated how an athlete responded to teammates and direction, what kind of commitment he had developed with his peers, and what his priorities were in education, sports, material desires, and personal relationships.

No, we didn't sit players down in a classroom. The "testing" was done casually. A coach would sit with a player at a meal and ask him questions in a relaxed conversation, so the player would be open and honest in his responses. We would discuss the test and our reasons for administering it, then ask the young man to take thirty minutes to complete it.

By comparing an athlete's answers to those of players already on our team, we could get a better feel of how he would fit into our organization.

We also used intelligence tests that were comparable to the SAT and ACT tests used for college admission. These were administered by our scouts, often while on campus for spring practice.

We conducted personal evaluations through interviews with assistant coaches and trainers, and then asked scouts their subjective opinions. These questions included: "How do you believe this player will be performing five years from now?" "How will he perform in his first year?" "Who is he most comparable to on the current Forty-Niner team?" "Who is he most comparable to on previous Forty-Niner teams?" "What role will he fill immediately?" "What role will he play in the future?" "What other players in the league have comparable ability?"

We had those reports categorized, so we could isolate and grade any player. Therefore, with a scout's subjective report, we had a solid profile on virtually every prospect available in the draft.

Forty-Niner scouts were treated as important members of the organization, not as second-class employees or men stuck in a scouting bureaucracy. When they arrived at a meeting, they were welcomed as full colleagues, and they participated in virtually every conversation about the team.

As a result of this communication, our coaches and scouts worked beautifully together over a period of years.

The coaches first evaluated college athletes by category, after lengthy discussions on our needs. Coaches were then given specific projects.

In one situation, for instance, we might have been very interested in a safety. So, Ray Rhodes, our defensive backfield coach, would evaluate the top fifteen safeties in the draft. But also, in a later round, we might be looking for a corner with outstanding speed but who might have been downgraded because he wasn't a hitter, a hard tackler. Ray's project would be to look for an early-round pick for a safety and then perhaps a middle-round pick for a cornerback as a high-risk project, so he had different categories to research.

We would always put a draft-pick label on each player, saying that one player would likely be a seventh-round pick, for instance. But even if he was expected to be a later pick, we would still give him a lot of consideration because that kind of player can make a team if he's evaluated correctly. In 1986, we were in need at the cornerback position. Consequently, Ray and George concentrated on evaluating every potential candidate. We drafted Tim McKyer in the third round and Don Griffin in the sixth round, and they became the starters almost immediately—both being named to the "All Rookie" team.

Our coaches, during the spring of each year, would travel to campuses across the country working with prospects. In one year, 1986, we determined that we needed a pass rusher, either one who could be drafted early or one who could be drafted later as what we call a "projection pick," a player with the physical potential to develop as a pro.

Most likely, the projection athlete is one who's played at a less-recognized school. If he's a pass rusher, he's usually a tall man without the requisite weight, but, through improved nutrition or weight training and a good conditioning program, he can add that weight quickly.

We isolated six men in that category for defensive line coaches Bill McPherson and Tommy Hart to visit. Charles Haley, playing at James Madison, was among the six. We expected Haley would not go high in the draft because he was a "tweener," in between the size of a defensive lineman and a linebacker, not big enough to play defensive line and not quick enough to play linebacker.

The film we had of Haley was crude and difficult to analyze, but we could see him covering the breadth of the field with great speed and making spectacular plays.

Tommy and Bill reported that this was the kind of man we were looking for. We knew he would have to gain weight, but he was very quick, and quick-witted. He had played in a lesser program, but we knew he had the potential we were looking for.

In the draft, we picked Haley in the fourth round. We put him on a weight program and monitored his nutrition in camp, and he's since been a Pro Bowl player, one of the great pass rushers in the league. With his positive, aggressive personality, he became a very effective pass rusher as a rookie.

That's a typical example of isolating your needs and then having your experts evaluate talent.

Our coaches were given a lot of latitude in working with our scouts. There was no competition between scouts and coaches, as there is in so many organizations. We created an atmosphere in meetings in which a scout or coach was able to express himself completely. If he overstated or understated in any category, he could change his opinion later without being criticized.

We were interested only in results. We wanted men to reevaluate and modify their opinions, instead of feeling they had to justify an earlier one. They could change their minds without being ridiculed. In an open forum, we could come up with a more comprehensive evaluation of players.

Technology also played an important role, especially in helping me make a decision. Assistants conducted exhaustive studies of tapes of players. Then, each coach would take an individual's ten best and ten worst plays and put them together. I would then have the means to evaluate a prospect quickly and to compare them.

With that battery of tapes, we would then reevaluate players at each position and for their ability regardless of position.

I had specific meetings before the draft with our scouts. We'd go over every prospect on the board without the coaches being present, so the scouts could express themselves without feeling forced to qualify opinions with the coaches present. Then, we would have meetings with the coaches to get their evaluations.

Following this there would be meetings with scouts and coaches in which both groups would offer their ratings. Between the scouts and coaches, we would come to a consensus, and then I would use my subjective judgment as to where I felt that player would go. Tony Razzano would direct his staff in finalizing everything including the most updated medical information. All reports would be complete, and further research necessary would be addressed at that time.

We put up players in several categories, some in the order we thought they would be drafted, others in a category of best potential. Still others were rated by position, or in a category of being able to play in their first year.

Before the draft, we would have a mock run to try to predict how other teams would choose, but those were usually an exercise in futility. The correlation between our mock draft and the actual one was usually very low. There were always big surprises, even shocks.

To help us, we got information from writers like Will McDonough (who later also became a broadcaster). *USA Today* often has good information, and Joel Buchsbaum in *Pro Football Weekly* has an excellent grasp of what teams are doing. We also culled information from other published sources, but even with all that, our predictions for other teams were usually no more than 30 percent accurate.

Before the draft we projected those players most likely to be available when we selected. We would have perhaps fifteen men who might be available, and we'd rate them in order of excellence. But we would have evaluations on everybody, because even if we were drafting last there was the possibility, as in '85, that we could make a trade that would move us up.

I worked for the 49ers through the 1989 draft. In my last nine years, with the exception of 1982, we were drafting either last or near the end, so we knew that, barring a trade, a player like Tony Mandarich wouldn't be available to us. Therefore, on draft day, we basically ignored what we thought were the top ten players, concentrating on the players who might be available to us after that.

When the draft got down to the two or three picks prior to ours, we would narrow our choice to perhaps four players, at least one of whom should be there for us. We would rank them, so when our turn came, we were ready to pick the best player available to us. The 49ers seldom spent much time before making a pick, because we had basically made the decision before our turn came.

It got more difficult in the later rounds because players tended to be very close in ability. When the few truly great prospects are no longer available, there's an argument for any number of men.

The more preparation you can do before the draft, just as the more preparation you can do before a game, the better off you are. You don't want to feel there's a time crunch when you're making your decisions, because your judgment can become distorted. On draft day, you might give too much credence to the last person with whom you spoke.

People outside football may think that the atmosphere is frantic at draft time, but in fact, our room was usually calm and relatively quiet (with the possible exception of 1986). It was established that only one person would be talking at a time and, of course, when the decision was to be made, I would make it.

Some teams say they draft the best available athlete. Others say they draft for need. We tried to do both. If a player had been rated very high but was outside our most basic needs, we would have to weigh his ability against our desire to fill a specific position.

Let's say we were looking first for a tight end, second for a guard, and third for a safety. We would say we were going to look for the top-rated player at one of those positions. The only development that would change that decision would be a very highly rated player at another position who would make a real impact immediately.

In this case, if we picked a tight end in our first selection, we most likely would eliminate that position for the next round and pick a top-rated player from one of the other two positions.

Prior to the draft, we would decide we would like to fill our needs at these three positions. As the draft progressed, we would make alternate choices at these positions. If, for instance, we took a tight end in the first round, we might take another one in the fifth. Or, if we went for a safety in the first round, we might take two more in later rounds.

We always drafted a speed receiver, if for no other reason than to give our defensive backs somebody to work against in training camp. If the receiver made the team, fine, but even if he didn't, he helped prepare our defensive backs for someone with sprinter speed.

We would pick a big fullback in the later rounds even if he was a lumbering runner, because we knew we'd want a big back in preseason games who could help control the game in the second half. We hoped he could make the team, but if he didn't, he still had value in the preseason.

In later years, we began to really check out players with senior-year injuries that cast doubt on their pro futures, looking carefully at their rehabilitation and the extent of surgery they'd undergone. So often, what appears to be a devastating injury may keep them out of action for a year, but following an extensive rehab program, the return to action can be with virtually 100 percent recovery.

A good example is Kevin Fagan. Kevin was a great defensive lineman at the University of Miami, certainly a first-round player and most likely among the top fifteen selections. But he had a very serious knee injury and his rehab wasn't coming along well, so teams completely overlooked him in the early rounds. We picked him in the fourth round.

It took an investment in time, planning, hard work and money with Kevin, because it was an entire year before he could even practice. Meanwhile, he had all kinds of complications with his original surgery. He is not only gifted physically but possesses an irrepressible determination. He's become one of the NFL's premier defensive ends.

The college draft is the very foundation of the National Football League. It is the point from which everything begins. Mistakes and miscalculations in this area cannot be easily rectified and can haunt a franchise for years into the future. Our formula proved to be extremely successful. We had talented people who were well organized and who felt a real commitment to their work.

11

Putting It Together

By early 1981, we were fully mobilized as an organization. We had people in place, in roles, and we had begun to work cohesively together, even as we had lost game after game in '79 and '80.

But it takes talented athletes as well as an efficient organization to win games and championships. We used every method to improve in '81, drafting key players, making an important trade, and signing a free agent who added the veteran leadership we needed. We finally were able to put together the pieces of the puzzle.

The free agent was linebacker Jack Reynolds, who had been known as "Hacksaw" from his college days at Tennessee.

In Jack's senior year, Tennessee had clinched the Southeastern Conference title but then lost to Mississippi, 38–0, which cost the Vols a chance to play in the Sugar Bowl.

Jack and some friends had an old car, a '53 Chevrolet with no motor, that they pushed around with a Jeep. Jack decided to get rid of his frustrations by sawing the car in half. He bought a cheap hacksaw from K mart and thirteen blades. It took him a day-and-a-half to finish the job, but he did it. When Jack Reynolds started something, he finished it. That crazy project gave him his nickname; he would be "Hacksaw" forever. The nickname also fit his style of play because he cut people down.

The Rams no longer considered Jack a topflight player. There were also contract differences and he was ultimately released. Buffalo and the 49ers were the only teams actively interested in him. He was seriously negotiating with Buffalo, because his original Rams coach, Chuck Knox, was there, and Knox appreciated Hacksaw's impact on a team. I finally persuaded him to join the 49ers, partly because we talked to him about coaching after he finished playing. At that time, Jack was thinking of playing two more years and then becoming a coach.

His agent, David Fishof, was even recommending that he become the defensive coordinator immediately, with no prior coaching experience. That was unrealisitc, but everyone in the organization was enthusiastic about the idea of Jack becoming a coach for us when his playing days were through. A future in coaching would be okay, but we wanted Jack to bring his playing intensity to San Francisco.

That trade was consummated while I was on vacation in Aspen, Colorado, at the home of my friend, Tom Guggenheim. In the football world, there is seldom the luxury of a total vacation. Even when I took a few days off to ski, or an afternoon to play tennis, there might be ongoing negotiations that would interrupt my leisure time. I couldn't afford to postpone something that could materially improve our team, as this signing certainly did.

Fortunately, I was the general manager as well as coach, so I could make that kind of commitment quickly, along with an excellent contract offer, so the deal was made at that point. I was thoroughly pleased with my conversations with Jack. We didn't have anyone on the squad who had such a work ethic and could set such a standard.

As it happened, Jack continued playing through the 1984 season, and he'd probably still be on the field if it were up to him. I tried to talk him into retirement before that season, but he convinced me he could play another year. I was concerned, as I was later with other veterans, that he could contract lasting physical problems by continuing to play.

Jack did come to training camp as a coach the next year, but it just didn't work out. We found that when we were looking at films, he was simply unwilling to criticize any of his former teammates. And Jack was not accustomed to a coach's work schedule, either. After training camp, he left the team and hasn't coached since. That is a real loss to the game, because Hacksaw Reynolds possesses more inherent football knowledge than any former player I've worked with.

So, in a sense, Jack's 49er career ended rather strangely, but his contribution in '81 was invaluable because he was such an unusual man.

Jack was absolutely the most competitive player I've ever known. He would get dressed in the hotel the morning of the game, because he didn't want to be distracted once he got to the stadium. For home games, he would often take a cab, dressed in his uniform, hours before the team buses were scheduled to leave. He laughed about that himself, saying that people who saw him going up the Bayshore thought he was just another "Forty-Niner crazy."

He was tough, barely six feet tall and about 235 pounds, very intense and extremely powerful, with great shocking power. He was explosive, able to "stuff" much larger offensive linemen. Jack's desire to win was so strong that it inspired his teammates and challenged them to play their best. In that sense, he lifted his teammates to a higher level. In my opinion, Jack should be ranked among the greatest to play his position.

This was the second straight year we had been able to acquire a veteran player who could give us both physical and emotional leadership.

In 1980, we had traded for tight end Charle Young. Charle had been a great tight end at USC and later with Philadelphia. His best years were with the Eagles, though he played well for the Rams after being traded there in 1977.

Charle supposedly had lost some of his speed, so the Rams were willing to trade him to us in 1980, because they didn't yet see us as a competitive threat. Though he may not have been the super performer he had been, he was still capable of playing well and, most important to us, he was a great leader.

When we first met after the trade, I could sense that he responded well to me, and I was confident he would work well in our offensive scheme. He was physically tough, and he could still make the crucial first-down catch.

Charle was a critical player and for three years had a real impact on our team. On draft day in 1982, I traded for Russ Francis. For a time, we had both Young and Francis on the roster, which wasn't good. It was like having two vying bathing beauties. One had to go. Russ was the superior athlete, so it was Young. I hated to see him leave, but the chemistry was bad between these two proud athletes.

Having Reynolds and Young in 1981 was extremely important because they gave us something we hadn't had before, leadership from top flight veteran players. We had men who would become premiere players in the future, like Joe Montana, Dwight Cark, Keena Turner, Randy Cross, and Dwight Hicks, but they weren't quite ready to assert themselves. To that point, the strongest source of leadership on the club had been offensive tackle Keith Fahnhorst.

Keith had been through the Joe Thomas years and somehow survived. His quiet strength and mature personality in combination with his solid week-to-week performances had set a standard for the entire squad. He ably represented the players during two strike years, keeping communications open and holding the team together. Keith was finally to get long-overdue recognition when named a consensus All-Pro in 1984.

Reynolds and Young had been acknowledged campaigners and they had been with winning teams. They were the embodiment of the true professional. Having played on other teams, they could compare our organization with those. Just the players are on the field, so the coach can only do so much without active, hands-on leadership from key squad members.

The third key veteran was Fred Dean, who joined us early in the season.

Dean was typical of many young players in the NFL at the time— players who had signed long-term contracts for relatively little money when they came into the league. Meanwhile, NFL teams were getting more and more income through the sale of dramatically increased television rights or higher ticket prices, and these players realized that, based on their production, their salaries should be two to three times higher, in line with the new contracts being signed.

San Diego owner Gene Klein had taken a hard line, insisting that players could not renegotiate their contracts, even if they were committed for as long as five years. The Chargers were notorious for negotiating long-term contracts with small yearly increments. Though he'd been in the Pro Bowl and was one of the best pass-rushing defensive linemen in the league, Dean had made only $70,000 in 1980.

Dean had convinced everybody that if he didn't get a new contract, he would sit out the year. He continued his holdout through training camp and well into the season, until Gene Klein decided he'd had enough.

The Chargers' general manager, John Sanders, contacted us, along with other clubs in the league, about a trade for Dean. His holdout was becoming a distraction. Every day stories about it would appear in the San Diego papers. There would be reports that Dean had driven by the stadium, exciting everybody because they thought he was coming back. But the follow-up would be that he hadn't stopped and was still holding out.

Some teams in the league were very reluctant to trade for Dean, who was an unusual man. He had a few very good friends, but he didn't exchange much with his teammates. He didn't seem to require the kind of attention that star athletes often crave. Other teams felt his contract demands would be outrageous and considered him a malcontent.

Ed DeBartolo, Jr., was totally supportive in our attempts to get Dean. When other NFL owners balked at Dean's demands, Eddie said, "If you think he can help us win, get him."

We saw Dean as a truly great player. He wasn't big, only about 225 pounds, but he had great explosion and upper-body strength. He could throw off much bigger offensive linemen and get to the quarterback. He wasn't a guy who could play every down, but he was a dominating force when he was on the field.

We finally completed a trade in the fourth week of the season. There were as many as thirty phone calls exchanged regarding this trade and the necessary compensation. The actual agreement was reached while I was playing tennis with three friends.

We were in the second set when the call came from John. He explained in detail the Chargers' final offer: our second-round choice in the 1982 draft plus an option to switch first-round picks, predicated on our success in reaching agreement with Fred. That was more than I'd hoped for. We might have been willing to give up a first-round pick. I said "John, go with it. If there are any problems, I'll be right here." I added that I'd call Eddie as soon as it was confirmed. I had total confidence in John's negotiating ability. To this day, he's one of the best I've seen.

I returned to my tennis game and remarked to my friends, "We just got Fred Dean. He'll make us a winner." Everyone in the league would soon learn how prophetic that remark was.

We had to modify our defense to use Dean. We now emphasized a three-man line with Dean as the wild card, set loose to rush the passer from the weak side, usually the quarterback's left.

One of the reasons we could do that was because Dwaine Board was at the other end. Board was probably our most underrated player. He had a great career for us, our most consistent and effective defensive lineman for years. He could rush the passer or defend against the run, even though he wasn't big, usually playing at about 250 pounds. Dwaine had great range; he could chase down even the faster running backs. He was a "coaches' player" and a "players' player." He provided a quiet, resourceful leadership. When he talked, everyone listened.

But it was Dean who could make the spectacular play. He was unstoppable that year, either sacking the quarterback or forcing him to pass too quickly—or simply chasing him all over the field.

With the addition of Ronnie Lott, Eric Wright, and Carlton Williamson, to go with Dwight Hicks, we also had a talented defensive backfield for the first time since I joined the 49ers. Very soon, it would prove to be a great one.

We made an early decision to start all three of our rookies together with second-year-man Hicks, rather than try to break them in one at a time. That way, they would begin to bond immediately. George Seifert and Ray Rhodes started them out together with fundamental teaching of the necessary skills. They developed as a unit. There was a camaraderie that was to carry them through two world championships.

We continuously emphasized explosive hitting. In early exhibition games, we used a conservative style, with the backs playing well off the line, because we knew they could close very quickly and really impact the receiver. In college, they had all been known as big hitters, and they soon established that they were going to make their presence felt. It didn't take long for opposing receivers to respect them.

There were times when we got burned by our inexperience. I remember one play in the NFC championship game against Dallas when Eric Wright came up in bump-and-run coverage on Tony Hill. The Cowboys quarterback, Danny White, called an audible. Eric didn't realize that when White audibilized, at that point on the field, he always called a fly pattern to Hill. On this play, Hill got a step on Wright and White threw a beautiful strike for a touchdown.

But even that kind of play eventually helped us. Eric wasn't going to let it happen again. As years passed, Wright was considered by many to be the best cornerback in the league. In later years, the knowledge gained from these experiences—from learning from our mistakes—helped the 49ers win added championships.

We didn't have a great team in '81. We lacked depth, our running game didn't meet NFL standards—Ricky Patton was our leading runner with just 543 yards—and we had one important potential problem. That was at left tackle, the most critical pass-protecting position in the offensive line because virtually all quarterbacks are righthanded and usually have their backs to the rush from the left side.

Our left tackle was Dan Audick, an intense performer and a real technician, but only 245 pounds, at least 30 pounds lighter than the average tackle at that time. He really should have been a guard, where he would have been considered small, but when we released Ron Singleton, we had to immediately locate someone to play left tackle, and we got Dan in a trade from San Diego. He had a history of emotional problems but dealt with them courageously that year.

So, at the most important position on the line, we had the smallest tackle in the league. We compensated in a couple of ways. We had our quarterback, Joe Montana, go only to his right when he was rolling out, to get away from the pressure from the left side. We had John Ayers, our very able guard on that side, help out when necessary with Audick's man. Around the league, people were amazed that we could play a 245-pounder at left tackle, but meanwhile, we were winning, week after week. It didn't bother Dan; he made up for his size with quickness and skill.

That team was greater than the sum of its parts because we had players who could make seemingly impossible plays, such as Montana on offense and Dean on defense. We had developed a solid passing attack, because Fred Solomon and Dwight Clark had matured into very good receivers. And we had a kicker, Ray Wersching, who had nerves of steel in the clutch, the steadiest kicker I've ever seen. Ray's kicking was the difference in four games that year, three of which we won by 3 points and one by just 2.

We had developed veteran leadership from Willie Harper, Archie

Reese, and Lawrence Pillers defensively. We claimed Lawrence Pillers after the 1980 season. He'd been a starter with the Jets but just wasn't compatible. We had the need and were quite willing to give him an opportunity. Soon Lawrence was an enthusiastic supporter of our approach to the game. He was to set a standard for aggressive, physical play.

As the year began, there were no indications that we were going to have a championship season. Around the league, we still had the same punching-bag image. In our first game of the season in Detroit, my good friend, Monte Clark, who was coaching the Lions, was admonished by the Detroit general manager, Russ Thomas, because he beat us only by 24–17. Thomas regarded that as an embarrassment. Monte reminded him of that when we arrived in Detroit, (before going on to Pontiac) for the Super Bowl after that season.

After our first three games, we were 1–2 and questions at the weekly press conference were becoming more and more pointed, with reporters demanding to know when they could expect a competitive team. One writer had prepared a four-part series on the impending demise of the 49ers. The first part ran, but then we started winning, so that was the end of the series. Presumably, that writer still has the last three parts in his file.

After the third game, I implored the reporters to give us a chance. "If we can't do it, who can?" I said. Well, that didn't work. They looked at my plea as just another excuse by the coach. I knew what they felt.

I thought the 49ers could help bring the community together, and the Bay Area really needed something at that time. There were all sorts of internal problems: gang violence, the escalating drug scene, clashes over gay rights. It hadn't been long since the San Francisco mayor, George Moscone, and supervisor Harvey Milk had been assassinated.

The 49ers were so closely tied to San Francisco because they had started there, unlike the Giants and the Warriors. That gave us a special, even sentimental status in the city. I really internalized that, having gone to college and started my coaching career in the Bay Area. It hurt me for the city that the media was unnecessarily holding our team up to national ridicule. Everything coming out of San Francisco seemed to be negative.

One night Geri and I were driving into town and I said, "This is such a beautiful city. Why won't they give us a chance?" Geri didn't know what I was talking about. "What do you mean?" I couldn't quite put it into words, but I thought it would be so important to have a team in which everybody could take pride. A successful sports team would cut across all social, ethnic, and cultural levels and give everyone something to share.

Later, after we won the Super Bowl, a half-million people turned out for a victory parade down Market Street and a rally at the San Francisco Civic Center, but that was a long way off when we were 1–2. The media was already preparing for the "scenario" of the coach's being replaced. I hadn't lost confidence in myself, but I feared that the team would never cast off the loser's syndrome and develop a positive image of self-confidence and pride.

When I could see some members of the press turning antagonistic, I felt it personally. I wasn't getting through. I thought, if they could only see that we were making progress. On the field, our statistics were better; off the field, we had a much better relationship with the public, and it should have been obvious that we had formed a class organization. To put a foot down on our neck after only two years wasn't fair. I exhorted the media to give us a chance.

My speech fell on deaf ears. In sports, only on-field results count. We would have to win before we would get any support—or respect.

Fortunately, we beat New Orleans in our next game to even our record at 2–2. It was a lackluster game. In fact, we were trailing at halftime, 7–0, and when Joe Montana (who had a sprained ankle from the previous week) threw an interception, I told Guy Benjamin to warm up. But Joe stayed in the game, and we finally won it, 21–14, when he threw a 10-yard pass to Freddie Solomon who turned it into a 60-yard touchdown.

The next game, though, against the Washington Redskins, showed what kind of team we would be. The Redskins were 0–4 in Joe Gibbs's first year, but all week the talk in Washington was that they were going to turn their season around that Sunday. Nobody took us seriously. But we went into Washington and beat the Redskins, 30–17, and it wasn't that close; we were ahead, 30–3, before the Redskins scored two meaningless touchdowns in the fourth quarter. This was the day our defensive backfield, led by Dwight Hicks, came of age, intercepting four passes. Hicks scored two touchdowns on a 32-yard interception return and an 80-yard return of a fumble.

We never looked back after that, winning twelve of our final thirteen regular-season games, fourteen of our last fifteen counting the postseason. Every game was important, but some stand out more than others:

• The following week's game against Dallas, at Candlestick. I reminded our players beforehand how the Cowboys had humiliated us the year before, running trick plays and throwing long passes in the fourth quarter, when the game had already been decided. The Cowboys did that often to teams they really outmatched, and their fans would gloat over the destruction.

The Cowboys were so good, they simply intimidated the weaker teams. They had sheer contempt for us.

Their mystique even included the uniforms they wore: Supposedly, they never lost when they wore their white jerseys. Fans called and wrote, and longtime 49ers beseeched me, to make them wear their blue jerseys—the home team always has the first choice of uniforms, colored or white, and the visitor must wear the other—but we just couldn't concede that they had any power over us. If we got beat, it wouldn't be because of the color of their jerseys.

As was always the case, as I stood on the sideline listening to the national anthem, I thought, "What a great moment this is." I loved it, feeling the thrill and the excitement of participating, and awaiting the drama that would unfold. The coaches and the players shared a closeness then. I would never lose the sense of that moment. Through the years, each Sunday, I would get a lump in my throat as "The Star-Spangled Banner" was played in all its variations. I'd reflect on how proud I was to coach this team and be part of this spectacle. All the frustrations and self-sacrifice of coaching would seem secondary.

I might begin to choke up, but only for a few seconds. Then I'd tell myself, "Here you go. Start pulling away, start computerizing. You must think clearly and remove yourself." The instant that moment of reflection during the national anthem was over, I became fully focused. It was like watching the game through a window.

I'm sure the Cowboys came into Candlestick certain this would be a typical 49er contest: We might be tough early but would cave in during the second half.

Meanwhile, we were ready. People like Ronnie Lott, Keena Turner, Dwaine Board, and Willie Harper had infused an energy that affected everyone. We were sky-high. We couldn't wait to play these guys. After our 1980 humiliation, we were primed. One team was overconfident and self-satisfied, the other intense and inspired. We exploded and they were flat. The result was a 45–14 win.

As in the previous week's game, we were even more dominant than that final score indicated. We were driving for still another touchdown late in the game when Amos Lawrence fumbled and Benny Barnes returned it for a 72-yard touchdown. We substituted freely in the second half; I wouldn't be accused of pouring it on.

We had acquired Fred Dean the Thursday before the Washington game, but couldn't get him on the field for that one.

He was ready for the Cowboys, though, and he absolutely ruined them, sacking White twice and forcing him to throw before he was ready on seven other occasions. The Cowboys' offense never got untracked. With Dean coming on the left side and Board on the right, we were too quick for their pass protectors.

After the game, the Cowboys' apologists said, "The real Cowboys didn't show up." That was the way they justified losses or upsets. I remember John Brodie said in response, "Who were those guys out there in the white shirts? Was it some other team?"

The next night on halftime of "Monday Night Football," the highlights of our game were not shown, though it was certainly one of the big stories around the league that week. There was an obvious reason, I thought: The Cowboys were playing the Los Angeles Rams next in a rare Sunday night game, and the league (or ABC-TV) didn't want to damage their image. That game would be up against Sunday night movies, considered stiff competition.

I felt it typified the NFL's mentality at the time: The 49ers weren't a factor, so why put them, or even their highlights, on national TV? I lashed out at the network during our weekly press conference at our headquarters in Redwood City.

"We're not accepted nationally, obviously," I told reporters. "The jockstrap elitists don't consider us in their comfort zone. There are power sources, influence sources in the National Football League, forty-five-year-old men who are football groupies who prefer that we not exist so they can hold onto their football contracts and associations or power groups.

"It's obviously a business and ABC needs the Los Angeles–Dallas game to be a big one, to compete with the other programming. It's obvious, it's blatant. In my opinion, it does a disservice to the game."

Was I sincere? Yes, it genuinely bothered me that nobody took us seriously, after we'd played so well against the Cowboys. More importantly, my remarks would spark even more determination on our part to overcome our past as a losing team.

There were other times when I did that, using statements made by other coaches and players to motivate the 49ers. At the same time, I cautioned our players against making statements that would incite the other side. For the most part, our players kept quiet. That was another lesson I'd learned from Paul Brown.

There was truth in my remarks, yet they were impetuous. We weren't on national television because we weren't a draw. Years later, we were to be the most popular and dynamic draw in the NFL. By that time, we had the opposite problem: We were almost being badgered by the networks.

Also, I let my emotions affect my judgment. The years of frustration were finally behind us, and I wanted people to recognize our achievement. Years later, as I read these quotes, I shock myself, feeling quite foolish.

There was a footnote to all this. Months later at the NFL spring meeting, Howard Cosell attacked me viciously in front of a large gathering. Apparently, he had felt I was criticizing him personally, though my remarks were directed at the network.

We were at a cocktail party, and Cosell was walking in my direction with his daughter, Hilary. He saw me and I knew he recognized me, but in his disdainful way, he pretended that he didn't, so I put out my hand and said, "Howard, I'm Bill Walsh." He looked at me for an instant and said, "So, you're the one. You're the one who dared to criticize me. Who do you think you are? Where do you come from, what have you done?"

He just went on and on. The crowd hushed, and there were four or five hundred people there; it was a large gathering. Everybody wanted to hear this. Ken Flower, bless his heart, tried to intervene, and Cosell started berating him as well. That was not unusual, of course. At that time, Cosell often took people on publicly, castigating them, abusing them. He had everyone intimidated.

Instead of responding, I listened. Whatever instincts I had in dealing with people came to my aid. I instinctively knew when to avoid an embarrassing conflict. He eventually finished his diatribe and moved on.

Well, I knew I couldn't let it stand that way, so I wrote him a letter—not apologizing, but explaining my remarks. We exchanged phone calls. Finally, the next year, on the evening before a Monday night game in San Francisco, we met for a private dinner.

We were compatible because of our views on college sports and the American sports scene in general. We found common ground. In his later years, he was most positive and supportive of me, and I appreciated that, but it took diplomacy to deal with his earlier remarks.

• Our win the following week against Green Bay was just as important as our win over Dallas. Typically, young teams who win unexpectedly against a major opponent lose their edge the next week. You expect the emotion to be there the second week, but it just isn't. That's when you need a standard of performance that smooths out the highs and lows, so you can play on a more consistent level from week to week.

It was a totally different day in Green Bay, and a totally different game. Instead of mild weather that would have allowed us to exercise our entire offense, as we had against the Cowboys, it was bitterly cold, which limited the offenses for both teams. But we won the game, 13–3. For the first time, we had shown that standard of performance we were seeking.

I remember reflecting on the plane home, this isn't 1980, when we caved in, this team can win the division. I certainly wasn't thinking in terms of the Super Bowl at that point, but at least I knew we could legitimately compete with anybody in the league.

• The two games against the Rams, both of which we won. For some reason, the Rams had dominated the 49ers; they led the series, 41–19 with two ties going into '81. Only four times in thirty-one years had the 49ers won both games in a season, and the Rams had won the last nine games in the series.

We didn't destroy them, winning by just 20–17 and 33–31; in the second game, we needed a Ray Wersching field goal with time running out. But it was the victories that counted, not the margin; we had demonstrated that the Rams dominance had come to an end. Counting those two wins, we beat the Rams eleven of the last sixteen games we played during my 49er coaching career, significant because they were usually the team we had to beat to win our division. We had become a much quicker team than the Rams, and that made the difference.

Fred Solomon, Dwight Clark, and Earl Cooper were weapons the

Rams simply couldn't deal with. They caught 29 passes among them in the two games.

The second win was significant because this was the first time we'd been able to use all the time left on the clock on our last drive—and that we had the nerve to go right down to the last seconds before kicking. If we'd missed that field goal, the contest was over and we would have lost.

Two Wersching field goals were the margin in the first game, too, but in that one, Ray kicked them when we were leading 14–10. As much as any other game that year, that victory demonstrated how important Fred Dean was to us.

I've always thought there are two keys to winning close contests in the NFL: being able to control the game with your running game in the fourth quarter while disrupting the other team's offense with a dominating pass rush.

In that game, the Rams had four opportunities to regain the lead in the fourth quarter, and Fred Dean was the key man in preventing them from even getting a field goal. Here's how those sequences went:

1. On third down from the San Francisco thirty-seven, Rams quarterback Pat Haden was sacked by Dean and Jim Stuckey, forcing a punt.
2. On third down from the San Francisco forty-six, Dean's pressure forced Haden to the other side, where he was sacked by Lawrence Pillers.
3. On third down from the San Francisco thirty-four, Dean sacked Haden, forcing another punt.
4. On the Rams last drive, Dean sacked Haden twice. The Rams still were able to get to the San Francisco thirty-one. On third down, Haden called a draw play, but Dean tackled Mike Guman after a 4-yard gain. Frank Corral then missed a field goal, and we won the game.

• The Steelers game in Pittsburgh. An NFC team hadn't won in Pittsburgh in ten years. It was really tough to go into the "Steel City," because they'd had those great teams, winning four Super Bowls in the '70s, and their fans were really tough. It would be an intimidating scene. I had experienced it firsthand a number of times when I was with the Bengals.

Talking to the team before the game, I told the story of the British soldiers in Burma during World War II, when the Japanese Army seemed unstoppable. The Japanese would capture retreating British soldiers and kill them, making it known that they were taking no prisoners.

Eventually, the British were backed up against a mountain in a small town. It was obvious that they would have to stand and fight because there was nowhere to run. They did, and they beat the Japanese back, forcing them to retreat. But they could do that only after they'd been humiliated for so long that they realized they had to fight the Japanese way or be killed.

In a sense, we were in that position. We'd been humiliated so many times, especially on the road, and it was time to stand and fight. It would be "forty-five against fifty thousand," meaning they'd have to take on the Steelers fans, too. And we'd have to do it the Steelers' way. Beat them at their own game.

They did. It was tough and physical. I particularly remember two hits by Carlton Williamson. In the second quarter, Steeler wide receiver Calvin Sweeney caught a pass in front of Williamson, and Carlton hammered him to the turf. Sweeney lay there for some time before getting up. On the Steelers' next possession, Williamson hit John Stallworth just as hard; again, Stallworth had to be helped off the field.

Carlton's hits epitomized the fierce intensity our defensive backs had established.

We won, 17–14, and I can't remember a locker room that was so wild after a game. We were just jumping up and down and yelling. The excitement was unbelievable. That was as emotional a win as I can remember. What a thrill it was to realize that this young team had done what others couldn't—outhit the Steelers. Privately, I hadn't been sure we could do it.

• The Cleveland game. Even though this was a loss, it was important because it shocked all of us into realizing how little difference there was between a win and a loss. We had to play our best to win, because we weren't going to overpower anybody. Our "standard of performance" had to be better. There were also some good things, even in losing; Paul Hofer had recovered from his 1980 knee surgery and was playing well, though he was later to reinjure the same knee.

• Cincinnati. I was too proud to share it with the squad, but this truly was going to be a once-in-a-lifetime experience for me. It was also a homecoming for Chuck Studley, our defensive coordinator, and for Sam Wyche, our quarterback coach. We had all given a substantial part of our careers to Cincinnati.

We had clinched our division the week earlier, so I indicated at our weekly press conference that we might rest some of our regulars. In a sense I was stretching the ethics of the game, the idea that you always play your best no matter what the circumstances. It was an impetuous attempt at "brinksmanship." I wanted to give Cincinnati the feeling that we wouldn't be at our best, and I also wanted to remind our reserve players they'd have a chance to play.

Howard Cosell jumped all over me on his radio show, saying it was a threat to the integrity of the game, and it created a lot of talk in both cities during the week.

Of course, we played our regulars, and we won, convincingly, 21–3. When we flew out of Cincinnati that night, I looked out the window at a sight that was so familiar to me, and I felt a great surge of relief and satisfaction. It wasn't gloating, and I didn't make any public statements about it, but it certainly was one of the most satisfying wins of my career. The last time I'd flown out of Cincinnati, I'd been embarrassed and in despair, wondering how I could ever return and face these people. The only face-saving gesture would be to come into Cincinnati and win.

There was never one particular point in that season when I felt that we had a championship team. I just had a growing feeling that we could be one of the better teams. Looking back, I'd have to say that it was my most satisfying season, because we had been down so far and suddenly we were on top of the football world.

And yet, even then, there was so little time to enjoy it. Each week, after a win, we'd enjoy the moment, but then we'd say, "Who's next?" And then we'd say, "Uh-oh," because it was almost always a team that had been beating the 49ers regularly.

We ended the season with a 13–3 record, the best in the NFL and, indeed, the best in the club's NFL history, but we had no time to think about that. We had to think about the playoffs and, specifically, the New York Giants and Lawrence Taylor.

12

The First Champion

A s I did before every home game, I drove to Candlestick Park
with Billy Wilson before our play off game against the New
York Giants.

Every head coach needs not only technical expertise from people
with very particular skill areas but the active involvement of a supportive, knowledgeable person who can act as friend and confidant and
soften the demands of the job. Someone who can present a rational
perspective even in the most severe and tension-filled situations.

Billy Wilson was that person for me. Billy, who had been an
outstanding Pro Bowl wide receiver with the 49ers, had joined us as
an administrative assistant and scout when I joined the organization.
He possessed a smooth, genial, and accommodating personality, and
combined with vast wisdom through many years in the NFL, served
as a sounding board for my varied moods and pregame concerns as we
drove to the stadium.

It was a ritual for every home contest. We would meet downstairs in
the hotel lobby, load our luggage and head up Highway 101. We
would speak of personal things, our families, our children, his golf
game, my tennis game, what was going on in the NFL, the college
prospects he had evaluated in recent weeks. As we drew closer to the
stadium, we would become more focused on the game.

As we got out of the car that day at Candlestick, Billy said, "You're going to get it done today." That wasn't just blind confidence; he was as sure as I was that we had the formula to deal with Lawrence Taylor and that intimidating Giant defense.

Joe Madro, the offensive line coach for Sid Gillman at San Diego in the sixties, was the first I recall who used a guard to double read for linebackers. He'd have the guard drop out of the line, looking first for an inside backer, then to the outside backer. If both blitzed, he'd pick up the inside backer, the one closest and the most dangerous to the quarterback, and the quarterback would quickly throw to a "hot" receiver. Most often, only the outside linebacker would blitz. That's how we would deal with Taylor. Instead of a running back blocking him, we would have a guard take him on.

Taylor had shattered teams that year with his blitzing. You may stop a blitzing linebacker like that on occasion with a running back, but the back is often giving up as much as fifty pounds, and Taylor would have a running start. You really can't expect a back to effectively get the job done, with consistency, especially late in the game. By the third quarter, a back would have simply taken too much punishment.

John Ayers was among the best pass blocking guards in the NFL at the time, so he would be assigned to Taylor. The Giants always lined up Taylor on the weak side, so there would be no tight end to block him. Since Ayers was the left guard, we set our formation with the tight end on the right side, so John would always be on the weak side. We had noted in film studies that the Giants didn't blitz their inside backer on Taylor's side, so Ayers could concentrate on looking for Lawrence. Offensive line coach Bobb McKittrick did a brilliant job in adapting to the Giants' defensive scheme.

With Taylor neutralized, we went on to win solidly, 38–24.

The next week was to become the greatest in 49er history. We would play the Dallas Cowboys for the NFC Championship. This game created massive national interest as "America's Team" was playing against those exciting young upstart 49ers for the opportunity to go to the Super Bowl once again. These were clearly the two best teams in the conference; we had finished 13–3 and the Cowboys were 12–4.

The 49ers had a sad history with Dallas. For three straight years, 1970–72, the Niners won their division but lost to the Cowboys in the playoffs. The last loss had been the most frustrating, because the 49ers had a 28–16 lead midway in the fourth quarter but couldn't hold on to it.

The last time San Francisco had beaten Dallas was in 1972 during the regular season; the Cowboys had won five straight since then. There was a lot of bitterness in San Francisco about those losses, and the Cowboys, with their contempt, aggravated it. They regarded themselves as the class of the NFL. We were a willing opponent, but if we could not stand up to the pressure of playing Dallas, we would be just like everyone else in the NFC.

When I talked to the team early in the week, I was more emotional than usual, because I was as sensitive to the supposed Dallas mystique as anybody. Here's how I was quoted:

"This goddamned Dallas team. They can't keep their mouths shut. They're doing the same thing again this week. They say, 'This time the Forty-Niners will be meeting the real Cowboys.' Their press releases are all about how they are going to kick ass. They're so arrogant, down there in the sports empire of the world."

I went on to say, "Nobody ever beats the 'real' Dallas Cowboys. If they lose, there's always somebody missing, the airplane food isn't just right, or their accommodations are wrong.

"Well, I'm fed up with this bullshit and everybody in the league is sick and tired of all this. So, let's just be ready for them. We're so much quicker than they are. They come out all fitted in those special uniforms. Well, so what. We're going to knock them all over the field."

We concentrated well during the week's practices. We had an excellent game plan. We would be ready.

On Sunday morning as Billy and I took our customary ride to Candlestick, I said, "Our quickness will have to make the difference." He agreed, but reminded me of that Dallas "front four."

I replied that I was sure Joe could get the ball off before they could get to him. Fahnhorst would have to "hit then cut" on "Too Tall" Jones or the big guy would be right in the way of everything thrown to the right. Everson Walls was a great ball hawk, but would jump at the first move a wide receiver would make. Dwight would get open on a "fake shake" pattern. Danny White is going to audible to a "fly" pattern the first time we go into a "bump and run" defense.

I said, "I think we will be okay. It's all we talked about during the week."

My first game as a 49er coach, against the Minnesota Vikings in 1979.

Huddling with the 49ers in overtime, during our record comeback from 35–0 against the New Orleans Saints—a key win for the team's future.

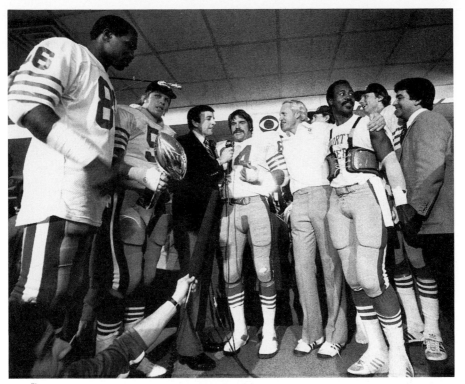

The first championship: a joyous postgame locker room after our victory in Super Bowl XVI, 26–21, over Cincinnati.

Three quarterbacks I had the chance to coach appeared in the 1982 Pro Bowl: Dan Fouts, Ken Anderson, and Joe Montana.

The Dallas Cowboys were a tough and arrogant football team, but we were able to beat them consistently in the 1980s. Here Joe Montana and I go over the offense during a 42–17 victory in 1983.

Preseason 1984: preparing for our greatest year.

Two halftime scenes during a 1984 win over the Saints: discussing some playcalling adjustments for the second half, and exhorting the offense not to let up.

I congratulate Ronnie Lott after a big 37–31 win over the Washington Redskins, who had been to the Super Bowl the previous two years.

Ed DeBartolo, Jr. and I laud the team after a 31-10 win over the New York Giants—our sixth consecutive win to start 1984.

A jubilant group of 49ers after a 31-0 blowout of our archrivals, the Los Angeles Rams.

Looking over my ready list on the sideline against the Saints.

Moments after our last regular season game of 1984, a 19–16 win over the Rams that gave us a 15–1 record, the best in football.

With players' emotions running high, a coach must keep his own in check and help the team to focus on executing the game plan—as I'm trying to do here, before a 1984 game against the Vikings.

Late in the game with Joe Montana, during our NFC championship win over the Chicago Bears.

During team introductions before the start of Super Bowl XIX.

After Super Bowl XIX, a 38–16 win over the Miami Dolphins, the culmination of the 49ers' greatest season.

At the half of a tough loss to the Vikings in 1986.

It wasn't all celebrating, as my grim expression shows during a 1985 loss to the Broncos.

Before each half the team would get together for a moment to focus their thoughts and emotions on the task at hand.

Two postgame portraits from 1988: sharing a victory with the team, and suffering a bitter defeat to the Phoenix Cardinals alone.

After a 6–5 start in 1988, we went on to our third championship of the 1980s. Here
I am with Joe Montana after beating the Vikings in the NFC championship game.

Retiring on a high note.

Billy asked who the officiating crew was. I said I didn't want to know.

He talked about how the Niners had blown the previous Cowboy playoff games, and this was the strongest Dallas team he had seen. I said Carlton Williamson and Dwight Hicks will take their receivers apart.

I said we're quicker than they are at every position, and the Cowboys just don't understand it.

Our locker room atmosphere was much the same as it was before any game, quiet, businesslike, some light humor, expressive of commitment among players.

Below the surface, coaches might be extremely anxious, but we had created an atmosphere that was rather sublime and relaxed. We didn't want to expend nervous energy that wasn't going to be related to the game. We might watch part of the other game that was being televised, and then, I'd take a short nap to pull myself out of the stress and tension and sort of meditate.

After that, I'd shake the hand of every player and coach, saying a positive word of a personal nature to everybody. Though players were moving about the room, I would know everybody whose hand I had shaken. That's how alive my senses would be before a game; my thought processes were so clear. As an example, I could miss Walt Downing or Craig Puki as I moved around the locker room but would then intuitively seek them out just before we left for the field.

I asked my coaches to do the same, to acknowledge each player and shake their hand, offer supportive thoughts, wish them the best. We wanted to go out on the field as a cohesive team, not just a collection of individual players who had no connection with each other or their coaches.

Having played Dallas three times in the past three years, we had an excellent grasp of what the Cowboys did and why they did it. We were confident we could move the ball; we had done it starting in '79. We matched up well, because of our quickness and our short, timed passing game, against the Dallas man-to-man pass coverage. So while Dallas had shattered the execution of other teams, we knew we could move the ball effectively.

The Cowboys were very predictable on defense. Their front four would line up the same way every time and their pass coverages would always make the same adjustments against specific formations. In effect, they were saying, "It doesn't matter if you know what we might do, because we're better than you are. Give it your best shot, but it won't be enough." And week after week they were right. They were extremely talented and thoroughly coached.

Their defensive front four was a dominating group, the best in the NFC, certainly bigger and more physical than our offensive line, but I felt we could take the edge off their pass rush by changing their reads. We'd pull linemen sometimes to simulate a running play, or use play fakes to freeze them, to keep them from getting to Montana. Plus, with our short, timed passes, we could get passes off before their linemen could penetrate. So, I felt we could offset their pass rush.

They only got to Montana three times, a real credit to the skills and tenacity of our offensive line. Dan Audick at left tackle, despite being outgunned, played beautifully.

We were quite sure we could force automatic adjustments in their pass coverage by using two tight ends and a man-in-motion. We could almost be assured single, man-to-man coverage, even forcing the weak safety Dennis Thurman to cover Dwight Clark. In effect we would force them to defend with their automatic adjustments rather than to defend with their basic defenses.

We could get anyone we wanted matched up with single coverage, whether it be Charle Young, Earl Cooper, or Lenvil Elliott. If we forced their weak safety into covering a receiver, Freddie Solomon or Clark had a cornerback to themselves.

As anticipated, we had a substantial edge in offense in the game, 393 to 250 yards, and could have won it convincingly but for some officiating calls that trouble me to this day. Many believe the officials were in a sense influenced by the Cowboys' mystique. I think subconsciously they may have believed the Cowboys were superior and deserving.

I remember one call in particular. We were leading in the fourth quarter when Ronnie Lott intercepted a pass deep in our territory. He was running with the receiver and saw that the pass was underthrown, so he slowed up and caught it, with the receiver behind him. Incredibly, he was called for pass interference. The official said he had interfered with the receiver's right to catch the pass. Well, if you accept that interpretation of the call, Ronnie would have had to step aside and let the receiver catch the ball!

That interception would have just about sewed up the game for us, but when the Cowboys got the interference call, they were able to position themselves for a field goal try and stay in contention.

At that point in NFL history, there were a few powerful men who virtually ran the league, which was probably a good thing overall. The league needed strong men.

Tex Schramm, the Dallas general manager, was one of those men. Schramm was invaluable to the league. And he managed the Cowboys with creativity and professionalism. Dallas had set a standard for everyone to admire and sometimes futilely emulate. But he also had an inclination to intimidate others in the process.

Schramm was a member of the competition committee, which is responsible for establishing a standard for interpreting rules of the game. Apparently he convinced his committee members that the Lott "interference" play be used by officials when they visited teams in training camp the next year as another example of pass interference that would be called. Well, I was told that our players and other players throughout the league just laughed when they saw that play. They knew the call was ridiculous. When officials showed it to us, players reacted very strongly, creating an uproar until the visiting official went on to another subject. Man, I would hate to have lost that game because of that call.

After being in control, we began to feel the game start to slip away. Dallas came back with a touchdown to go ahead 27–21 with just a little over five minutes to go.

After the ensuing kickoff, we found ourselves backed up against our goal line and facing that damned Dallas "Doomsday Defense." That front four of Too Tall Jones, Randy White, Jethro Pugh, and Harvey Martin would be teeing off to get to Joe. Late in the game our smallish offensive line would be at a real disadvantage. Bobb McKittrick and I immediately reminded each other on our headsets that "18 and 19 BOB," our sweeps, could take advantage, as planned, of their nickel defense. We were only a few paces apart, but the crowd noise was so intense that the only way to communicate was by head set.

The Cowboys would be in their "nickel" defense, with either one or two extra defensive backs in the game. Most teams would play a very predictable offense against that defense in this situation. They would substitute one or two wide receivers and start throwing. The quarterback would be expected to hold the ball until pass patterns developed down the field. The Cowboys would totally disrupt these tactics with their great pass rush, using only an occasional blitz.

But because their linemen were charging hard up the field, we could get excellent angles to block them on the sweep. We had the best pair of pulling guards in the league in Randy Cross and John Ayers, who were as critical to the success of that last drive as the men who handled the ball.

Meanwhile, the Cowboys defensive backs, certain we would be throwing the ball, were concentrating on pass coverage. By the time they realized we were running the ball, they were out of position to support quickly.

For that game, I had activated running back Lenvil Elliott to complement Ricky Patton, our starter, which put defensive lineman Pete Kugler on the inactive list. Our defensive coaches understandably argued against the move, but I had to set priorities. Kugler deserved to be activated but we needed Lenvil's poise and his experience offensively.

Lenvil, who played at Cincinnati when I had coached there, was somewhat past his prime; age and injuries had robbed him of his once-outstanding speed. But I knew he was a reliable ball carrier, who knew when to make his cuts on our running plays. His experience and savvy were vital at this point. He was outstanding at reading blocks and breaking off them. He knew when to go down, when to protect the ball, to avoid fumbling, and he knew when and how to go out of bounds, to save time off the clock.

Without great premiere backs, our running game was effective because we had our guards run full speed courses. This was something I had learned from Bill Johnson at Cincinnati.

Linemen can become hesitant as they release, pull around the tackle and head downfield to the corner. They slow down, looking for a defender to block, causing the running back to slow down. We taught our linemen to run full speed courses and taught our ball carriers to maintain a constant relationship to the blockers. Defenders would be forced to come to the blockers to get to the ball carriers. Our backs knew exactly what to expect, so they could run at full speed, cutting off the linemen's blocks.

The very essence of the running game is to run full speed courses and to cut people down. This is developed and refined only through hours of repetition, much of it established in training camp. Now we would depend on what we had acquired during those long hot days in July and August.

Four of our first seven plays on that drive were sweeps by Elliott for four, six, seven, and eleven yards (see Diagram B, page 269). When we got to the Dallas forty-nine, we ran a reverse with Fred Solomon—another play that took advantage of the hard charge of the Dallas line—for fourteen yards.

By that time, the Dallas pass rushers were becoming frustrated, seeing Elliott sweep outside them time after time. This forced them to slow their rush, to look for the run as well as the pass. Consequently there was less heat on Joe, and we went to our passing game, Montana passing to Clark for 10 yards and Solomon for 12. The final play before the winning touchdown was "19 BOB," another Elliott sweep, this time around the left side for 7 yards. With 58 seconds left, we had third down on the Cowboys' 7-yard line.

At that point, we went to a pass we had used effectively all year (see Diagram C, page 270). Solomon lined up inside Clark, and quickly broke to the sideline. Meanwhile, Dwight went to the end line and then slid into the corner. Joe would look immediately to Fred and then, if he were covered, look to the back of the end zone for Dwight. The design of the play called for Solomon to brush very closely to Clark as they passed, which would pick off the man covering Solomon. Dallas covered Solomon perfectly.

As Joe rolled to his right, he started looking for Clark. The pressure was really on as Joe finally located Dwight. He threw it high so no one but Dwight would have a chance for it. Dwight leaped to make a spectacular catch, and we had the touchdown. Ray Wersching then calmly kicked the extra point.

After the game, there were people, including Paul Brown, who questioned whether Joe was just trying to throw the ball away. That bothered us because we knew it was an integral part of the play. Joe and Dwight did exactly what they had practiced many times. We were to score on several occasions in ensuing years with this tactic.

Everybody remembers that catch, but few remember that Dallas got the ball back. The Cowboys only trailed by a point, and they had a solid, reliable place kicker, Rafael Septien, so if they could get to our thirty-yard line, Septien could still attempt a field goal which would beat us.

The Cowboys got to our 44 with a 31-yard pass to Drew Pearson, and Eric Wright made a tackle that kept it from being an even bigger play. At this point our pass rush was desperate. On the next down, Lawrence Pillers really unloaded on Dan White and knocked the ball loose. Jim Stuckey was right there, recovered the ball, and that was the game.

Just as our two wins over the Rams had shown a shift in momentum in our division, our two wins over the Cowboys showed a shift in power in the league. Again, it was because we had become so much quicker than Dallas. We continually beat them to the punch. That championship game was between two teams going in the opposite direction.

Clearly, we had deserved to win, but the Cowboys just couldn't face it. The Cowboys remained defiant; they just couldn't accept the fact we had beaten them twice in 1981 after they had dominated the 49ers for so many years. Tony Hill was quoted as saying, "I don't feel the Forty-Niners are the caliber of the Cowboys. If we played them tomorrow, we would beat them." Danny White said, "We feel we have the best team in the league." Even Tom Landry in frustration was quoted as saying, "The Forty-Niners are not a better team than us, but the game ended at the right time for them. Montana has to be the key. There's nothing else there but him."

I was upset at the time by those remarks, but in later years, I realize how devastated he must have been, almost assuming he'd go back to the Super Bowl, only to find his season ended in such a shocking manner. In previous playoff games against the 49ers, the Cowboys had always managed to win, and I'm sure he was confident they would do it again.

His reaction was to serve me well later when I had to deal with the media after devastating losses, particularly the NFC Championship game after the 1983 season, when we lost to the Washington Redskins on a late field goal. I was bitter and frustrated by the loss, but recovered to be totally complimentary toward the Redskins. I must admit I did have some critical words about the officiating.

As years passed, Tom and I were to become good friends. I will always be one of his biggest admirers, as he is one of the great coaches in the game's history. The very basis of coaching is the knowledge you possess and how well it is imparted. The bottom line is: Did the athletes under your direction reach their full potential? I believe both the Dallas Cowboys and the San Francisco 49ers coaching staffs personified this quality.

The Cowboys' remarks made no difference in San Francisco where 49er fans were so excited about finally beating Dallas, they called that game the biggest win in our history.

But we still had the Super Bowl to play. We couldn't stop now; this was when you rebuild your dedication. And it would take every bit of concentration and discipline we had acquired to meet the challenge.

For the first and only time in my coaching career, I didn't travel with the squad. I was being honored as "Coach of the Year" by the Touchdown Club in Washington, D.C., so I went there first and then on to Detroit. I arrived about two hours before the team. As I was waiting in the hotel lobby, I don't know what got into me, but I impulsively decided to loosen everyone up. I saw a bellhop who was about my size and gave him $20 to let me wear his uniform for a few minutes. It was pretty gamey; I don't think it had been laundered all that many times over the years, so I suffered for my gag, believe me.

When the team bus arrived, I greeted the players in my bellhop's uniform. At first, none of them recognized me. There were tussles when I tried to take suitcases from them, and when I held out my hand for tips, they reacted with disgust. Soon, Lawrence Pillers recognized me and then Joe Montana, and then everyone started laughing. It turned out to be a lighthearted way to start the week, with a little humor, because it quickly became one of the most difficult weeks we'd ever experienced.

Part of it was the attention and hype that is lavished on a team in the Super Bowl. We had never been even remotely exposed to that kind of hype and chaos before, and there were times when it was hard to handle. But that wasn't the only problem, or even the biggest one.

The NFL had placed us in a rather small and very remote hotel. (We later realized it was the only one available near the Silverdome.) Consequently players were existing in crowded, cramped conditions, and there wasn't any place to escape. You couldn't go outside because of the freezing weather. There was just snow and ice everywhere you looked. I established a later curfew than players had expected, but it didn't make a lot of difference. I knew they couldn't get very far.

Both teams were expected to practice in the Pontiac Silverdome, where the game would be played. The NFL had decided that the fair way to do it would be to flip a coin to decide which team would work out early and which team would have the facility later. We lost the coin flip, so we were assigned the early workout, at 9:00 A.M. A press conference would be held daily at 8:00 A.M. before the practice. Meanwhile the Bengals won the coin toss, and chose to work out in the second session, about 11:00 A.M. The afternoons were reserved for all game entertainment rehearsals.

It may have seemed fair to the NFL, but in fact, it turned out to be grossly unfair. The Bengals were coming from the same time zone, so they really had no change in their daily routine. But we were coming from the Pacific time zone, a three-hour differential. That meant that we were getting up at the equivalent of 3:30 to 4:00 A.M. in order to have breakfast, attend brief meetings, and get taped before being bussed to practice. It would have been one thing if we'd had to do that for a single day, but we were expected to do it all week. The players never really did adjust. By the third day we were functioning on nerve alone. We just couldn't get enough sleep.

It was just as bad at night. To get enough sleep, players should have been going to bed around 10:00 P.M., but that was only about 7:00 P.M. Pacific time, so that wasn't very logical either.

I made every effort to use our plight as a further source of motivation. I told the team it was just another "example" of the NFL not giving the 49ers the respect we deserved. There was one other development which served us well that week. Fred Solomon had twisted his knee very slightly in practice, so we notified the press and placed him on the injured list. Fred was virtually 100 percent by the next day, but we hesitated in changing his status on the report. If Cincinnati wanted to think Fred was not 100 percent, that was all right with me. You work for any little edge you can get, anything to distract the opponent. This would give the press something to question the Bengals about all week.

Finally, another development was to serve as an advantage. I was reminded of this during practice when kickoffs would take wild, skidding bounces off the artificial turf. In our league opener with Detroit, Ray had pulled a hamstring and was forced to "squib" kick. The Lions' return men had difficulty handling the ball, and it was on their home field. So, we had Ray work on low trajectory kicks which would skid when they hit. During the actual game it was to cause the Bengals all kinds of problems.

As the game approached, Howard Cosell, Jimmy "the Greek" and other "experts" had decided that our win over Cincinnati during the regular season should be discounted because the Bengals were physically much superior and it would be demonstrated in a championship game.

In truth, the Bengals were a very talented team, with great players like Ken Anderson and Ken Riley at cornerback. They had a big offensive line, with men like Max Montoya and Anthony Munoz. They had an excellent coach in Forrest Gregg, who had played for Vince Lombardi on the great Green Bay Packer teams of the '60s. Lindy Infante had developed a beautifully conceived offense. Their passing attack was the most potent in the AFC.

We were blessed with enthusiasm and confidence. It made some difference that we weren't meeting an established team that was accustomed to playing in championship games. The Bengals were a young team like us and, also like us, this was their first experience in a game of this magnitude.

But we knew we "belonged." We had beaten the Cowboys twice, we had beaten the Giants twice, we had beaten the Rams twice. We had gone into Pittsburgh to beat the Steelers. And we had beaten the Bengals.

But I have to say that in a sense, we really did win with "mirrors" as we were accused of doing all season. Physically, the Bengals were bigger and stronger and they ultimately outgained us by a good margin, 356 yards to 275. While preparing for the game, I racked my mind for anything that might work, passes off reverses, anything. Not desperation plays; they were things we had touched on throughout the year. But they were also plays we wouldn't have resorted to in a typical weekly NFL game.

Well, the game finally arrived and we were relieved to break from our impossible living conditions. Now all we had to do was play the game.

Because of the extreme weather conditions, just getting to the stadium became a major problem. There were two team buses, and I was on the second, with about half the squad. The early bus made it to the stadium without any serious trouble, but our bus got stuck in a massive traffic jam. We found out later that it was because of a motorcade for then-Vice-President George Bush, but we didn't know what the problem was at the time. We could communicate by radio telephone to the players in the locker room who were already dressing but we had no way of knowing when we'd get there.

I was becoming very concerned, and I could feel the tension on the bus. Players have their routine before a game. They spend a certain amount of time getting dressed, for instance, and they have their own rituals, whether it's meditating by themselves or talking to teammates or listening to a Walkman. They wouldn't have the time to do this now, and they were out of their comfort zone.

We couldn't even see the stadium because there was a hill between our bus and the Silverdome. I thought we might have to walk to the stadium, over that hill and through the snow, for about a mile. That was not a prospect that thrilled me.

But I couldn't let the players see my concern. I first amusingly remarked that we would join arms and hike cross-country. Then I got on the bus PA and told the players that the game had already started and we were ahead, 7–0. I said that Chico Norton, our equipment manager, was calling plays and Ted Walsh, his assistant, was playing quarterback. The players laughed and it broke the tension.

Meanwhile, I very seriously was scouring the countryside for the best route that would get us to the stadium on foot. It looked as though this might be the toughest decision I would make all day.

Finally the traffic broke, and none too soon. We didn't get to the stadium until twenty minutes before scheduled warmups. Players were frantic, trying to get dressed quickly to get on the field.

The group which came earlier were anxiously waiting for us in the locker room. There was all kind of nervous joking about our arrival. But then everything started to get serious.

Joe Montana had picked out a song by Kenny Loggins, "This Is It," to play in the dressing room because it had a message. One of the lines in the song was "This is your miracle," which certainly applied to us. Most players listened to it for a moment, then turned it off, but I insisted they keep playing the music. It was important to do anything possible which might relieve the tension.

We were almost traumatized. We had been exhausted during the week because of our workout schedule, and the delay in getting to the stadium had further disrupted our psyche. It seemed we had no control over our own fate.

And then, we got in the hole immediately when Amos Lawrence fumbled the opening kickoff after returning it to the twenty-six. It really wasn't his fault. The "wedge" blocker in front of him made the mistake of turning to the outside at the last instant, so an unblocked tackler hit Amos right after he caught the ball. Amos never even saw him coming.

At that point, we seemed very vulnerable and a Cincinnati touch-down might have been difficult to overcome. But on the sixth Bengal play, Dwight Hicks intercepted Ken Anderson's pass and returned it to our 32. Finally, we had some breathing room, and were able to drive 68 yards for a touchdown.

On reflection, there is one particularly satisfying play on that drive. With a third and one on the Cincinnati forty-seven, I called "Triple Pass," which started with Joe Montana handing off to Ricky Patton running to the right, reversing to Freddie Solomon who ran to the left, tossing the ball back to Montana, passing to Charle Young for a first down.

That was an old Paul Brown play. Paul, in the press box, had to watch his old "Triple Pass" used successfully against him in the Super Bowl. At that point, I remembered his constant admonition to use your own trick plays first. I had done it, but in this instance Paul probably didn't appreciate it.

We did everything we could to keep the Bengals off balance. One tactic was the use of an unbalanced line, which several Cincinnati defensive players admitted later really surprised them. They didn't really adjust to it until the second half, and we were able to drive for another touchdown and two field goals before the end of the half, while outgaining the Bengals 208 yards to 99 in the half.

After the game, Montana told the media, "Coach Walsh is really amazing with the game plans he comes up with. When we go over the game plan during the week, it doesn't look like it will work, but when we get into a game and use it, it seems the plan always works."

The plan worked because of people like Joe and because a "standard of performance" had been achieved.

There were some key plays in that first half. On one Cincinnati drive, for instance, Eric Wright stripped the ball from Bengals receiver Chris Collinsworth and Lynn Thomas recovered on the eight. We then drove 92 yards for a touchdown.

That touchdown was a perfectly executed play. Earl Cooper came out of the backfield through the center of the line, then broke to the left. The Bengals lost him in the traffic and didn't react to him, and he made the catch completely uncovered (see Diagram D, page 270).

Our last field goal of the first half proved to be significant because we had practiced those squib kicks by Ray Wersching during the week. The payoff came when we kicked off after a field goal had put our lead at 17–0. Archie Griffin couldn't handle the ball; Rick Gervais and

Amos Lawrence hit him, knocking the ball loose at the 15. The ball
continued to bounce all the way back to the 4-yard line where Milt
McColl recovered it for us there. We had only five seconds left. If
there had been even seven, I would have tried for one quick pass for
the touchdown, so we settled for the field goal. But those three points
were very important when we went into the dressing room with a
20–0 lead.

At that point, you could look at it two ways. You could say that we
could go on to win, 40–0. Or you could say that the Bengals should
come back in the second half. Sam Wyche wrote on the blackboard
in the locker room, "This game is not over yet." Everyone understood
because we had great respect for the Bengals. I told the team we would
need 10 more points to win.

The Bengal offense got untracked and they scored on their first
possession of the second half. Two possessions later, they drove to a
first down and goal on our three. We put up a fierce goal-line defense
in what is probably the best remembered play sequence of that game.
On the sideline I was in awe of the incredible character demonstrated
by our defensive team. We had come so far since 1979 when we would
regularly collapse in the second half. Men who had been inept losers
were now playing like true champions.

That critical sequence of plays began at our 3-yard line. Looking at
first and goal, the Bengals had all the momentum; in the second half
they had stuffed our offense and were now cutting up our defense.
They must have felt exhilarated, but we were cool and fierce, determined to stop them. On first down Pete Johnson, their 250-pound
fullback, dove straight over left tackle, but John Harty, Dan Bunz and,
of course, Jack Reynolds stopped him at the one-yard line. Second
down, and Johnson plowed over right guard, but Reynolds and Bunz
downed him with the help of Archie Reese, who undercut their
guard's legs. On third down, the Bengals made a good call: Anderson
faked to Johnson and quickly threw to Charles Alexander in the flat.
Again Bunz was there with a picture perfect tackle for no gain on the
play. Cincinnati then called a time out to discuss their fourth down
options. On the biggest play of the game, Pete Johnson followed
Charles Alexander into the line, where he was consumed by Reynolds,
Puki, and Lott over the top and Reese, Pillers, Choma and Board
underneath. The Bengals trotted off the field in disbelief. Turner,
Williamson and the others came to the sideline, hands on hips, heads

tilted back, filled with pride. They awaited the next onslaught. The Bengals would be back, and with their great pass offense, would take control of the game. That brilliant defensive effort would prove of vital importance. The Bengals had taken almost six minutes off the clock without scoring, which seriously curtailed their capability to utilize long, time-consuming drives to score.

But what people may not recall about that goal line stand is that Cincinnati came back on its next possession to close the gap to 20–14. We were in serious trouble. We hadn't made a first down yet in the half. We continued to have poor field position and were reduced to avoiding a critical error and taking time off the clock.

Cincinnati had changed its style of defense for the second half, going to a blitzing, attacking style of play that began overpowering our offense. I hadn't wanted to take a chance on an interception or a quarterback sack that could turn the game around.

But on second-and-fifteen from our twenty-two, Montana hit Mike Wilson for twenty-two yards on a play we had prepared for difficult situations such as this. Wilson started what looked like a go pattern but then planted his inside foot and drove to the sideline at twenty yards to catch the pass. Mike was barely in bounds in front of the Cincinnati bench.

That was what we called a "drift" pass for Joe. He dropped straight back, hesitated for a moment, then rolled out to get away from the rush. Our receivers hadn't been able to get open quickly enough, and Joe hadn't had time to pass, until we finally counteracted the blitz in this way.

That was the biggest play of the game, because it finally gave us some breathing room, improved our field position and got us un-tracked. From that point, we went to our running game, to take time off the clock, running the ball seven straight times and using up five minutes.

We couldn't score another touchdown, but Wersching hit a 40-yard field goal to make it 23–14. That normally was approaching the outer edge of Ray's "automatic" range, but kicking off the artificial turf in an indoor stadium extended his range, as it does for any kicker.

Then came another very big play. On the Bengals' first play after the kickoff, Anderson tried to hit Chris Collinsworth but Eric Wright made a brilliant interception at the Cincinnati 47 and ran the ball back 25 yards. The Wright-Collinsworth matchup was one of the great features of the game, both superb athletes and great competitors.

At the end of the play, Wright tried a lateral. Oh, my God! The ball bounced around on the turf. My heart was in my throat. Here, Eric had just made a play that should have almost clinched the win for us, but he might be giving the ball right back to them. Then Willie Harper fell on the ball for us, and I could breathe again.

We used almost another three minutes, getting a key first down on a run by Johnny Davis, before Wersching kicked another field goal, from 23 yards out. That was really the game. The Bengals came back to get another touchdown on a beautifully orchestrated drive, but we had forced them to use up too much time, leaving only sixteen seconds remaining when they scored. Dwight Clark fell on the onsides kick, and the game was over.

And so was our Camelot season.

13

Dealing with the Genius Label

After the 1981 season, when we had surprised everybody by winning the championship, I first began to hear the term "genius" applied to me. My reaction to it was quite different than I had supposed it would be before I became a head coach.

Naively, I really cultivated the idea of receiving special recognition when I was an assistant coach. For an assistant coach, it's gratifying to know you have a creative talent that has an impact on the NFL. I felt most positive about that in the seventies with the Cincinnati Bengals and the San Diego Chargers.

I very much appreciated acceptance by coaches and players who had dealt with our style of offense. I remember being absolutely inspired when Don Shula, one of the greatest coaches in the game, who was in Cincinnati when his Dolphins played the Bengals, approached me and acknowledged my existence.

This acceptance was most important to an assistant football coach who had played a major role in developing a passing attack that had been measurably different from the style of football accepted for many, many years. I felt positive about that. As time passed, TV commentators and sportswriters from other cities became most complimentary.

Assistant coaches were rarely recognized in those days. In one sense, it was gratifying, but in another sense, the head coach takes the public heat, so he should receive the credit.

Now, when I became a head coach, the term "genius" took on a completely different cast—someone who had a special talent or gift in coaching itself, not for just being creative in offensive football. When that began to happen, I became quite uncomfortable. It came at a time when I was just establishing myself as a head coach. I think everyone is sensitive about how your contemporaries react to you. That kind of tag made it seem that I was attempting to gain attention for myself, and that just wasn't the approach we took with the 49ers.

From the standpoint of the style of football itself, I took pride in that recognition. But as a coach, I wasn't anywhere near being established enough to be considered with the recognized men in the field.

When it was said positively, no harm was done, but you could almost assume that as soon as there was some failure or frustration the term would be applied in a negative way. That did hurt. Something that was started as a positive thing became almost a matter of ridicule when we fell during the 1982 season.

There were two or three general managers in the league who took real satisfaction in labeling me "the genius" and, of course, making it a joke, because our team struggled and stumbled in 1982. I knew that was happening, and it was an embarrassment, but I never allowed it to dominate my thoughts because I was so involved in the challenge of bringing the team back.

Really, when you're working, you don't have time to relate to a term like that. The life of a football coach is so intense, it doesn't make sense to give much thought to your reputation, or to what people are saying. It's a high-profile job, but so much of the time is spent in isolated meetings with your assistants or the players. You just don't have the option of worrying about personal identification.

Obviously, "genius" can be thrown around because people don't always have a developed vocabulary. There are all kinds of terms: great, super, genius. People go right to the strongest kind of label, often grossly overstated and temporary in nature. A player isn't truly great unless he is a "superstar."

I took pride in our offense as it was being developed. If there were positive responses to it, I was pleased. But when the genius label came up, I didn't give it a lot of thought until it was turned on me.

I can remember exactly when that happened. As I left after one of the 1982 Super Bowl press conferences, a writer—I honestly can't remember who it was now—stopped me and asked, "How do you feel about being called a genius?" I was already late to a meeting, so without thinking, I said something on the order of, "It's not my term. If people are using it, you probably should ask them." Somehow, that got turned around so it came out that I felt personally that I was some kind of genius.

There were some who decided I had an ego. Those who knew me realized it was much more likely to be insecurity, because of the years I had spent as an assistant coach not knowing whether I'd ever get an opportunity to become a head coach.

There is no question I have always had a strong drive to meet my career goals. That sustained me during the frustrating years in Cincinnati. In going to Stanford, I took a pay cut. That wasn't important because I was going to be the head coach at a great university with a solid football reputation.

But there is a distinct difference between drive and a kind of arrogance that overwhelms people.

People use the word ego, not differentiating between it and arrogance or selfishness. On occasion, I was labeled egotistical by some writers—not so much by San Francisco sportswriters as those in other areas who didn't know me. Even my game day sweater seemed to some to be an attention-getting device. Traditionally, 49er coaches had worn white sweaters, and I was just following the custom. I wore what the equipment manager put in my locker.

On occasion, that stereotype did trouble me, because I didn't know how I could ever address it. I realize that people need to write and they need a subject, and it's much easier to take a critical view of someone from a distance. But there wasn't any way I could address it.

This subject never came up with my coaching staff, because we were so intensely involved in everything we were doing. We simply didn't have time to talk about it, or even think about it. But even my attitude toward my assistant coaches played a part in this.

If you're primarily an administrative coach, if you're not directly involved in the makeup of a game plan or the strategizing, it's easy to seem humble by saying, "My offensive coordinator was responsible for that," because it's true.

I couldn't operate that way. I had to be directly involved. We would work together, well past midnight many times a week in formulating our game plan. I wouldn't deflect responsibility.

Often, I used the term "we" because it was "we." I'd say "we did this" or "we did that," and writers occasionally would inquire about the constant "we." In truth, so many ideas and suggestions come out of a staff that no one can be concerned about whose creation it was. The final decision would naturally be mine, but only after significant input from the others.

The public scrutiny even extends to a coach's family, and is sometimes even more telling on them. This is something we never considered when I began in coaching.

When I began coaching, the aspirations of my wife Geri and I, like many young couples, were filled with anticipation about the adventure and excitement the future held. The thought of continuing my future in sports, as a coach, after leaving the playing field was most comfortable because I felt at home with the life-style.

Almost overnight we were thrust into a situation that demanded considerable adult responsibilities. As an example, Geri's first exposure to the life of a coach was dealing with my schedule: I had to drive the high school team in a school bus after practice, delaying our dinner hour well into the evening. Not only did I arrive home after 7:00 P.M., but I also brought home all my job-related anxieties. At age twenty-five I couldn't exactly depend upon vast experience in dealing with each problem as it came up. Geri found early on that a nice meal she had prepared before our night game would be gulped down; I hardly realized what I was eating.

Later, when I became a college assistant at Berkeley, Geri was exposed to an even more demanding work schedule. Now, I would be away, living in college dorms for two weeks of training camp, and arriving home at 10:00 or 11:00 P.M. many nights during the season. Also, of course, there was the continuous athlete recruiting schedule, which required many nights away from home in the off-season.

Above and beyond this, Geri was quickly exposed to the frustration and exhilaration inherent in sports. This became part of our very existence. At that point in time, young women were not typically exposed to the volatile emotions of sport—the stark reality of life based on winning and losing each week. The resulting wild swing of emotions of the stadium now prevailed in our home.

As my career in professional football evolved, all of these forces became even more intense. The difficult life of a coach and his family is compounded by the haunting concern over job security.

When I finally achieved my ambition of being a head coach, there was the added public exposure related to my work. During our winning years, this was most often very positive and flattering. But in those difficult years, there were the natural resulting criticisms and consequential gossip. Our children, as well as Geri, were subjected to some unfortunate experiences in such places as school, the supermarkets, and restaurants.

For example, our daughter Elizabeth, at a very vulnerable age in about the fifth or sixth grade, was told by one of her classmates at school that I was going to be fired. That remark had come from her parents who, at a cocktail party, has visited with one of the employees of our organization. As you might guess, Elizabeth was embarrassed, Geri was upset, and I was livid.

As time passed, we conditioned ourselves to account for public scrutiny and found ways to insulate the family from it. Our sons Steve, now a radio and television broadcaster, and Craig, a commercial real estate executive, have survived the pressures and are doing well professionally.

Few wives can identify with this life-style. There are those who can't understand how women can deal with the demands and effects on the family and with others who might be envious of the public notoriety.

In contemporary life, it is critical that a woman develop her own career. She then has a vehicle to direct her concentration on her work and is less susceptible to the ebb and flow of the coach's career. Geri returned to the University of Cincinnati, majoring in interior design, and has since embarked on a very successful career.

Geri and I were ultimately able to blend two careers and thrive under these conditions. The original sense of adventure has sustained itself as years passed. Each season was a beginning and ending of a new chapter, and with it came the anticipation, excitement, and ultimate gratification. This sense of accomplishment was infused in the entire family. That sustained me as I dealt with the public scrutiny.

* * *

I think in a sense it's inevitable that a coach's relationship with the media becomes more strained and confrontational over time, whether it's conscious or not. Just by being associated under the same set of circumstances with the same men and women, you're bound to have people who notice idiosyncrasies, and, in their minds, find flaws in your makeup, and who find remarks redundant that seem to be made week after week and year after year.

The media becomes bored with a coach who is around as long as I was, ten years. Reporters think they see a person who is less than direct, less than concise, who is consistently hedging or manipulating the press. That's typical of anybody who's been with the same press corps for several years. I was warned of this by Sid Gillman.

Sid said, "They'll get tired of you after five years. If you lose they'll be after your job. If you win they'll start looking for anything that can create controversy." To make his point, he purposely overstated his point, but not by much.

In later years, there were those who questioned whether I gave Joe Montana enough credit for success, though whenever asked, I'd elaborate at length on his specific areas of greatness.

There was one instance when, after our weekly media conference, one writer decided I had criticized Montana, and I challenged him: Fifty fellow journalists attended the press conference and none of the others reported in this way. Why did you?

Also, in a sense, I was a victim of my own success. When I first started coaching the 49ers, we didn't have many reporters covering us, because the team had had so little success and, consequently, had a reluctant following. But as soon as we were in contention and then won a Super Bowl, that changed. So did the expectations of the media.

We had as many as seventy-five people covering the team on a regular basis, and after that first championship, everybody was thinking in terms of more championships. As we won consistently in the '80s, at the very least making the playoffs, there was a natural tendency among reporters to look for the "downside" stories.

On an individual basis, I had grown to appreciate and thoroughly enjoy the company of most sportswriters. But collectively, there is a lemming mentality that develops, almost a herd instinct. When a topic was hot, often initiated by a more prominent or controversial writer, virtually everyone chased it, each looking for a different angle or insight.

There was one writer in our local press corps, who is no longer in San Francisco sports, who showed virtually no ethics or respect for anyone. When you have one who does that, many of the others almost feel obligated to slant their writing to stay competitive.

For instance, I don't know how many times writers would approach me and say either another coach or other players had said our offense was outdated, the league had caught up with it, and what will we do about it? It was becoming common knowledge that "the game passed me by." That would happen every preseason, over and over, because naturally, in the preseason games, we were limiting the number of plays we would use, and we were calling plays to give players an opportunity to demonstrate their abilities, regardless of the circumstance. We had not researched our opposition as we would in the regular season. I would tease writers: Didn't they recognize that they were writing the same thing they had in previous years?

As an example, members of the media, especially those with less seasoning, fail to remind themselves what the coach has just experienced before a postgame press conference starts. They expect answers and responses to be very natural and normal and succinct. In fact, the coach has just been taken to the very depths emotionally. His emotions are spent and his nerves are momentarily shattered, because his whole being is exhausted. He may not be able to respond and express himself as clearly and concisely as he'd like. Things could be understated. Things could be overstated. There could be a giddy laugh, or almost sobbing. In this state the coach is a study of a person who is emotionally exhausted.

By the end of a given week, the coach has spent as many as seventy hours preparing for the upcoming game. He finds himself physically, mentally, and emotionally exhausted. As the game progresses there are literally hundreds of hard, stressful decisions that must be made.

As years passed, I found this exhaustion affecting me more and more. Following the game almost anything could set me off. My nerves were so frayed, I was impatient with anything. A honking horn, slow traffic, a caustic reporter, gawking guests at the DeBartolo's postgame gatherings.

It wasn't just losing. I could be just as vulnerable after a win. Those around me over a period of time learned how to offer their support and shield me from expectant or demanding situations. I couldn't handle any surprises.

The night following the game was always spent at home. Immediately after home games, my family and I would gather in Eddie's quarters, discuss the outcome and visit with our friends and guests of the organization. The accolades were nice but I couldn't wait for the traffic to clear so I could get home. A sleeping pill would be necessary because I would inevitably wake up and relive every decision I had made, getting no sleep whatsoever.

I have never experienced a game after which, hours later, I couldn't accurately second-guess myself after reanalyzing information that had become available to me. Of course the most satisfying moments were during the flight home, after a victory. I could relax, reflect, and at least momentarily take pride in our success.

There were also occasional brushes with the more fanatical fans. I can remember one early in my 49er career. We'd lost the game, but we'd played well and I was pleased with our performance. As I was about to drive off, a fan yelled at me, "Bill, we've met before! I'm a friend of so and so. Please stop for just a minute. I need to talk to you."

So I stopped the car, rolled down the window, and as soon as I did that, he started to beseech me, "Listen, you dumb son of a bitch, you just blew another one. You're making stupid decisions. How can DeBartolo keep you on? If we could get rid of you, we might have a chance. Yes I've met you, but I'm telling you . . ."

With my emotions as they were, I wanted to stop and get out, but Geri convinced me to roll up the window and drive off. He was still trying to run along with the car. That's the kind of reaction you get sometimes with that fringe mentality. Anything can happen and a coach can be quite vulnerable.

I remember a columnist wrote right after I was hired by NBC that since I can't even express myself after a game, I cannot put two sentences together, how could I ever be a television analyst?

Her most recent experience with me had been after games during a very emotional 1988 season, games such as the one against the Raiders, in which we could not score a touchdown. I probably didn't make much sense in those instances, but as a television analyst, I'm not emotionally involved with the teams or the games. It's not nearly as difficult to be profound and expressive in that role.

The coach is very vulnerable dealing with the press and the public because of the stress involved, unless he's conceded the season. If he is only expected to do fair-to-average, he could conceivably be very open and upbeat with the press. That happens. You can get some gregarious coaches who feel that an 8–8 record would be acceptable. But after our first Super Bowl, an 8–8 season would have been a major disappointment for the 49ers. Except for the strike-ridden '82 season, we were at least 10–6 every year in the '80s.

Both as a 49ers coach and as a TV analyst, I'm often approached for autographs. That's not a problem for me. It's a very nice feeling to know that I'm respected and appreciated. If it takes just thirty seconds to sign an autograph, why the fuss? It becomes part of the obligation that goes with notoriety.

I'm especially pleased when minority youngsters acknowledge me. To them, someone with my age and my appearance could only be an authority figure, feared and not to be trusted. When I'm approached, I make an effort to respond warmly and demonstrate I'm quite human, someone they can feel comfortable with. When I see black and Chicano youngsters approach me in an enthusiastic way, I'm very happy to share that moment with them. I believe it to be a hand across a huge generation gap.

Fortunately, the 49ers did well in my coaching years, so virtually every contact I've made publicly has been positive.

There have been times when I've had to say, "Wait until we are through with dinner or wait until I've finished what I'm doing." There have been instances when I've been on the pay phone at the airport and people have walked up and started talking to me while I'm trying to talk to somebody on the other end of the line. Or, even worse, there have been those occasions in a rest room when I've been handed a piece of paper and expected to sign while I continued to do other things.

That part of it is sort of humorous. But I've been fortunate because we were successful. I doubt I would have handled constant criticism as well as some others have, but fortunately, I was able to get through my career without much of it.

14

The Repeating Problem

The optimism, the disappointment, the anxiety, the excitement of football is a true challenge before the season starts. Once the season begins, it becomes a crusade to focus those emotions.

Twice I had teams that won Super Bowls but could not repeat as champions. That wasn't unusual; until the 49ers repeated by winning the 1990 Super Bowl, no NFL team had repeated in ten years. The teams that followed us as champions in '84, the Chicago Bears and New York Giants, were great teams in the years that they won and I'm sure they expected to repeat. But they couldn't do it either.

In retrospect, the failure in '82 is much easier to understand. We were so pleased with what we had done, because it was unprecedented that we had accomplished so much so quickly, that we were over-confident and self-satisfied. We felt we would sustain this accomplishment and had established ourselves as one of the best organizations in football.

We were seasoned enough to realize it would be tough to repeat, but we hadn't won a championship because of a fluke. We had battled through some tough times and beaten the best teams twice.

But we failed to fully understand how fortunate we had been the year before. We hadn't suffered key injuries. We had won close games because of Ray Wersching's field goals. Without his consistency and poise we might have lost some of those.

We also weren't cognizant of the fact that we lacked the depth to sustain that kind of success.

And then, as the 1982 season began, we were hit by an abnormal number of injuries, starting with Randy Cross breaking his leg in a fall during a rope-swinging act in a show at an amusement park. Cross's injury was a freak, but he shouldn't have been involved in such a risky venture. This was a product of our newfound image. Other injuries may have come because players weren't as well conditioned and mentally prepared coming back after the Super Bowl. I can recall a game against Denver when we had 14 of our 22 starters out with injuries, and we didn't have anywhere near the quality of players we needed to replace them.

There were times, too, when the team played lethargically. I knew we had a drug problem on the team, but I didn't know how much that was hurting us. I did know that we were losing the close games we'd won the year before. It didn't help, either, that the season was interrupted by a players strike, which cut the schedule to nine games.

One of the games which hit me the hardest was against Dan Fouts and the San Diego Chargers in a "shoot out." We had taken the lead late in the fourth quarter, only to have Fouts complete five passes, drive his team the length of the field and beat us, 41–37. Joe Montana had a great game but we couldn't stop them at all defensively, primarily because we just didn't have our top players on the field.

In the locker room immediately following our stunning loss, I broke down. The other coaches stepped out to allow me privacy, and I let it all go. It all hit at once. The world champions, all of the recognition— and now, once again, we were losing week after week by close scores, as we had in my first two years with the 49ers. The game itself truly tested my ability to orchestrate a game offensively. We had to score on each possession just to stay with Fouts and company. There was the sheer frustration of not being able to slow down the Chargers, even on their final drive. Now, the reality set in. We were champions of the National Football League but we still "weren't there yet." I got up, fixed my shirt tail, washed my face, combed my hair and went to the postgame press conference to deal with the obvious questions.

The final blow was the loss to the Rams. Before the game, I asked our special teams coach, Milt Jackson, why he hadn't practiced against the Rams "field goal block." He said the Rams hadn't run a defense specially designed to block a field goal all year, so we had nothing to practice against. So, of course, on the final play, the Rams blocked our close field-goal attempt to knock us out of the playoffs.

That was another shattering experience.

Going into the season, I had felt that the frustration of the past was behind me. After having spent so many years as an assistant, I had finally become a head coach. Then after two frustrating years, when we won the championship, I felt vindicated. All of my hard work had come together and I had established myself.

Then to see the '82 season coming apart at the seams took more of a toll on me than anything I could expect to experience. This kind of absolute distress was to occur again, under somewhat different circumstances, in 1987.

It was embarrassing to me. I was far too emotional, to the point that, by the time the year was over, I had become cynical and bitter. I didn't want to continue. I'd had so many agonizing experiences in football. All those years when I thought I would never be a head coach. The stress of playcalling throughout my years with the Bengals. A crushing loss to USC when I was coaching at Stanford. The downside seemed too much to take. Losing those close games in '82 were exhausting, devastating experiences.

Following that '82 season, I had decided I was through with coaching. I would retain only the general manager's job. The years in both roles were really taking a toll on me, and I resolved that if I were to give up one, it should be coaching. After all, I didn't want to hire someone who would immediately become my boss as general manager.

I felt I could get the right man to coach and that I could continue to administrate what we were doing by providing strong leadership and management skills, and by concentrating on acquiring and developing championship level personnel.

Eddie DeBartolo had said many times that he would support me in whatever decision I made. He preferred that I stay as the coach, but if I decided I wanted only to be the general manager, he would agree to that.

So I had made the emotional decision to step away.

I took everything as humiliating personal failure, which I would have to say is a characteristic that is not particularly desirable. I was too sensitive. I suffered too much with the losing.

Among other things, there was a haunting feeling because of a drug involvement that not only permeated our team in '82 but also every other franchise in the NFL. Players' performances were affected by cocaine and marijuana. There were a number of players involved. The use of drugs had become so accepted that it was commonplace at social functions, including team parties.

I didn't know if I could deal with that, on top of everything else. I was troubled by the fact that it was my obligation to act publicly as if nothing like that was occurring, at the same time that I was expected to take full responsibility for the team losing.

When the team lost, I sensed there were members who were so involved in drugs that their performance was affected. I didn't know how long I could live with that inequity, but I was obligated by my personal code not to go public with it, and in fact, I denied over and over that we had a drug problem.

The majority of our players were not involved but there was almost a social code that this was a player's business and they weren't concerned that it would affect their performance. There was no peer pressure to stop it. I didn't get any response when I made an effort to address drug use with the players.

That really frustrated me. There were at least twelve men from our championship team whose lives were dramatically affected by drugs. Again, I want to remind people there were an even larger number on many other NFL teams.

Following the Rams' loss, in a very emotional state, I decided I'd had enough. I had met with the team after the game and remarked on what had happened in 1982, and why and what they could expect the next season. There was a typical end-of-the-season meeting scheduled with the players the next day, at which we would get their off-season addresses and attend to routine business. I was so distraught, I decided I'd better not meet with them, so I had John McVay preside over the meeting.

My failure to attend was unquestionably very poor judgment, but I was so emotionally upset that I wasn't going to make a very good impression on anybody. Later, I was criticized by certain prominent players, but none of those players had actively supported me in our efforts to address the drug problem that existed on the squad.

I privately met with many people, among them Lou Spadia, the former president and part-owner of the 49ers, looking for guidance and affirmation. They were all sympathetic. I think they all felt if I waited long enough, I'd be rejuvenated and ready to get back with coaching, but at the time, I'd had it.

So, I contacted three people about the coaching job—Mike White, John Robinson, and Terry Donahue. Eddie indicated that any one of them would be acceptable to him. Mike could well have become the head coach of the 49ers but he preferred to stay at the University of Illinois. John had left coaching at USC for an administrative position. He decided that he'd rather stay with that, though he later changed his mind and became the coach of the Los Angeles Rams. Terry would most likely have been interested, but soon after visiting with him, I decided to remain as the coach.

The reason White and Robinson balked, I think, is that they didn't want me to quit, that they felt I should continue coaching. So, they didn't "cooperate." These men were among the very best in football. All had been extremely successful at the college level.

Then, my thinking was heavily influenced because of an exchange with two good friends, Jim Finks and Jim Hanifan.

Collegiate scouting was an integral part of my responsibilities, so while I was debating my future, I was at the Senior Bowl at Mobile, Alabama. I was bitter and cynical, in a terrible state of mind. I sat in a restaurant with Finks and Hanifan and told them, "I don't even want to go out and see tomorrow's practice. I don't want to look at another athlete, I don't want to time another athlete, I don't want to decide whether this one is good or bad. I just don't want to see another football player."

Finally, Finks said, "You're full of bleep. You get your ass out there. You're the best there is. Go out and do your job." And Hanifan said, "That's right. We're both sick and tired of this kind of crap. Quit feeling sorry for yourself. We'll see you out there in the morning."

That really jolted me. As I returned to my room, it hit me. They were right. I got up the next morning feeling differently about everything. I told myself to quit the self-deprecation and go back to what I do. Finks and Hanifan had shocked me back into reality with expletives and straight, hard talk between friends.

That evening when I called Eddie in Youngstown, he said he too had had enough and expected me to continue as coach. As I began committing myself to coaching again, I began to feel much better and anxious to get going.

During my days of indecision, I had talked to my assistants and told them it was likely I'd be stepping down and that I couldn't assure them of their jobs, because I'd give the new coach the latitude to choose his own staff. So, in the time before I decided to return, several coaches had left. Billie Matthews, who had done an excellent job with the running backs, left for Philadelphia. Milt Jackson moved to Buffalo. Chuck Studley took a comparable job as defensive coordinator with Houston, with the possibility of taking over as head coach. Sam Wyche went to Indiana as the head coach, although that had nothing to do with my status; Sam had an opportunity, and I urged him to take it. He was ideally suited for the top job at the collegiate level.

I had four men leave, so I immediately directed my energies to hiring coaches and training them, which pulled me out of the doldrums. The coaches who left had done an outstanding job, taking us from obscurity to a championship in three years, but the idea of a new, revitalized coaching staff appealed to me. It would be exciting to put together a group that had something to prove. It was an opportunity to get started again. We refocused our attention and changed our defensive philosophy, to include a more comprehensive approach. With Chuck Studley, we had been known as a solid, sound team that was extremely tough against the run. The emphasis had been with our defensive line and linebackers. As the game evolved offensively with the implementation of multiple receiver formations with a stress on the forward pass, I decided much of our attention should be given to the "nickel" defense and the multiple coverage options that had become so vital.

In retrospect, I'm not sure if I could ever have been happy solely as a general manager. At one point, it seemed that it would be an absolute relief, but I doubt that I could have sustained myself for another ten or fifteen years in management only.

After our total domination of the NFL in 1984, everybody predicted that we would repeat in '85. It was a major disappointment when we didn't. Of course, a great Chicago Bears team that was just finding itself was lurking out there. They had gifted players—Walter Payton at running back, Jim McMahon at quarterback, Willie Gault at wide receiver—a fine offensive line and a great defense, led by Mike Singletary, Otis Wilson and Dan Hampton. They were peaking, as were the New York Giants.

Many things happen to a team that wins a championship. Other teams will research more and give much more concentration in their preparation, and players feel it's more of a challenge to play a champion. Psychologically, once you've accomplished your goal, it's harder to keep working to improve. There is a sense of self-satisfaction that can finally result in complacency. There are new contract demands. Everybody wants to be compensated now. These demands lead to holdouts and in some instances, real animosity.

We worked hard in training camp in '85 to avoid those pitfalls, but we still self-destructed. I'm still not quite sure why. I can't really say it was a lack of effort. We'd play well, but then make critical mistakes.

I didn't realize it at the time, but our 1985 opener in Minnesota was an indication of the way the season would go. We literally fumbled away the game. We gained almost 500 yards (489) and outgained the Vikings by more than 200 yards, which shows how we dominated the game. But we fumbled twice in the fourth quarter, giving up a chance at two more touchdowns, and giving Minnesota new life.

When we took the field for what we thought would be the drive that would put the game away—because Minnesota hadn't really stopped us all day—I warned Wendell Tyler about fumbling at this time of the game, to be sure to put the ball away. Then, on his first carry, he broke through the line, had a collision with a teammate, and simply dropped the ball. Naturally, the Vikings recovered.

Wendell was really an enigma. He was a great player, an explosive, elusive runner, but those fumbles would seem to come at some of the most critical times. We won in '84 with Wendell as a major factor, but in '85, we started to have problems with his tendency to lose control of the ball.

But, even after the Vikings scored, we were still tied and could have won the game on our next drive. Before the kickoff, I reminded Derrick Harmon, "Now, protect the ball at all costs. Just kneel down at the twenty if you have to." But Derrick took the kickoff and, when he was hit, fumbled deep in our territory. The Vikings went in to score again to take the game away from us.

Those kinds of games take so much out of you, they're such a shock to your system, to be a proud champion and then lose to Minnesota after totally dominating the game. What can you say to a team after a game like that? The loss didn't really reflect a lack of team effort, because the team played well, only to give it away.

I can remember a play in that same game when the Vikings ran a counter for a 60-yard gain because Mike Walter wasn't yet familiar with his position as inside linebacker and he was momentarily fooled, recovering too late to get to the ball carrier.

That kind of thing just kept happening in '85. The team was prepared to play and desperately wanted to repeat. Now, whether we could have repeated, with the Bears playing so well and the Giants coming on, I can't honestly say. But we kept self-destructing.

That tendency wasn't obvious when, after the Minnesota loss, we recovered and won the next two games. And in fact, the second game, a 34–10 win over the Raiders, was one of the most gratifying victories of my coaching career, because it came in the Los Angeles Coliseum.

Throughout my career—whether it was as an assistant at Cal, an assistant and later head coach at Stanford or assistant with the Cincinnati Bengals—whenever we'd travel to Los Angeles, we'd lose.

During those years, USC, UCLA, and the Rams were among the best teams, and going in representing Berkeley and Stanford and Cincinnati was an awesome task. There was a mystique about those teams, and about the Coliseum.

Much of my youth was spent in southern California. My parents, Ruth and Bill, who still lived there, attended every game in which I was involved. I could recall how many times I had walked up the long ramp leading from the Coliseum dressing room, to meet my family after still another loss. I particularly remembered the defeats to USC, with that damned horse running around the track.

This game matched the winners of the two previous Super Bowls, the '83 champions against the '84 champions. When I noted the game on the schedule in April, I knew it would be one of the biggest games of the year. Why did it have to be in the Coliseum?

It was an important game in still another respect: Even though they'd moved from Oakland four years before, the Raiders still had a big following in northern California, so in a sense, it was the "Battle of the Bay."

As we drove from our hotel to the game that day, I was reminded again of my personal history with the Coliseum, because we drove down Vermont Street, which was the street I traveled to see USC and the Rams play, when as a youngster I first became interested in football.

There was a huge crowd at the Coliseum, and it was a very hot day. When people talk about the effect of weather on a game, they generally think of the cold weather in the Midwest and East late in a season, but they underestimate how difficult it can be to play in the heat and smog of Los Angeles. The Raiders made it even more difficult with their physical, violent style of play. They intimidated teams.

I wasn't concerned that they would intimidate us; the 49ers have great pride, and they rise to the occasion. We knew we would have to play a physical game to beat the Raiders, and we also knew we were capable of it.

Still, because of my own history in the Coliseum and the importance of this game, there was a great deal of apprehension before the game. Because of the respect I have for Al Davis, we talk frequently, but with all the tension that day, Al and I didn't speak as our teams warmed up. We both wanted this one.

Our quickness really showed in this game. By the third quarter, some of the bigger Raiders began wilting in the heat. The big play came at a time when we were leading, 20–3. After being hit by Jeff Stover, Raider quarterback Jim Plunkett fumbled. Milt McColl picked up the fumble and ran 28 yards for a touchdown, and as he was running, I thought, "I'm finally going to win a game at the L.A. Coliseum."

The celebration in our locker room, with me leading it, was really something, and for the first time I enjoyed my postgame walk up to meet my family.

Late in the game a Stover sack of Plunkett had injured Jim's shoulder, which was to affect his career. Everybody on our team felt bad about that, because Jim was not only a great player, but a true gentleman. But I have to say that if the Raiders had had the chance to get a shot at Joe Montana, they certainly would have taken it.

Overall, Stover had a great game. When healthy, he was one of the best defensive linemen of his time.

Unfortunately, that was the last time we looked like the team of the year before. We lost three of our next four games and, though we played well in the second half of the season, winning five of our last six games, we had so many injuries, we couldn't sustain our drive in the postseason.

We beat the Cowboys to get into the playoffs as a wild card team, but then lost to the Giants, 17–3, in the Meadowlands. We were so banged up, we just couldn't field an effective team. So many players were injured but played hurt, guys like Russ Francis, John Ayers, Wendell Tyler, and Dwight Clark. Joe Montana was hurting, too. The combination of our injuries and the fact that the Giants were playing so well was too much to overcome.

But, really, I don't know what we'd have done if we'd won that game, because our injured players couldn't have made it another week. I doubt that Montana could have suited up the rest of the year.

Our troubles continued into 1986, even though we made the playoffs again.

Joe Montana played beautifully in the first game against Tampa but wrenched his back when he was running left and threw to the right. He didn't complain after the game, but in the next couple of days, it really began to bother him. Joe had suffered through a series of back problems in his career. The diagnosis this time was ruptured and bulging discs, putting pressure on his spinal cord. Finally, it was decided that surgery was absolutely necessary. It would be major surgery, and Joe's career would be in jeopardy.

Fortunately, we had acquired Jeff Kemp in a trade with the Rams in the off-season. I had been impressed with Kemp's strong arm and mobility when I'd seen him play with the Rams. When Los Angeles signed Dieter Brock out of Canada, Kemp was expendable, so we were able to trade for him during the draft. I thought he'd be a capable backup for Joe. I certainly didn't envision him starting for us, but with Joe out indefinitely, there was little choice. We were to be very fortunate to have Kemp's services.

Jeff is the son of Jack Kemp, the former NFL quarterback who became the Secretary for Housing and Urban Development in the Bush administration. Jeff had played at the Ivy League level, at Dartmouth, and had started only seventeen games for the Rams before being traded. But he adapted well to our system and consequently, we were able to remain competitive.

We rested Joe the next week and used Kemp against the Rams in Anaheim. We could well have won that game, but the Rams scored on a 65-yard return of a blocked field goal. Replays showed that the ball was illegally lateraled forward to LeRoy Irvin, who scored the touchdown, but it wasn't called that way in the game. Kemp had played well, completing 19 of 24 for 252 yards, one of those completions a 66-yard touchdown pass to Jerry Rice.

The team thought Kemp was just replacing Montana for that game. That wasn't unusual; injuries had kept Joe from starting a game in each of the previous two seasons. But it had been decided prior to the game that Joe would have surgery the next week. I announced that to the team after the game; not only had we lost to the Rams but we had lost the best quarterback in the game. At that time, we couldn't be sure that Joe would ever play again.

Our goals didn't change when Montana went out with his surgery. We still were aiming at the playoffs. I reminded our team that, so often in battle, the best soldiers are killed early and the ones who replace them are the ones who win the battle. I often used specific battles to more graphically make that point. For instance, as the Battle of Midway developed, many of our best pilots were lost in initial raids that brought no results. Later as our other pilots arrived on the scene, the enemy had been committed and spent. Because of this, we dealt a devastating blow with those who participated late in the action. In football, too, the best players are often injured early in a season, and it's their replacements who must take over and carry the team to victory.

In this case, Joe Montana had been injured and basically removed from our plans. We didn't expect to have Joe again that year, so it was up to everybody else to play their best football and to compensate in any way necessary for the inexperienced Jeff Kemp.

As it turned out, Jeff performed admirably and everyone closed ranks around him. It was a real tribute to the team that we were able to play so well in Montana's absence. It was a complete change from '82, when every little thing hit us so hard. Here, we had lost Joe but the team continued to play championship football. The team's character and personality asserted itself, as it did later when I left. The camaraderie and standard of performance that we had established demonstrated itself.

Jeff was short for a quarterback, just under six feet. If we first faked a run and he could get back and get some clearance between himself and the pass rushers, he was okay, but once the defensive linemen read pass, they'd close on him and it was difficult for Jeff to release the ball if he telegraphed it in any way.

Our linemen were asked to engage their pass rushers earlier and stay in front of them. In a sense, they sacrificed their ability to sustain their blocks, but if they stopped the rushers early, Jeff could get some clearance and his height disadvantage wouldn't be a factor.

Jeff was told, and everybody understood, that if linemen were to engage their opponents early, there was a chance they could lose them and the pass rushers would be, in a sense, unloaded on Jeff. But he could stand up to that because he possessed great courage and had a solid physique. He was tough and durable, and he feared no one.

We also emphasized the play pass because faking the run would take some of the heat off the pass rush. We had always stressed play fake techniques, and Jeff's ballhandling soon became as adroit as Montana's. But any time you play fake and the offensive linemen drive out much as they do when they're run-blocking, they can lose their men quickly. So, we always reminded our quarterbacks, if we play fake, you're going to get quick clearance but expect somebody to get free and take a shot at you.

In Jeff's case, he'd get the time he needed to get the ball off, but he'd be hit right after he threw, almost without exception. Still, we had great success throwing to Jerry Rice deep downfield, after our running backs did a convincing job of faking when they didn't have the ball. At one time, we were throwing the ball about as well as we ever had, with Kemp throwing primarily to Rice. Jeff's running ability was comparable to Joe's, so he was always a threat to run if the pass protection broke down.

With Kemp, we won our next three games, before losing to Minnesota in overtime. But then Jeff got hurt. He wrenched his hip playing in a 10–10 overtime tie against Atlanta. He demonstrated great courage, having his hip twisted and torn and yet playing the rest of the game with it, but that was virtually the end of his brief 49er career. When we acquired Steve Young before the next season we had to make room on our roster, so we traded Jeff to Seattle, but I'll always appreciate how much he meant to the 49ers that year.

When Kemp was hurt, we went with Mike Moroski. Mike was a very bright man and competitive, but he had only been with us a couple of weeks, so he couldn't be expected to know much of our system.

We beat Green Bay in Milwaukee with Moroski at quarterback, but then, we lost to the Saints in New Orleans, 23–10. Ed DeBartolo, Jr., was terribly distressed over that loss, and we had a confrontation in the locker room after the game, the first time that had happened. It took another forty-eight hours before we got back together on the phone to smooth things over, reminding each other how hard we had worked to get where we were, and that we could deal with bad times like these.

That was a real crisis. The chemistry wasn't right. The combination of my emotions being totally drained by the game and Eddie being distraught over a frustrating loss had created a volatile situation, so the flight home was a most difficult one for me, on top of losing and dealing with these injuries. I couldn't be sure what my future held.

Joe Montana recovered so well, being very fit going into the surgery and having doctors who knew exactly what the procedure would be. Following the surgery, he improved significantly. It was a relief to him that the problem had been rectified, and he was really upbeat. The pain was gone. He took his rehabilitation as a challenge and made an almost superhuman effort to come back. Suddenly, we realized Joe might return this year.

Dr. Arthur White, who had done the surgery on Joe, had given him clearance to practice and possibly play the week before the New Orleans game, but we didn't suit him up. I insisted on being as safe as possible, giving him an extra week of work before he played. The next week in practice, Joe looked very good. He was throwing the ball, and though he was 5 to 6 pounds lighter than he'd been before the surgery, he was strong and active. I announced that he would start against the St. Louis Cardinals. He now was stronger and much more fit than before the surgery. His rehab program had gone beautifully.

But then, just forty-eight hours before our game, Dr. White had a press conference and stated that if it were up to him, Joe wouldn't play. When that word got to me, I was stunned. We had been given the okay to play Joe and, at the last moment, it appeared the doctor had sidestepped the responsibility for Joe's well-being and had put it all on me. At that point, I really felt the heat.

Joe wanted to play. He was fully prepared to play. I anguished over that decision because it could look as if I were an absolutely ruthless, calculating coach who would use a player who was vulnerable to further injury. If I didn't play him, it would have a major impact on the team because we had nobody but Mike Moroski available. So I was in a difficult position, to say the least.

As it turned out, Dr. White's remarks had been misinterpreted. He had said that he didn't see how anyone could play football. Why would anyone play such a dangerous game? So, naturally, when he was asked about Joe Montana, he said he didn't understand how Montana could play. That was a long way from saying Joe shouldn't play because of his surgery. When he was told how his remarks were being interpreted, the doctor quickly restated his position. He also told me privately that he was confident Joe was able to play without abnormal risk.

Still, if any problems had developed, our judgment would have been seriously questioned. Fortunately, Joe played well against the Cardinals and had no aftereffects from his surgery.

In part, that was because of the Cardinal players and their coaches. There isn't any question that the Cardinal players weren't going to try to punish Joe that day, probably because of the counseling they'd gotten from their coaches. You could see they didn't want to be accused of purposely trying to knock Joe Montana out of football. They were intense and making every effort to win, but they also displayed great sportsmanship.

Now, I can't say that about every team and every player. Washington's Dexter Manley, the next week, told the press about what he was going to do to Joe Montana. Some people took that in a humorous vein, but I'm not sure Dexter was joking. From the way he went after other quarterbacks, we had to take him at his word, that he really intended to put Joe out of the game.

Dexter had a way of circumventing the rules. When he jumped offsides, he would continue in and hit the quarterback flush. He'd get a five-yard penalty, but that was a small price to pay for getting a shot at the quarterback. I remember an instance when he knocked a quarterback out of the game in this manner. It got to the point where coaches were demanding that Art McNally, the supervisor of officials, tell the referee to throw Manley out or at least make that a personal foul, which is a fifteen-yard penalty.

After those remarks, to neutralize Manley and protect Joe, we installed a special play. Tight end Russ Francis lined up as a wide receiver and went in motion to the inside. As the ball was snapped, the six-five, 250-pound Francis would blindside Manley as he crossed the line of scrimmage.

Russ couldn't wait to do it, and Manley was meanwhile intent on getting to Joe. The ball would be snapped and Manley would come flying up the field, only to have Russ Francis catch him under the helmet and knock him flat on his back. The first time it happened, Manley had no idea where Francis had come from. He was hit so hard and just flattened. A couple of plays later, we did it again and Russ knocked him flat on his back. That time, Manley looked over at me and nodded his head, as if to say, "You're one up on me."

That was the good news. The bad news was that we made history against the Redskins, but in an unfortunate way: We became the first NFL team to gain 500 yards (501 total) without scoring a touchdown. And we lost the game, 14–6.

We simply threw too many passes in that game. I couldn't resist it. The Redskins were playing man-to-man, and our receivers kept getting open. But Joe really became fatigued as the game went on. He threw sixty passes, and by the time we got into the fourth quarter, he was so tired, he could have been vulnerable to further injury. After the game and since, I've felt bad that I called so many passes and extended Joe to the limit.

Joe hung in there and threw well, and my feeling was that if we'd just hit one more deep pass, we could win the game. But I'd like to have that game back. Even though Joe wasn't hurt, I wish I hadn't taken that chance.

15

Good-bye to the Veterans

Following the '82 season, it became evident that we had not acquired the necessary depth, nor did we have enough impact players to establish ourselves as a perennial contender. We had done it with enthusiasm and attitude in 1981, but a number of our players were either at the end of their careers or had just had one big year.

The first step was to improve our running game, so we drafted Roger Craig and traded for Wendell Tyler. That in itself gave our offense much more punch.

It's rare to see a team make a significant trade within its own division, because you don't want to strengthen a divisional rival. But, there were special circumstances behind this trade. The Los Angeles Rams had traded to get into position to draft Eric Dickerson, which made Wendell extremely expendable. He'd been a star at UCLA and with the Rams, and he obviously wouldn't want to sit on the bench behind Dickerson.

The Rams knew that, and they wanted to get a trade completed quickly so there would be no public debate over Wendell's future. Other teams were interested, too, but we pursued Tyler more aggressively. The Rams didn't have experienced people in their front office at the time. John Shaw, a businessman who was somewhat naive about the implications for the Rams if Wendell Tyler made a big difference for the 49ers, was the executive in charge of negotiations.

We were working all angles to make the trade. I was in Eugene, Oregon, scouting Mike Walter, an Oregon defensive lineman we thought we could use as a linebacker. I had two or three telephone conversations a day with John McVay, who was talking with Shaw. Finally, I got a call from John, giving me the final Rams position, and we agreed to go with it, though the final details weren't to be worked out until draft day.

It was a great trade. Although we gave up a second-round pick for Wendell, we exchanged our fourth-round draft choice for their third. That was an advantageous point, because there is—or should be— quite a difference between a third- and fourth-round pick.

Unfortunately, we didn't make the best use of that draft choice, and it was my fault. Going against the advice of our scouts, I drafted Blanchard Montgomery, a linebacker from UCLA, who didn't work out as I'd hoped.

I had wanted to draft Mike Walter, but Dallas selected him ahead of us in the second round. We had felt Walter would be a legitimate NFL starter, having the intensity of Jack Reynolds but with more size and speed. From what we could gather, the scouting combines had not rated Mike very highly. We assumed that was because other teams were thinking of him as an undersized lineman, instead of as a linebacker prospect. Consequently, I was shocked when Dallas picked him. Having lost Walter, I had it in mind that we needed a quick, active linebacker, and Montgomery had had some very impressive games his senior year, including the Rose Bowl, when he made three consecutive tackles on the goal line.

But that would have to go down as one of the really poor choices we made. Others had confidence in my judgment and went along with it, thinking, "Bill must know something we don't," when, in fact, I was making too much of limited exposure.

Ironically, we later got Walter. The Cowboys released him, and we claimed him. I still don't understand that, because we had been trying to trade for him. I had offered a fifth-round draft choice, but I certainly would have offered more if we'd kept talking. But the Cowboys didn't pursue the trade. Soon thereafter, they were forced to release him to meet a required cut-down date.

It puzzles me that we were one of only two teams to claim him.

The Raiders did also, but because we were in the same conference with Dallas, we had first crack at Mike. Nobody else in the NFC claimed him.

The Raiders had been sitting and waiting for Mike, too. I had cut our roster down to just six offensive linemen temporarily, to make room for him. Al Davis called me and teased me, saying that nobody could go with six offensive linemen. He immediately offered to trade for him, but I wouldn't do it, of course. Since then, Mike has become one of the finest linebackers in 49er history.

Meanwhile, even if I didn't make proper use of the third-round pick we acquired from the Rams, that trade was great for us. Wendell sometimes hurt our offense with his fumbles, but he gave us a quickness and explosion in our running game that we'd never had. He was one of the quickest backs into the hole the game had ever seen. He was also a great blocker for a running back, one of the best in the NFL, and, though not a naturally gifted receiver, he made a number of critical receptions.

Complementing Tyler, Roger Craig had an outstanding rookie season with his high-stepping running style. He was also a solid blocker in his first year, but as he became more successful as a runner, his blocking became less effective, so later we shifted him to running back and placed Tom Rathman at fullback. That's proved to be the best backfield for the 49ers since Joe Perry, Hugh McElhenny, and John Henry Johnson in the 1950s.

Roger had had one great running year at Nebraska, gaining more than 1,000 yards, but when Mike Rozier came along, Roger was shifted to fullback and used primarily as a blocker. As a runner, he was one of the few players I'd compare to a Hugh McElhenny, with his high-kicking style. He also had size, in the 220-pound range. Everybody agreed he was an outstanding person, very competitive, very intense.

We drafted him in the second round. In the Fred Dean trade, we had wound up with San Diego's first-round pick. We then were to trade that pick to the Chargers for two second-round picks. One of them went for Wendell and the other for Craig.

The Craig pick was one of the best choices we ever made. But, even after we'd drafted him, there were those in the NFL who said he'd never make it.

We had worked him out before the draft and had seen that he had an instinct for catching passes, even though he had rarely been used as a receiver at Nebraska. He was big and could reach for the ball, and with his deceptive running style, I thought he could be extremely effective coming out of the backfield, even more effective than Earl Cooper had been, because he had more lateral quickness than Earl. So, when we moved Earl to tight end, with Roger and Wendell in the backfield and a maturing, improving offensive line, we had the makings of a potent offense.

We had drafted Bubba Paris in '82. At 300 pounds or less, Bubba would have been a Hall of Fame tackle. He was quick, active, bright and he had a mean streak. He would have been a great player if he hadn't had so much trouble controlling his weight.

We were told by the Michigan people that Bubba had a weight problem, but I thought I could deal with it. I was wrong. I had experienced Hollywood Henderson, but I had yet to experience Bubba Paris.

As his weight got over 300, I began to clamp down. He was upset at me because he thought he could get down below 300 any time he chose. But he couldn't. It's hard to believe now that he was upset— and so was I—when he was 307 pounds. He's gone far beyond that since.

We tried everything: a fine for being overweight, a bonus for reporting at the right weight, and a clause in his contract specifying a substantial amount of money if he sustained a mutually agreed-upon weight. We even sent him to the Pritikin clinic in Santa Monica during the '88 training camp. An intelligent man, Bubba kept trying new exercise and diet plans himself but nothing worked, because he would quickly stop both exercising and dieting. Ben Parks, a capable high-school coach and physical fitness expert, came to Bubba's house to take him to one of their programmed off-season workouts and found the drapes closed, and nobody answering the door. Bubba had retired from the program.

As time went on, it became obvious that Bubba simply couldn't deal with his weight problem. He would say all the right things about losing weight, but for whatever reason, he couldn't stick with it. I'd have loved to have seen Bubba play for fifteen years at 300 pounds. He would have been the best in the game.

Our willingness to sign and trade for veteran players did not always work out perfectly. There were those who joined our club after outstanding careers elsewhere who simply could no longer play, men like Bob Horn, Wes Chandler, Fulton Kuykendall, and Tom Cousineau. In putting together a winning football team, one must be decisive in acquiring talent, be willing to take calculated risks, and then be equally decisive in moving players if they cannot contribute.

Rebuilding a team also involves releasing veteran players who have passed their prime, and a number of such moves in the '80s brought me into conflict with media and fans—and sometimes, even with my fellow coaches.

The Pittsburgh Steelers are thought to have suffered because Chuck Noll stuck with his veteran stars when they should have been replaced. When Vince Lombardi left Green Bay, the once-champion Packers were but a shell. The Miami Dolphins also went through this, to some extent. I knew we would have to have the resolve to make changes and then depend heavily on our ability both to select players and to coach them to the level of those who had departed.

A coach has to be very strong in his player moves. If he becomes overprotective of a player's feelings or sentimentalizes his history with the team, he can damage the team over the long haul. Nor can he afford to consider how a move looks to the press and public, or to give too much consideration to how a player's teammates will react. There's always the possibility that you'll release a given player a year or two before it's absolutely necessary, but in making decisions for the future, you'll find you're right much more often than you're wrong.

So often coaches will stay with veteran players because that's more comfortable. My real lesson with that was when I was with the Cincinnati Bengals and Sam Wyche was the quarterback.

After months of developing Sam's skills, we drafted Greg Cook. The moment Greg took the field, he was superior to Sam, but I had spent so much time with Sam, I was determined he would be the quarterback until Greg had learned some of our system. Paul Brown had no such problem. He said, "Greg Cook is our quarterback." Paul said it so strongly that I knew there was no recourse. So, out came Sam and in went Greg, and of course, he played brilliantly. There's no question Paul was right. His position was that if the man can play and he's your future, he should play now. Don't justify a decision for the sake of expediency.

That's been my philosophy since. If a young player can perform as well as an aging veteran and can be expected to perform at that level for several years, he should be in the lineup. Or if there is a specific situation in a game better suited for the younger player, he should be utilized without hesitation.

Coaches are often more comfortable with veteran players who understand the system, but they fail to realize that the younger player thrust into that role will develop rapidly and will assume the responsibility. On a number of occasions I had to hold out against a very persistent assistant coach who was campaigning to keep an aging veteran, similar to how Paul Brown handled me.

I was also determined as we built the team to remind myself at the proper time that a number of key players came to the 49ers late in their careers—players such as Charle Young, Jack Reynolds, Russ Francis, and Wendell Tyler. I knew they would have short-lived careers for us, but I also knew they could make the difference between good years or great years.

So, as each of these men passed rather quickly through their 49er careers, it was my obligation to tell them that it was time to leave football. That was almost a campaign in itself. It took planning, it took timing, it took preparing the athlete for that moment. I used every bit of wit I had, and also encouraged others in the organization to contribute, to prepare the athlete for the time when he should step away from the game.

As a result, we caught some hell from newspaper writers, who claimed we had a cold, indifferent, calculating organization that simply disposed of athletes on a whim. It wasn't whimsical at all but the result of an objective evaluation of veteran players. No veteran we released ever again played as well as the man who replaced him on the 49ers. Most, in fact, retired shortly after they left the 49ers.

The early signs of a player coming to the end of his career are chronic minor injuries, or injuries sustained early in a career that now start to bother him. This shows up primarily in his lack of practice time. At first, he misses Monday and Saturday. Then, it becomes a matter of giving him light workouts on Wednesday and Friday as well, working him hard only on Thursday. Finally, the player is reduced to hardly practicing at all, and then playing effectively for only part of the game, or even every other week.

Yet, even then, the player may play effectively when he does, so fans will see him miss a couple of games but then come back and play well in the next one. Fans appreciate the athlete and are excited by his performance, and they don't understand what is really occurring.

At that point, it is up to the coach and general manager to make a judgment. There may well be a younger player on the squad who can play as well as the veteran, or at least close to that level, but who can play more and has a future. Fans can afford to be sentimental about the aging veteran, but a coach cannot.

There were several particularly tough decisions that had to be made. Every one was an experience in itself because each player handled it differently. The ones I remember most vividly are:

Jack Reynolds. Jack told me on joining the 49ers that he would like to play two more years and then be a coach. As I said before, that was a selling point to Jack, but he still had a lot of trouble leaving the game he loved so much.

He attempted briefly to work with linebackers in training camp in '85, but he could not criticize another player. It was almost an unwritten code for him. He was uncomfortable in our staff meetings because we talked candidly about players. Jack had a brutal time with that. He felt despondent and just left.

Later, Jack had trouble talking to me because he had told others that I had shortened his career by forcing him to retire too early. In fact, Jack just could not play any longer. As grand a campaigner as he was, he just couldn't continue.

Wendell Tyler. We tried everything to avoid releasing Wendell in 1986. We offered him a retirement incentive of $50,000, but Wendell couldn't give up the game. Even with an arthritic knee, he continued to play.

I didn't want him to play with that knee. I was concerned about his life after football, because I had seen too many former players who had played too long on bad knees and were forced to live with severe physical restrictions. But Wendell demanded publicly that he play. He had doctors independent of the team claim that, though his knee was arthritic, it was sound enough for him to play on.

We put him on injured reserve, and there was a public outcry that he should be playing. We activated him for the New York Giants game, and he performed well in the first half. But he was badly fatigued by the second, and on one key play, he just wouldn't hit the hole, so we lost yardage. At that point, I think the fans began to realize that Wendell couldn't do it any longer, and I think Wendell did, too.

But before that, there were some incredulous moments. Writers claimed we were trying to save money, which has certainly *not* been a factor since Ed DeBartolo, Jr., bought the team.

Wendell was quite popular, and some fans became maudlin over what he had meant to the team and simply blinded themselves to the reality of the situation. For instance, I received a scathing letter from a law firm in the East Bay suburban town of Pleasanton, signed by forty-two men and women, saying I had insulted Wendell, that releasing him was an imbecilic decision and I was ruining the team.

It showed how high emotions were, that members of a law firm would take the time to send me such a letter. I'm sure not too many weeks passed before they understood my action, but they didn't write another letter.

Fred Solomon. Following the '84 Super Bowl, there were several decisions that had to be made on veteran players, including Fred Solomon. The '81–'84 era basically came to a close then, and we had to start rebuilding for the future, though we were still a playoff team.

Fred had been one of the original 49ers who had seen us through our hard times and had provided most of the big plays that were to bring us two world championships. He was an extremely quick, explosive, heavily muscled athlete.

Unfortunately, Fred had had continual muscle pulls that really reduced his playing time in '84, and just as important, sharply reduced his practice time. He was so tender, with hamstring pulls and calf muscle pulls, that he was just unable to function. In the past, he had come through for us in key situations but now, at the end of the game, when we needed a big play, Freddie often would have cramps.

Freddie was a big fan favorite. He could still catch the ball, he could still make a play. They'd wonder why he didn't play more. They didn't realize that he couldn't play very much anymore.

When I drafted Jerry Rice, I decided that Freddie should sit down and that Jerry should step in, though I knew he would make many rookie mistakes. I felt that Jerry would make at least as many big plays as Freddie, that he would be productive while gaining the experience necessary to be a great player.

That pushed Freddie into a retirement mode, but he handled the situation well because he was truly a team man. He retired gracefully after the '85 season.

But during that season, there was a tremendous amount of controversy over the fact that Jerry Rice was starting. Jerry had a hard time in the early games. He had to learn so much so quickly that he had problems concentrating and dropped a number of passes. There were some writers who insisted I had made a mistake in starting Rice, and others who thought I had made a mistake in even drafting him. But that kind of criticism ended when Jerry caught 10 passes for a team record 241 yards against the Rams.

Paul Hackett of my staff was also troubled by my benching of Solomon, and by his subsequent retirement. He thought Freddie should have played one more year. I think that was an indication of where Paul was in his career and I was in mine. I had learned enough to know that there are times when a coach must make the decision to go with a younger player.

It's not an easy decision. So often, a coach will feel more comfortable with a veteran player because the veteran knows so much more. You can work much more easily with a veteran because he can adapt more quickly. Even emotionally, a veteran can adjust more easily. But when the physical breakdowns come, it doesn't matter how much the veteran player knows; he can't function at the level a championship team needs.

John Ayers. Ayers was especially popular, but we felt he no longer possessed the quickness to run-block. Because of the emphasis we put on our sweeps, the pulling-guard techniques are absolutely vital. John was simply unable to get to where he needed to be fast enough. John could have been the most underrated starter on our team. He was able to nullify such great players as Lawrence Taylor and Fulton Kuykendall. It was difficult for me to release John, who was a true gentleman and one of the most respected men on the team, but it was necessary.

You don't release an aging veteran unless you have a young player with talent and intensity to replace him. In this case, we had Guy McIntyre, an outstanding prospect.

John was picked up by Denver, and we endured newspaper stories accusing us of disposing of a fine man who had done so much for the 49ers and who could still play. As it turned out, John was with the Broncos for only a short time before retiring.

Keith Fahnhorst. Fahnhorst was much the same as Ayers. His pass blocking was still reasonable, but he had lost the explosion he needed as a run blocker. That became more apparent as he began to miss so much practice time.

I had first talked to Keith about retirement before the '86 season. In 1987, we drafted Harris Barton and I told the press on draft day that I expected him to ultimately replace Fahnhorst. That didn't make Keith happy, but it was obvious that with his natural ability, Barton could fit in very quickly on the offensive line. He is a quick, smooth athlete. He learns easily, and has a lot of poise. He replaced Keith, and Keith had to step away.

Keith was troubled because it was so difficult to accept. He was one of the 49ers' great campaigners and had been named to the Pro Bowl late in his career, finally receiving the accolades due him, only to have to leave the game shortly afterward. He also went through a hard final year, emotionally and physically. As the team player representative, he had to deal with the ramifications of the players' strike. When the strike ended, he had injuries that had never quite healed all season—the sign, as I said, of the declining veteran player.

Two other players, Randy Cross and Fred Quillan, sensed the time had come to retire.

Randy had been a great guard, making Pro Bowl teams, but he had been an outstanding center at UCLA, so he knew the final years of his career would be at center. (In fact, he had played his first two years with the 49ers at center.) By 1987, he had lost some of the quickness he needed to play at guard, but he was still valuable for his leadership.

Quillan had had a brilliant career, had been one of the fine technicians at center, and had been a Pro Bowl player. He completely sacrificed himself for his team and would go year after year without missing a play. His skill level was at the very top of the National Football League. But by 1987, he seemed to have lost some of his explosion and strength, so we made the anticipated switch of Randy to center in midseason. It would have been most difficult to retain both players at center. These were two established Pro Bowl performers, and neither could stay on the bench very long. So we arranged a trade, sending Fred to San Diego before the '88 season. He retired soon after that.

Randy played well at center, but before the end of the '88 season, it was obvious that this should be his last season. Randy knew that, too.

Before I could even bring it up, he decided that this would be his last year, and he announced his retirement during Super Bowl week.

Randy must be considered the best all around offensive lineman to play for the 49ers in the '80s. He was not only a talented player but among the toughest physically I've ever been associated with. He served as a team leader throughout his playing career and has become just as successful in the business world since he stepped away from football.

We won the world championship with Randy at center, so he was able to leave at just the right time.

When we asked a player to retire, in virtually every instance we had developed a suitable replacement, a player who could play close to the level of the veteran and had a future.

Jerry Rice for Fred Solomon was the most obvious, but the changes made in the offensive line were just as important. Harris Barton stepped in for Keith Fahnhorst at tackle, and Guy McIntyre and Jesse Sapolu replaced John Ayers and Randy Cross at guards.

Sapolu, who moved to center in the '89 season, had been only an eleventh-round draft choice in '83 and had twice broken his leg since. But he had recovered physically and offensive-line coach Bobb McKittrick had faith in him—and I had faith in Bobb McKittrick. Sapolu went into the starting lineup, and he has played well.

Why is it so difficult for players to step away from football? We have to remind ourselves what this game has meant to them. They have given so much to it, and it's difficult for them to finally let go. Football has been the center of their lives, the basis of their existence. It has been the source of their satisfaction and gratification, and also the center of their social lives and day-to-day existence. The game is their very identity. It's what they live for. So, there's a real loss, a real grieving when they have to leave.

This shouldn't be surprising. Throughout their lives, these men have been recognized only for their athletic accomplishments, not for any other talents they may have. They naturally come to the conclusion that football is all they have to offer. When they are then deprived of that, they are at a distinct disadvantage. They haven't developed other facets of their lives.

Often players were indifferent or even hostile to me for a year or two after leaving, but as time passed, most had a better perspective and understanding of the inevitable separation.

It's difficult for athletes to be objective about themselves. An older player looks quite the same in the mirror and with more intense weight training he actually looks more fit and stronger than some younger players. He certainly knows more. But the accumulation of minor injuries and the loss of quickness and reaction response are too much. He can perform in a given game, or for a brief period of time about as well as he ever could. He convinces himself that as soon as these nagging injuries clear up, he'll be all right, that it's just a run of bad luck. He'll remind the coach that he has played ten years without problems, and now when a few minor injuries crop up everyone gets down on him. But when they do clear up, he finds that the years of physical wear and tear have taken their toll.

Often these men find themselves with family and friends who want them to stay in the game, because it has been their life, too. Sometimes, wives have a harder time than the players, because they are used to a certain life-style, a certain feeling of social importance. When a player retires, he and his wife find they are no longer included in the activities surrounding the team. Domestic difficulties, even divorces, have resulted when a wife cannot adjust to her husband's new identity. Feeling isolated and rejected, she vents her feelings on her husband, who is in the meantime going through his own life crisis.

In many instances, players have done virtually nothing to prepare themselves for life after football. So, when they retire, they have no viable alternative. Suddenly, they're living in a vacuum, depressed and confused, not knowing exactly what to do next.

They soon come to the conclusion that their life-style can't be sustained, because they no longer have an income even approximating what they were accustomed to. If they try to live in the same manner, their savings rapidly dwindle away. After years of interacting with many people on a daily basis, the former player now finds himself home in his solitude. He becomes moody, restless, with nowhere to go. From the comfort of his small cubicle in the locker room he now feels completely trapped in his spacious home.

You become accustomed to the zany teasing and lively horseplay, to the bonding, the tight friendships, the sacrifices, to the daily excitement. In addition, you are used to the attention and adulation of the fans. In one quick stroke it's over; you are no longer needed and not included. The guys remaining on the team actually seem to avoid you. They're clearly uneasy talking with you. It's as though you have a disease and they might catch it. They just don't want to be reminded of the inevitable moment when they will meet the same fate.

You find yourself saying just one more year, I'll save every penny, I'll concentrate every second and I'll truly cultivate and cherish every moment with those guys, with my teammates. God, do I love every one of them. The coach didn't have to do this. I used to think he was a good man. I'm still better than that dumb bastard they drafted to replace me. I busted my ass to take this team to the top, and now these new guys are strutting around, basking in the glory.

It's tough, but true. Yet the former player has forty years of productive life ahead of him. They should be glorious years, after what he has been through and has accomplished. But first he needs help. Often, he enters a new field at ground zero, feeling insecure, inadequate, and indifferent. He has already given much of himself to football, while his contemporaries in that new field are highly motivated, extremely enthusiastic and career-driven, just as the player had been when he entered professional football.

To begin his new career, the player needs active support from his family, but, as I've said, the family often feels empty and rejected, too, and fails to provide what the athlete needs most.

I could only see that in full perspective when I retired from coaching and experienced that haunted, lonely feeling—not so much a feeling of being deserted as of no longer feeling a part of the team and the organization.

16

The Triumphal Parade

We always played extremely well in December, year after year the best in the NFL. Starting with our first Super Bowl team, our December record was 26–4. Two of those losses came in the disastrous '82 season, and another at the end of the '88 season to the Los Angeles Rams, after we had clinched the division. Otherwise, we were nearly perfect.

Why did we do so well in December? There were two reasons, one positive, one negative.

Our style of practice and approach to the game did not take too much out of the team. By the time you get midway through the season, you have to have developed the confidence that the team can play well on Sunday, so you don't have to prove yourself in practice.

Often there were weeks when we didn't wear our pads in practice. While other teams were having a lot of contact, we were working long hours but without the physical contact. So, late in the season, we would appear to be fresher than other teams. The wear and tear seemed to affect defensive linemen more than anyone. With that in mind, we had more on the roster. Down the stretch, it's the pass rush that makes the difference.

Our style of football didn't depend on the run as much as teams like the Rams, so it didn't take the same toll on our players. Also, our kind of play was resourceful. We had more things we could do, so we weren't stereotyped. After they've played half a season, teams will have demonstrated what they can do and cannot do. You're much more aware of their strengths and weaknesses and consequently you can make decisions more quickly in your preparation. Our style became so fully dimensional that we could continue to maintain an offensive edge right through the conclusion of the season.

But there was also the downside. We often found ourselves slumping at some point in midseason because we lacked the physical strength to sustain ourselves, so we were forced to win in December to get into the playoffs.

It was the same pattern in '83. We played several good games early, flattened out in midseason, but then came back in December to finish very strong.

We had some devastating losses that really shook us up, that were totally unexpected. In turn, those losses had a clear effect on us the following week.

For instance, there was our game against Atlanta.

We completely dominated that game until Renaldo Nehemiah was knocked unconscious by a tackle the instant after he had caught a pass, just before halftime. Russ Francis came to his aid, which unfortunately meant he stopped playing football. The ball was knocked loose as he was hit, so it was still in play. But Russ ran right by the ball to check Renaldo, and it was then picked up by Blane Gaison and run 64 yards for an Atlanta touchdown.

So, we were tied at halftime, 14–14, in a game in which we should have been ahead by at least a touchdown.

Still, we were leading, 24–21, with one play left in the game, when a defensive flaw cost us: We didn't put heat on Atlanta quarterback Steve Bartkowski from the middle. We had a three-man rush with both defensive ends coming up on the outside. Bartkowski was able to step forward between the two pass rushers, set his sights, and throw a nice, lobbing pass downfield.

After that game, we changed our defensive strategy. When three wide receivers lined up on one side, we would have three linemen rushing there, so the quarterback wouldn't have an open lane to throw a pass to that side.

But that was after the fact. In this game, Bartkowski threw a pass that was batted toward the ground by Keena Turner. Billy "White Shoes" Johnson had fallen down, and the ball came to him while he was on the ground. He scrambled for what was called a touchdown. When we reviewed the play on film, it was clear that he was down. His knees had touched, and he reached with the ball over the goal line. But the referee awarded a touchdown. Suddenly, our win became a loss.

I cannot recall ever being so stunned and sickened by a defeat. We had played an inferior team and allowed a game to be taken away. You have to figure that fortune will decide some games, and this was one of them, but that game should never have been left to luck. If Russ Francis hadn't been distracted by Renaldo Nehemiah, instead of looking for the loose football, Atlanta wouldn't even have been in a position to win with that desperate late pass.

When we went to the dressing room, there was really nothing I could say. No use pointing fingers, just live through the agony, let's get out of town and regroup. Ed DeBartolo came in and was terribly distressed and wanted to vent his frustration, but everybody was in such a state of shock, nobody could pay much attention.

That game affected us the whole week. I was still trying to recover, and so was the team. When we went back to Chicago the next Sunday, we just weren't really ready to play. I had been told of the "46 defense," but I was trying to bring the team back psychologically, and I didn't pay as much attention to our preparations as I should have. I felt we could handle the 46 defense rather easily with our passing game, but because of the weather, we couldn't throw the ball effectively. It was so cold that the rain turned to sleet, and because the wind was blowing so fiercely, the sleet was almost parallel to the ground. So, we had to run against that defense, and they stuffed us.

It was a competitive game. We ruined our own chances early when, after we had driven the length of the field, Wendell Tyler mishandled the ball on the one-foot line and we failed to score. They went on to win, 13–3. The Bears were an excellent young team, and would eventually become world champions in the 1985 season. That experience was etched in my mind, and I knew that ultimately we would have to solve the puzzle of the 46 defense.

But the loss was also the result of our not preparing as well as we should have because we were still in a state of shock from the Atlanta loss.

We had to come on strong to win our division, taking our final three games following those back-to-back losses. Then we had a tough playoff game against a Detroit team that really shouldn't have matched up with us well. Again, after taking command we didn't put the Lions away. After we scored to go ahead, Detroit came storming back against our prevent defense, but Eddie Murray missed a field goal with a few seconds remaining and we won, 24–23.

It would have been frustrating if we'd lost that game, because earlier, we had the same play set up that won the 1982 championship game against Dallas. But Tyler, faking a run into the line, broke through and wanting to help decided he would be a receiver on the play. In the process he knocked down Mike Wilson! The game would have been put away there, but with Mike out of it Joe had no place to throw the ball. Otherwise, as usual, Wendell played beautifully as both a ball carrier and blocker.

We then met the Redskins in the NFC championship game, and it seemed everything was in their favor. We had lost Clark in the last regular-season game against Dallas, when he wrenched his knee. The Redskins, meanwhile, had been proclaimed one of the best teams of all time. They had won the Super Bowl in the previous year, in the strike season, and had sustained that success in 1983, with the best record in the NFL.

We misfired through much of the game. We'd move the ball, only to overthrow a pass, or have a penalty at a critical time. We were only down, 7–0, at halftime, but the Redskins had figured out our pass coverage and came out to hit some bombs, so we found ourselves trailing, 21–0, after three quarters.

There will be an ebb and flow in every close contest; now it was our turn.

We began our move in the fourth quarter with Joe hitting strikes all over the field. We scored 21 points on three Montana touchdown passes, two of them to Mike Wilson, to tie the game. It appeared we'd stopped the Redskins on the next series, only to have Eric Wright called for pass interference on second-and-five. If you viewed that play now, it would appear harmless, but in those days, pass interference could be called based on an insignificant brushing of bodies. Neither man had a play on the ball; possibly Eric had a hand touching the receiver, but you couldn't find anything that might affect him.

That's an example of the kind of thing that infuriated me as a coach: the tendency of an official to get caught in the moment and to participate in the drama itself. All too often, an official can be seen rushing forward and throwing a flag, on a highly subjective or even the notorious "phantom" call, which will directly affect the outcome. That intrusion of the official into the game action distresses every coach.

Regardless of how proper sounding it is to say you treat the entire game with uniformity, I much prefer the philosophy in the NBA, where officials are very prudent with their calls in the last seconds, because they are cognizant of what hangs in the balance. In short, they let the players play. I think football officiating should consider these dynamics.

The official should be there to monitor the game, not to direct the course of it. They are there to protect the safety of the players, and to enforce the rules, so the game is played within the parameters expected by the participants and by the public.

That's part of a larger problem: In the NFL, officiating has not stayed abreast of the skills and talents of the players and the overall speed of the game. While football operations have become more and more specialized and sophisticated, utilizing the most contemporary managerial and business practices, officiating has the same preparation format that has existed for many years. Administration has done a competent job, but I don't believe we've asked enough of the officials themselves.

You're not going to find a better group of men to handle these games; they're professionals with careers that afford them time for officiating. They're mature, they're knowledgeable about sports. You'd have to say that collectively they're a very good group. But we need more consistency. Part of the problem is the frequent changes in rules and interpretations. The interpretation of pass interference alone might change three times in three years. But the point I have made as a member of the Competition Committee, and during NFL spring meetings, is that officials should be asked to give more time, and naturally compensated for that.

I think the ideal concept would be a yearly camp, three weeks in length, where officials would go through the same kind of training format that a football team does. There would be an intense seminar on rules and interpretations. Extensive time would be alloted for on-the-field situations and examples and in officiating crew mechanics.

In our 1983 NFC championship game, the penalty against Wright was followed by a defensive holding call against Ronnie Lott. Although the Redskins failed to move the ball, those calls took almost two minutes off the clock. We lost that game on a Washington field goal in the fourth quarter, but we had proven something to ourselves.

We were now back among the football elite, one of the top three or four teams in the league, having revitalized our team, while retaining the original nucleus of Montana, Clark, and Solomon, our gifted defensive backs and our quick, intense defensive line. Men like Keena Turner, Milt McColl, Ron Ferrari and Riki Ellison would give us the hitting power to make it happen again.

I remember when we lost to Miami on a Roger Craig fumble in '83, a writer asked me, "How can you ever beat a Don Shula team?" That was the image Shula had at the time, that he would find a way to win the close games. I began to believe it myself. But Roger was developing, and we found more ways to utilize him. By '84, we had two runners who could gain 1,000 yards, and we had Russ Francis and a fine defensive line, quick and nimble. Our outside running game was among the best in football. With Dwight Clark making the tough, third-down catches and Fred Solomon as our deep threat, we had a fully dimensional offense.

Defensively, we had utilized a group of people. Dwaine Board was one of the best defensive ends in football. Lawrence Pillers was a solid defensive lineman. Jeff Stover, a gifted athlete, gave us a solid pass rush in key situations. Riki Ellison had become a solid inside linebacker. Dan Bunz, converted to strong-side linebacker, had become a truly championship player; he made a great combination with Keena Turner, who had another outstanding season. Manu Tuiasosopo was a midseason acquisition who played ably at defensive end and nose tackle; in 1984 he would get a big sack of Dan Marino in Super Bowl XIX. Another veteran, Gary "Big Hands" Johnson, served as a pass rush specialist and was extremely effective in that role. Here were two veterans, deemed expendable by their parent teams, who were revitalized as situational players with a winning organization.

Then, we had our defensive backfield, one of the best that's ever taken the field, with Eric Wright and Ronnie Lott at the corners, and Dwight Hicks and Carlton Williamson at safeties. They were all Pro-Bowl performers, and Lott will be a Hall of Fame player. Wright was the ultimate at cornerback, with size, speed, and intensity. A recurring groin injury would later keep him from having the great career he was entitled to, but in 1984, he was outstanding. And Ray Wersching was one of the most consistent place kickers in NFL history.

Drafting Michael Carter was important, too. In a sense, he was dismissed by the rest of the NFL because he was competing in the Olympics—he won a silver medal in the shot put—and would be late reporting.

Because of his shot-putting, he had not participated in spring practice, and other NFL teams felt he was primarily dedicated to developing as a shot-putter, but when we saw him play, he displayed incredible strength, explosion, and quickness that were truly something to behold.

When he played at SMU, he demonstrated a tendency to jump around and try to make blockers miss. At times he got caught during his move and driven off the line, and runners would break up the middle for sizable gains. As a result, scouts felt that Carter wouldn't be stable enough inside as a nose tackle. But Bill McPherson and Fred von Appen thought that could be dealt with through drill and with a sound team concept.

He arrived late because of the Olympics but once in camp, Michael impressed everyone. There was concern that a track-and-field athlete couldn't thrive in the physical, violent world of the NFL, but Michael calmed our fears immediately. He was extremely quick and agile, and also as intense and aggressive as anyone in our camp. We had solid people like Jack Reynolds, Riki Ellison, and Jim Fahnhorst at inside linebacker to offer stability and compensate for his quick-committing style often getting him out of position. He was to become one of the great defensive linemen of the '80s.

Carter was part of one of our best drafts, in which we also acquired tight end John Frank, guard Guy McIntyre, safety Jeff Fuller, linebacker Todd Shell, and running back Derrick Harmon. All made significant contributions, not only to our 1984 world championship team but to future teams, though a serious neck injury curtailed Shell's career.

That 1984 team will go down as one of the great teams in NFL history. We came into the season with real momentum and confidence. We had been bloodied in '83. As it turned out, our shattering loss to the Redskins would give us impetus in 1984. We were bitter about that loss, yet had come to the realization that we could very well have the best team in the league.

Our only loss was a close, hard-fought game to Pittsburgh decided by a "phantom" goal-line pass-interference call on Eric Wright. We had led throughout the game and appeared to be on our way to our seventh straight victory, only to be shocked. We missed a long field goal as the gun went off and lost, 20–17. Chuck Noll was very gracious about that later. He, too, questioned the call but told me, "You're going to go all the way." This loss may have sharpened us for the remaining games because it reminded us that anything could happen.

We were to "blow out" most of our stronger opponents and struggle in so-called "routine games." When we played the Cincinnati Bengals, Sam Wyche brought his team in very well prepared and brimming with determination. Joe had one of his rare erratic days, throwing four interceptions. If he had a weakness at that point, it was his penchant for forcing the ball to Dwight Clark. These are the kinds of games that require a high standard of performance to overcome an inspired opponent. To become a champion, you can't lose games to teams like Cincinnati, which came in without an impressive won-loss record. The Bengals were actually ahead at halftime, 17–7. It took a supreme second-half effort to pull out the victory, 23–17.

We dominated the Bears in the NFC championship game. We had lost the year before, of course, and this was a much better team than the one that had beaten us, but by this time, I had some very definite ideas on playing against Buddy Ryan's 46 defense. I had been embarrassed by our loss to the Bears in Chicago. This time around, we were really ready.

In the '83 game, Mike Singletary's blitzing up the middle tore us apart. A back had been assigned to block Mike and was simply unable to get to him quickly enough; when he did, Mike simply bowled him over. For the '84 game, we assigned our guards a "double read" to account for him. Either John Ayers or Randy Cross would quickly check for a Singletary blitz. If he didn't blitz, they would immediately look for an outside-linebacker blitz. At that time, the Bears didn't blitz both Singletary and an outside linebacker, so the guard knew he would have only one man to block.

The most critical area in protecting the quarterback is between the offensive tackles. It is almost impossible to avoid an unblocked man coming up the middle. These tactics accounted for the inside rush. Any unblocked defenders would be coming from the outside.

Our plan called for Joe to throw quickly, before these outside rushers could reach him. Everything depended on our receivers beating their cornerbacks quickly with Joe taking three steps and getting rid of the ball.

Those who had been destroyed by the Bear defense had not accounted for all eight potential pass rushers located near the line of scrimmage or for the lack of time for the quarterback. The Bears had a combination of outstanding personnel functioning in an unfamiliar style of defense. Ryan and his defensive staff had utilized their talent beautifully, highlighting Singletary, one of the great players of our time. As an example, with people like Richard Dent pressuring from the outside and Dan Hampton up the middle, an opposing quarterback just didn't have time to set up and throw his normal patterns.

We speeded up that process, with Montana throwing the ball to a wide receiver or running back before the pressure could develop. The only player who could upset that strategy was a blitzer, and we had taken care of that.

Actually, we could have won the game by 30 points or more. We moved the ball extremely well in the first half but because of breakdowns, left the field with only a 6–0 lead. Our defense dominated, and our offense picked them apart in the second half, going on to win, 23–0.

While the 46 defense had received much national media attention, the 49er defense demonstrated on this day that in 1984, it was the best in football. It was a very satisfying win.

In the media, everyone was writing of Chicago being a "revenge" game for us. That kind of talk comes from a misunderstanding of the coach's priorities. Every NFL game is so important, you don't have room for any special feelings. You really have to control yourself, rather than relying on a special surge of emotion. You get out of sync trying for too much. After a win, there may be great satisfaction, but during the game, your concentration is on the playing field, not on an emotional high. Regardless of opponent, a championship game is all one needs in the way of motivation. Words like "vendetta" or "revenge" can become counterproductive.

Yes, I was aware of Buddy Ryan's belittling remarks before the game and I thought how sweet it would be to take apart that defense, but a momentary thought was all I could give it. You simply cannot allow yourself to believe emotions alone will win the game. You have to remind yourself that the other team will be sky-high emotionally, too. Execution is the difference.

The Super Bowl that year was played at Stanford, where I had coached in college. People asked me how I felt about returning to Stanford. Really, I couldn't afford to give it much thought. The stakes are so high in a game like that, there isn't room for anything else. There's so much drama in the game itself. Playing at Stanford, wonderful. Playing in northern California, fine. But the game itself was so important, you could play in Alaska and it would still be fine. Relying on sentiment and considering it an advantage is a mistake. The one factor that I did appreciate was that I knew it would be an excellent playing field.

The game was also unusual because we would be playing in our home area, just about thirty miles south of Candlestick Park. That had happened only once before in Super Bowl history, when the Los Angeles Rams played in the 1980 Super Bowl in Pasadena.

Was that an advantage? Not really. We did have an advantage at practice, because we could work at our own facility in Redwood City. But during our championship years, we played better on the road than we did at home. In only two of my last eight years did we have a better record at home than on the road. In fact, the only game we had lost in the '84 season had been at home. Overall, for those last eight years, we were 40–20 at home, 45–14–1 on the road.

We put premium importance on our away games because I had always felt that to be a champion, a team had to consistently win on the road. We were fully mobilized on the road. We had specific meeting times and a full daily schedule. We gave the entire weekend, from our arrival on Friday through the game on Sunday, to football. We were well rested, and we could prepare ourselves for the game without distractions.

When we returned home, players had to deal with their social and domestic concerns. They had more free time, and would spend much of Friday and Saturday meeting other responsibilities. Players need to totally focus on the game and often at home don't have the solitude and privacy they need. For single players, an early evening can become a very late one if they meet someone attractive and interesting.

In the big cities, like New York, Los Angeles, Chicago, and San

Francisco, there are many diversions for players, too. Now, if I were coaching a team in Green Bay, there wouldn't be as much concern, but in San Francisco, there was. The many distractions could subtly affect our concentration.

Over the years, I was more concerned with our home games than our road games because when our concentration lapsed it demonstrated itself at Candlestick. In the disastrous 1982 season, for instance, we were 3–1 on the road but 0–5 at home.

Trying to minimize social inclinations and family commitments, we stayed at a hotel the Saturday night before home games, one of many innovations begun by Paul Brown and later adopted by all NFL teams. But even that had its problems. On two occasions, we changed hotels because they had so much convention business and disco activities, it was like a carnival. At times, it seemed as if we were in the middle of Mardi Gras.

For the Super Bowl, all the distractions were multiplied. Family and friends of the players traveled to the Bay Area for the game, so players had to deal with parties, gatherings, reunions and monumental ticket requests. Overall, there were probably more distractions for this game than for either of the other two Super Bowls in which we played.

So, though we enjoyed not having to travel and adjust to a different time zone, there was certainly no special advantage for us playing at Stanford.

The game appeared to be a great matchup, because it brought together the teams with the two best records in football. Miami had broken every passing record with Dan Marino, and most people felt it would be a real shoot-out.

In any Super Bowl, or any big game, there are some lasting impressions, and mine that day came in the pregame warmups. As I walked through the Dolphins, I could see a distinct difference between the two squads. We were a much more physical, more athletic football team than Miami. Maybe it was just the color of their uniforms, but the Dolphins didn't look physical. We weren't a really big team, but we were very athletic. At that moment my confidence soared.

I felt that we matched up well against the Dolphins. We truly feared Dan Marino and his battery of receivers, but they were a one-dimensional team offensively, with no running attack to worry us, and I thought we could attack their defense effectively. It wasn't difficult to recognize that they didn't have outstanding speed and quickness.

Without a potent pass rush, Miami was forced to cover the receivers tightly. The Miami defense depended on locking their linebackers into man-to-man coverage on running backs. That had worked well for them during the season, but I doubted that they could cover our backs, particularly Roger Craig, coming out of the backfield.

We had one play in particular that was ideally suited to work against that defense: On "20 Bingo cross," both backs would release between guard and tackle just past the line of scrimmage and then cross. The Miami inside linebacker couldn't cover Craig when he broke sharply away on that pattern, and that was exactly what happened (see Diagram E, page 271). Roger caught 7 passes for 77 yards, added 58 yards running, and scored 3 touchdowns, a Super Bowl record.

In preparing for Miami, it became apparent that Joe Montana could run effectively against this defense. I declined to remark on it until just before the game, because I didn't want to preoccupy Joe with this option and preferred it to be as spontaneous and instinctive as possible. Just before the game, I told Joe, "If you see it, take it." With the linebackers chasing the backs, there would be nobody to take Joe. This is an example of the confidence I had in him; he would know when to throw and when to run. He ran five times for 59 yards, and his runs set up two of our first three touchdowns.

The run I appreciated most was a 20-yarder down the sideline in front of our bench.

Craig was running a pass pattern down that sideline with the linebacker chasing him. Joe sensed it and quickly took off, so the three of them were running in a line down the sideline—Roger, followed by the Miami linebacker, followed by Joe. The linebacker had no idea that Joe was right behind him, almost on his heels, and it was a defensive back who eventually came over to force Joe out of bounds.

The game went much as I had anticipated. The Dolphins kept it close for a while, leading 10–7 as they caught our defense off balance for a short time with a no-huddle offense, but then we took control and turned it into a lopsided game by halftime.

We had known that field position would be vital because Miami lacked a running game to get out of a hole. If we could back them up against their end zone and force them to punt, we could gain the initiative.

We got an unexpected bonus because their great punter, Reggie Roby, had three successive mediocre punts, of 37, 40, and 39 yards, while punting from deep in his own territory. We took over after those punts at the Miami 47 the first time and then at our own 45 and 48.

On the sideline, we were almost celebrating because, operating from midfield, we could use all the weapons in our arsenal. Working against a physically weaker Miami defense, we knew that getting the ball at midfield meant an almost automatic score. In fact, we scored three touchdowns on those three possessions to turn the game into a rout. We eventually won the game, 38–16, and set a Super Bowl record with 537 yards of total offense. When you're moving the ball that well, there's real excitement and enjoyment because you can use everything in the game plan.

I realized that Don Shula had done it with mirrors, because he didn't have the physical ability we had. For the Dolphins to have gone 14–2 and won two playoff games was a real tribute to Don.

It was nearly a perfect game for us, though two misplays still stick in my mind. The first was the kickoff to Guy McIntyre just before the end of the first half, after Miami had finally kicked a field goal to break up our scoring run of three touchdowns.

We'd told Guy to hit the ground if the ball came to him, and he did as we'd told him, but then rookie Derrick Harmon came running up and said, "Get up, get up," and McIntyre got up just in time to get hit, and he fumbled. Miami then kicked a field goal as the half ended. That only cut our lead to 28–16, so we were still in control, but it marred the game for me. I guess that's a perfectionist talking.

Then, in the fourth quarter, we were driving for what could have been a touchdown. A fourth-down play at Miami's five-yard-line was Roger Craig over the top, which after being called twice previously I almost assumed would be stopped. At that point, there was no reason to run up the score.

When we won, we felt we were one of the great teams of all time. Flippantly, I said in the postgame media interview, "We are clearly the best football team competing today, including some of the major universities."

One other event made the game very special for me: The players awarded me the game ball, with Dwight Hicks making the presentation. I didn't think as much of it at the time, being overwhelmed by all the excitement, as I did later, when I realized how much it meant to be awarded the game ball for the world championship. It was the nicest acknowledgment the players could give me.

17

Triumph and Tragedy: The 1987 Season

I f the 1987 season were a play, it would be a Greek tragedy. We had moments of high drama, and great triumphs, but in the end, one game ruined everything.

Going into the season, everybody in football assumed there would be a strike. There were no negotiations between the Players Association and the Management Council, which represented the owners. The only question was when the union would call the strike.

I was a member of the NFL Competition Committee, and during our meetings in Hawaii that spring, Dallas general manager Tex Schramm was adamant about continuing to play through a strike. Not everybody agreed. Some were concerned that it couldn't be done, that we couldn't mobilize quickly enough to field another team and that the public wouldn't accept it. There was also a fear of violence around the stadiums if we continued to play.

There were strong arguments on both sides. Violence by militant players was a real possibility. We also wondered whether we could get adequate players for replacement teams, but those who wanted to continue to play pointed to the USFL, and all the athletes who ultimately had become established in the NFL. That made it clear there would be enough good players for replacement teams.

There was also the cost of paying these players to consider. So, there were financial and ethical concerns, and, certainly, the question of whether the public would support these games.

The NFL fortunately listened to Tex and others who believed the NFL should stay in business through a strike. Guidelines were established so teams knew who they could sign and how to commit players to binding agreements as they were released, so these players could return to the team. Obviously, it would be best to sign men who had been in your training camp and knew your system of football.

It was recommended that teams sign more players than usual, and that we evaluate them more carefully. We had players sign letters of agreement that committed them to us, for a nominal figure, when they were released.

More than most teams, the 49ers worked very hard to be ready when the strike occurred. We established a complete subprogram to secure and develop replacement talent. That took much more time and effort by our coaches and staff, but it ultimately paid off.

We signed so many players that we rivaled teams like Dallas and Denver, who were known for bringing abnormal numbers of players into camp. Again, it was because Ed DeBartolo, Jr., was willing to commit the 49ers to whatever it took. There were other owners who were not willing to do that, and their teams later suffered.

When the strike hit, we were ready with men who had been on our squad previously or who had been in our recent training camp. We had spent extra hours after regular practice with some players we knew couldn't make our team but would be needed for a replacement team. We had scouted other men in the league who might be available when the strike came. We had a "ready list," and we assigned administrative assistant Neal Dahlen to put together a strike team, based on scouting reports from Allan Webb, our director of pro personnel. We had a contingency plan that gave us a distinct advantage over our competition.

But before that, we had to deal with the regular season. During our annual organizational meeting in Youngstown, I had projected the remainder of the '80s in this way: we would be in transition in 1987 and '88 and could expect to return to the Super Bowl in 1989. Our draft of 1986 had set the stage for our eventual return to the championship level. We could see that some of our great veterans were at the end of their careers, so our team would be evolving and the composition of the squad would change dramatically in the next two seasons. It would take two years to get this team to the level of our 1984 champion.

Our 1987 season started disastrously. We were pleased with our preseason progress, but we were flat in our opener in Pittsburgh, mostly because I had overtrained the team, and lost to the Steelers, 30–17. Every conceivable break went against us, and somehow Mark Malone completed a couple of key passes.

Then came a game in Cincinnati that ranks as one of the most incredible in my career. I still can't quite believe it. We seemed destined to lose our second straight, 26–20, but through some excellent, spontaneous plays on our part and a strategic mistake by the Bengal coaches, we pulled out a win on the last play of the game.

We had punted to the Bengals, even though we were trailing with just over a minute left, because I felt the only way we were going to score was for Cincinnati to make a mistake. I hoped they would fumble the punt, or we would somehow get a turnover. We just weren't protecting the passer. We had fourth-and-eighteen, so we punted.

I can't say that was my bravest moment. I suppose we could have dropped back and thrown one more long pass and hoped for the best, but I made an instinctive move to give the ball back to the Bengals and hope for a big play, a fumble, a blocked punt, whatever. With two time-outs left, we still had a chance to get the ball back.

We did not get a great punt, and the Bengals got the ball at their own forty-five. Trying to avoid a fumble, Sam had his quarterback, Boomer Esiason, carry the ball on the first two downs. We stopped Boomer for a loss each time, and called time-out after each one. The clock was now down to forty-five seconds, but we had no time-outs left. On the next play, Esiason just fell on the ball at the thirty-five, and the Bengals let the clock run down to six seconds, taking a delay-of-game penalty. The clock stopped on the penalty.

Around me on the sideline, there were coaches and players who were understandably shaken and in shock, assuming we'd lost the game. But I saw that they were going to run a play and not punt, and I said, "We're going to get the ball back." Ronnie Lott was screaming at the other players to stay in the game, because we still had a chance to win it.

Then, our defensive coaches came to life and called a short-yardage defense that turned out to be the key to our victory.

Bengal coach Sam Wyche had decided not to punt the ball away because he was concerned about a possible block. He called a sweep, thinking time would run out on the play, but he didn't have the right blocking combination against our short-yardage defense. He had blockers who were reach-blocking against guys coming hard off the corners, and they couldn't block everybody. Kevin Fagan, slanting to the inside, was not blocked at all. With his unusual quickness, he was able to hit running back James Brooks five yards behind the line, before the play even started. With another blocking combination, Sam might have been able to use up the time.

We got the ball back on the Cincinnati twenty-five. Two seconds left. We had time for one play, and it didn't have to be a "Hail Mary" because we were close enough that Joe Montana could easily throw to the end zone.

Now the Bengals were in a state of shock. *My God, how could this happen to us?* They failed to call a time-out to get organized. So, we ran out on the field quickly to get our play off.

We were prepared and our call was ready—"tandem left 76 all go," which began with three wide receivers to the left and Jerry Rice to the right. Joe would drop back, look to the left, and pump-fake in that direction to get the safety moving and then turn to fire to Rice on the other side.

Joe did it beautifully. He pumped left, their safety bit on the fake, and Rice was in the end zone, with rookie defensive back Eric Thomas, who was much shorter than Jerry, behind him. Without a defender in front of Rice, the Bengals were at the mercy of two great athletes. Joe threw the ball high, Jerry caught it, and suddenly, we had won the game.

But even in my joy, I felt terrible for Sam. He came over before the extra point was kicked, and he was in a state of shock.

Sam and Jane Wyche were very close to Geri and me, going back to when we'd both been with the Bengals. We'd have dinner together often, and we resumed that relationship when Sam joined the 49ers coaching staff. By the time of this game, we'd known each other almost twenty years.

Jane had spent time with Geri before the game, which wasn't easy. Jane had said she'd get together with the 49er coaches and their wives after the game, and she did. She was a real trooper, coming down with Geri after that absolutely shocking loss. She handled herself beautifully, as did Sam.

As soon as the 49ers plane landed in San Francisco, I called the Wyche home. Sam was already asleep, so I talked to Jane and told her that Sam had done the right thing.

I called Sam the next day and was supportive. Whether I would have or not, I assured him that I would have done the same thing, that he'd had every reason to call that play. I blamed the loss on a breakdown in individual blocking, rather than on a strategy that had blown up in his face. I told him the game was history, he had a fine team and they would have a great season.

As the game ended, there were two humorous off-field incidents.

The first involved my son, Craig. He was in a men's room, which was naturally crowded with Bengals fans who were celebrating and laughing. Somebody had brought in a radio, and through the noise, everybody heard, "The Forty-Niners have the ball . . ." The place suddenly hushed. Migawd, what had happened? Then, the announcer said, "Touchdown, Forty-Niners!" Everybody shuffled out in stunned silence. One of the last remarks Craig heard was, "They did it to us again."

In the other, Ed DeBartolo, Jr., and his group had left the stadium and were in the parking garage preparing to drive to the airport to meet their plane. Bill Moses, a senior vice-president with the DeBartolo Corporation, was trying to tell them the 49ers had just won. Others said, "Bill, are you trying to be funny? Ha, ha, ha." Eddie was terribly upset, thinking that Bill was teasing him. Then, they all heard it on the radio, and back they came.

In my years with the 49ers, we had some incredible dressing-room scenes, but that particular dressing room rivaled the one after we beat the Steelers in Pittsburgh in '81. It was absolute mania. Everybody was wild, jumping and screaming. You couldn't believe it. It just went on and on, players screaming and hugging each other, lying on the floor and kicking the lockers.

Eddie came into that scene. Until that final score, he'd been very upset with his team. We had lost to Pittsburgh, and Pittsburgh is close to his home town of Youngstown, Ohio. Now, just when it appeared we were going to lose to another team close to his home, we had pulled it out. It was unbelievable, and Eddie was as dazed as the rest of us.

So, what could have been a disastrous start instead left us at 1–1, and when the strike was called after that weekend, we knew we'd be in better shape than most teams when we had to field a replacement squad.

Some teams thought that if games were played by replacement teams, the results wouldn't be counted in the standings. But being on the Competition Committee, I realized that the league was very serious about playing and counting these games.

We moved very, very quickly and put together a representative team that included people like Bob Gagliano, a quarterback who later started for Detroit, and running backs Tony Cherry, whom we had drafted in '86, and Del Rodgers. We also had other players who were to remain with the 49ers even after the strike ended: Harry Sydney, Brent Jones, Terry Greer, Darryl Pollard, Chuck Thomas, Clyde Glover, and George Cooper.

Because we largely had men who had been with us at one point, they knew our system when they came in as a replacement team. We had a positive atmosphere. They were proud to be with the 49ers, one of the great teams in the league.

We spoke to them of taking the 49ers to the Super Bowl. Whether they played the rest of the season or were replaced when striking players returned, they would have been part of the team.

So, we were fully mobilized. All of our practices had planned for this development. We had a contingency for every logical scenario.

Not every team was willing to do this. Because of Schramm, Dallas did it, of course, but some teams, like the New York Giants, refused to be a part of it. The Giants and others did not want to do anything to distract their regular squad. The Giants assumed the strike wouldn't occur or that the NFL wouldn't play if there was a strike, so why disrupt their normal operation by putting together a strike team? But the strike did come, and we had a game with the Giants in which we were totally superior to them, both in the amount of coaching the players had received and the level of talent. Rather than disdaining these replacement players, our coaches did an enthusiastic job of preparing them. Neal Dahlen was invaluable throughout this process. But in the meantime, we had to face a serious problem. Because of loyalty to the team, and because of desperate financial need, a number of 49er players chose to return. That was a most sensitive situation, and it took care and tact. I had to handle it almost intuitively, based on my relations with our squad, meanwhile accounting for the league directives. My priorities had to be first, Ed DeBartolo, Jr., second, our players, and third, the National Football League.

Each week of the strike, it was expected that it would be settled. The issues weren't ones that many players felt strongly about, and the union was making unrealistic demands, fully aware that management wouldn't agree. At some point, it was obvious that we would either have to total the season or the players would return, agreeing to resolve the issues through continuing negotiations.

We had a bye, which gave us two weeks to establish a team, while players were wondering whether the strike would hold. Some people from other teams began to return. We had a major group of eleven who wanted to come back, including stars like Joe Montana, Dwight Clark, Roger Craig, Jeff Fuller, and Russ Francis.

I had been in contact with leaders of the team. The morning they were expected to return, which was the deadline for being able to play that Sunday, I had met with Keena Turner, Dwaine Board, and Pete Kugler. They were among those ready to report, but they were team leaders, and they feared that if a large group returned, the team would be permanently divided.

Ugly things had been said in team meetings and workouts. Some players had taken a hard, militant line and were physically threatening some of the others. It wasn't so much that these players believed in the strike, but they felt that it was important to support the union. Others felt it was important to go back. So, you had two polarized groups, those saying, let's stick together and stay out, and others saying, let's stick together and go back.

I met with Keena, Dwaine, and Pete. They had given me an impassioned plea to keep players from returning, saying that, if I could wait, a larger group would come back the next week and possibly even the whole team.

I left that breakfast meeting, went by the office, talked with Eddie LeBaron and others who were NFL liaisons on the strike, and with Ed DeBartolo, Jr. I decided to talk to the players who planned to return; they were meeting at a shopping center near our practice facility, and I would ask them to wait another week. We were going to beat the Giants, anyway, and if we could wait a few more days, maybe the whole thing would be resolved.

On my part, it was almost an evangelistic approach, that somehow we could work this out. I got in the middle of the storm, thinking that if we could get through this, we could be a stronger team. The bottom line was winning football games and winning the world championships. At the same time, I had to account for all parties involved. I met with the players and talked to them about waiting until next Tuesday. In a sense, it was a real conflict of interest for me, because the league was doing everything it could to persuade people to return. NFL executives were in constant contact with each team, and particularly those with solid morale, to convince them to persuade men to report. There were isolated instances of individuals reporting. In two or three cases large groups returned en masse. The NFL expected us to entice our players back, to break the strike, but I didn't want to break the team, to affect the camaraderie and compatibility of our squad. Nor did I want the union broken, because it had an integral role in a "balance of power." I was caught between the two sides.

The 49ers were unusual because of the personal interest that both Ed DeBartolo, Jr., and I took in individual players and in the squad as a whole. We were determined to do what was best for the 49ers and not blindly accept the dictates of the National Football League. Naturally, we would operate within NFL guidelines. Ed had complete confidence in me, and I felt that, however I dealt with this matter, I would get the organization's complete support.

Because I had a sense of what would be in the players' best interests, I counseled those who had chosen to report not to return until the next week. But some of these men had families and were already exhausted financially.

Football salaries are usually structured so that players receive one-sixteenth of their total salaries each week of the season. That meant players had received just two paychecks, after the Pittsburgh and Cincinnati games, since last season. For the players at the lower end of the salary scale, who had house payments and all the other normal living expenses, that wasn't nearly enough to sustain them. They had planned their family budgets assuming that they would receive their entire salaries during the season. Because of this, many of them would be deeply in debt until their weekly flow of income could resume.

I felt a responsibility for them. If they wanted to earn a living, how could we stop them? We had very little time—perhaps only forty-five minutes before the noon deadline to be eligible to play in that week's game and qualify for their salaries.

There was a media circus at our practice facility, with television trucks and reporters from every paper in the area. It was expected that some men would return, and that would be a major, major story.

There was a demonstration in progress outside our facility. There were players with placards, supporting the strike in threatening ways. If returning players passed through them, we didn't know what might happen. So, there was the possibility of abuse between teammates, plus the media crush. I was going to do everything possible to avoid public ventings of our problems.

I said, "Look, I can't pay you for not returning, that just doesn't make sense, because then we'd have to pay everybody for striking. But I will find a way to get you a loan for half of your week's salary." I implied that the loan wouldn't have to be paid back. So, those in crisis had a choice.

There were big, big dollars for Montana, Craig, Clark, and Francis, but they weren't concerned so much about the money. The guys on the lower end of the scale were, so I told them I'd get them that loan and that, if everything worked out, they wouldn't be expected to repay the loan. The basis of my formula was that we could support these players in dire need and yet, they'd still be sacrificing half of a week's salary for the sake of team morale.

That ultimately got me in real trouble with the rest of the team, but the group would remain out another week. They left, agreeing to come back on Tuesday following our game against the Giants.

When I arrived at our Redwood City facility moments before noon, I was hit from every angle by the mass of reporters. What had happened? Where were Montana and the others as rumored? I tried to honestly explain without misleading people, but naturally, I couldn't tell them everything that had been agreed upon.

Then I caught hell from the rest of the league, because everybody had been waiting for a substantial number of 49ers to return. We were supposed to break the strike, but we were also supposed to accept our team being divided by some players reporting and some remaining out. Nobody seemed to care about that. They just wanted the 49ers to lead the charge.

I got on the phone immediately with Eddie and he responded with, "I don't care what the NFL tells us to do. We're going to do what's right for our squad and the Forty-Niners. If this is the way you want to do it, we'll take them on."

Then, I talked to Eddie LeBaron. I didn't tell him about the deal I'd worked out, but I did tell him that the players would not be returning, that we were going to play our game against the Giants without Joe Montana and other stars.

There would have been another concern if those players had returned: we weren't sure what would happen to our team bus going to the Meadowlands if it was known to have regular players on board. Unions outside football were joining the cause and threats were being made.

When we went to New York without regular squad members, there were some demonstrations, but they weren't militant, though they were vocal. It was a crazy game. We used the Wishbone, to lighten the atmosphere. More fans showed than anybody expected, but the Giants were really hapless, absolutely unable to compete with us.

The next week, Montana and that group did return against Atlanta. They weren't a strong team and I didn't want to use these players against the Falcons. I didn't want a total mismatch. But one thing was for sure, we couldn't afford to lose the game. So, we used our top men sparingly. Montana threw eight passes. We won easily.

The next week, as the strike continued, we played the St. Louis Cardinals. This time, I didn't have to worry about a mismatch because the Cardinals were a team that had over twenty players return. So, I played Montana the whole game. He had a great day—31 of 39— which was just barely enough to win 34–28. This was an extremely well-played game. The replacement teams, after four weeks of practice, were beginning to become cohesive units.

The strike actually broke the week before the St. Louis game, but the players didn't return until late Thursday. The league declared they couldn't play unless they reported on Wednesday, so most of our men couldn't play until the following week, although they could use our facilities to work out. League executives felt that the players would need three full practices before they could safely participate in this potentially dangerous game. I agreed completely with the NFL's position. At least three days were needed to gauge the athletes' physical condition and readiness to play.

We had a 4–1 record after the strike, which put us on top of the NFL. Had the strike not occurred or had we not fielded a winning replacement team, our season could very well have gone in another direction. Every one of our replacements got a plaque with a team picture on it, a token of our appreciation. They had been an eager, enthusiastic group of guys.

But then I was faced with the entire squad, which was one of the most difficult meetings of my career. There were a number of emotionally volatile players who confronted me because they were still really angry that Montana and his group had returned, and that I had manipulated their decision.

Some players had returned because of their loyalty to the San Francisco 49er organization. Others had come back because they simply did not agree with the union's position. Still others had returned because of dire financial circumstances. But whatever their reasons, their reporting had offended many members of the team. Some felt they'd been betrayed and that I had duped players into returning.

We had a meeting with the team in the middle of the practice field, with the media just out of earshot. I was put on the spot in an emotionally charged exchange with the players, with Ronnie Lott and Guy McIntyre in particular warning about the destruction of the team. I had planned a meeting indoors following practice, but Ronnie wouldn't wait.

Some players said they could never feel the same way about their teammates, that they'd always have contempt for them because of the way they'd broken the strike. Naturally, Russ Francis was ready to take on anybody and everybody, because he said he'd do what he wanted to do, and nobody would dictate to him.

I began systematically to explain everything to the team. The pressure was intense; I had a lot of explaining to do. Emotions had run unbelievably high. I was personally attacked for my actions. I thoroughly re-traced every step. I couldn't afford to let the meeting end with players in this mood. I slowed the process and made every attempt to be conciliatory and justify my actions. It was important that everyone be allowed to vent his feelings. Then, players might be willing to listen to my position. I think the vast majority of them understood my stance of trying to keep the team together, but there were some who were really hostile.

During my presentation, positions began to soften. I told players of the loans, and why we'd done it that way. When that meeting ended, there was still some animosity, but most of it had begun to subside.

Later, I had a problem with the loans, which reminded me, once again, of how differently athletes see the world.

As coaches, we have to remind ourselves that players have been protected, isolated, and coddled because people needed their services on the athletic field. Others have taken on responsibilities for players, so athletes are often naive, unaware of the many services a coach or general manager may provide for them.

Coaches have to realize that players aren't necessarily going to appreciate what you're doing for them. The player assumes this is part of your job. Because he is part of a select few, he feels that someone else should deal with the mundane details of his life. As soon as you resolve one problem, he tends to forget that and comes into your office with another. A coach who expects that the player will be appreciative or demonstrate more loyalty or will be more motivated on the athletic field as a result will very likely be disappointed. A coach should take these actions because he feels they're in the best long-term interests of the athlete. The coach should believe that his advice, counsel, and actions on behalf of the athlete are ethically and morally right. He should not expect service in return.

In this case, I heard nothing from the players I'd helped but only from those who felt slighted because they didn't get loans. To keep the team together, I said we'd make the same loans to everybody, but once players began receiving their weekly checks, there was no need to take advantage of that assistance.

To demonstrate our loyalty and sensitivity to the entire squad, and to diffuse whatever resentment remained, I asked Eddie to consider doubling our first playoff check, which also might serve as further motivation for the remainder of the year. Eddie immediately agreed with this suggestion. By the time Eddie made this offer, we were 5–1, so we could be almost assured of making the playoffs. The players eventually received an extra $10,000.

Before we committed ourselves, John McVay had contacted the league office to see if that was within the rules. In one part of the NFL constitution it states that you can give a bonus if everybody receives it; you can't just give it to one player or a few players. Another part of the constitution states that you cannot give anything beyond the basic playoff shares as a further incentive to win. But we did get reluctant approval from the NFL for what we were going to do.

All hell broke loose when the rest of the league heard about it. NFL commissioner Pete Rozelle eventually ruled that the players could keep the money, but he fined DeBartolo $50,000. The players later banded together to pay the fine, because they were appreciative of what Eddie had done. Then and since, others have attempted to say we've succeeded because of Eddie's deep pockets. We've had to remind people that in 1981, we had the best record in football and won the Super Bowl with a salary schedule that was at the very bottom of the league.

That wasn't the end of the matter, though. At the Competition Committee meetings the next spring, Don Shula and Tex Schramm accused me of being disloyal to the NFL, of coercing the players, of being unethical—right at the dinner table. It was a very uncomfortable experience. Later, when I was to explain the entire scenario, both softened their position dramatically.

Should we have acted any differently? I don't think so. We could have stayed out of it, which would have been simpler, but we were trying to keep the team together and reward the players for their loyalty and accommodate their financial needs.

It cost Ed DeBartolo a lot of money, and we had gone through a lot of pain to get everybody together, but we had mobilized, we had kept going, and now, after the strike, we were together and playing well.

We finished the season with the best record in the NFL, 13–2. That was gratifying. Going into the season, we were not favored to win even our division, but now, at the end of the year, we were considered the best team in football.

Moving Roger Craig to tailback and putting Tom Rathman at fullback had improved the offense, and Jerry Rice was the most dangerous receiver in football. Ronnie Lott was much more of an impact player at safety than he'd been at cornerback. Linebacker Mike Walter and strong safety Jeff Fuller had come of age. Though this team really wasn't to reach its peak until late in the 1989 season, we had successfully made the transition from the '84 team that won the Super Bowl to a team that seemed on its way to another championship. We had destroyed the Chicago Bears, 41–0, and handily won a showdown game with Cleveland, 38–24.

But, all that was forgotten when we were shocked by the Minnesota Vikings in the first round of the playoffs.

How did that happen? It was a combination of meeting a Minnesota team that was playing very well and not being ready for the game ourselves, for a variety of reasons, many of them originating with me.

Minnesota was at its very peak. Their defense was awesome. They had three outstanding defensive players, linemen Keith Millard and Chris Doleman and safety Ross Browner. Their offense was functioning very effectively. They were one of the best teams in the league; they'd destroyed a fine New Orleans team in the Wild Card game.

We had capped our season with a 48–0 win over the Los Angeles Rams in our final game. In retrospect, I can see how that win was one of the primary reasons we lost to the Vikings, because we became too emotional over a game we would certainly have won just by throwing our jocks on the field, so to speak. The Rams were decimated. Jim Everett had been injured, so they had Steve Dils playing quarterback, and they weren't the same team. They had just lost a Monday night game that knocked them out of the playoffs, so they were emotionally spent as well.

We substituted and played reserves as the game developed, but I just kept the offense in motion. I can recall that before the end of the game, we ran the slow draw for good yardage and then faked and passed for a touchdown to make the score 41–0. Those unnecessary calls were made because I was trying to prove a point to myself.

I was adamant about beating that Ram defense near the goal line. They had been extremely effective against us in the so-called red zone because they'd utilized a well-executed zone defense and disrupted the things we would normally do against a man-to-man or a blitzing defense in that situation. We'd beaten the Rams 9 of our last 13 games, but I had had to spend more and more time devising ways to counteract their tactics. That zone had given us so much trouble in the past, I was almost consumed with proving that we could beat it.

By the time we played them, we really had their number. We threw play-action passes to destroy their defense. We'd fake the run, so defenders couldn't drop as quickly into their zone, and then throw hooking patterns. We'd done that with Dwight Clark for a touchdown.

Then, we went into overkill. My conscience bothered me later because we scored on that fake draw and pass when the game was already lopsided. I was determined to prove—to myself—that I had the Rams' number. That was poor judgment. I talked to John Robinson after the game. John is a real gentleman, and he didn't seem upset at all, but it bothers me to this day. Our philosophy has always been to stick with our plan; when the game is completely under control, run the ball, expend the clock. I found myself trying to prove something on this day, I'm not sure what. I found myself feasting on the carcass, in direct contradiction to what I've represented. We ended up winning 48–0.

Before the game, too, we'd had some impassioned speeches by players. Keith Fahnhorst reminded everyone he was playing his last season, and he talked about how the Rams had always been our chief rival. Ronnie Lott and Keena Turner made stirring speeches. We came out to play our best game that night and we did, but we drained ourselves emotionally. We played a perfect game, but in a sense it was too much, too soon.

I knew it would have to be a methodical, mechanical, game against Minnesota. I knew we couldn't expect to play at the same emotional pitch that we had against the Rams. It would have to be a game of execution and strategy.

As I now reflect, I realize that I worked the team too hard in practice. The first week following the Rams game, we threw deep pass after deep pass to our receivers, trying to refine those patterns. We practiced too hard and too long, so we took too much out of our team physically. We had practiced in this way before our Super Bowls and it had worked very well, but it wasn't right for this team.

We were so sure of ourselves. It had been predicted that we would beat Denver in the Super Bowl by three touchdowns—as we most likely would have—but we weren't mentally prepared to take on a team that was among the top two or three in the league. As they proved, the Vikings were the toughest kind of team for us to play. It was their physical, attacking style of defense against our offense, stale from too much practice and lacking intensity. Compound that with an excellent day of throwing by Viking quarterback Wade Wilson and an incredible receiving performance by Anthony Carter, and we were doomed. Keith Millard destroyed us. That day may have been the Vikings' high watermark.

On defense, we stayed with—and I must say this was a miscalculation on the part of our defensive coaches—our bump-and-run, man-to-man style of pass coverage, which allowed Wilson to have a near-perfect day throwing the ball. We didn't get untracked with our pass rush to get pressure on him, and our corners got taken apart by Carter. They were victimized by a great athlete having the best day of his career. There were plays on which Carter seemed to be covered, but he'd still make an acrobatic catch.

We weren't moving the ball and they were. Then, we had a key interception, on a forced pass by Joe Montana, with Reggie Rutland returning the ball 45 yards for a touchdown that put the Vikings ahead, 17–3. It's just possible that sentiment figured in that play. It was Dwight Clark's last season, and Joe threw an "out" to Dwight almost blindly. They had worked together so well through the years, but it was not a good decision, because we wanted Joe to get the ball to Jerry Rice, who was wide open on the right side of the field. The Vikings were running a four-man, undershifted line, their typical defense. Three pass rushers were to Joe's left, so the "out" pattern to the right would be there. But Joe instead threw to Dwight.

It was a poor performance by all of us, very uninspired considering the stakes. Before the half, we had driven in close but missed a routine field goal. It was as bad as that. We couldn't even get points on the board. When somebody as reliable as Ray Wersching missed a short field goal, something that was a "gimme" for him, it was all the more obvious that we weren't in sync.

As we left the field at halftime, my mind was racing rapidly, trying to formulate how I would handle our halftime break. From past experience, I knew all too well that only big plays could pull us out. The Vikings were beating us to the punch, and that wasn't likely to change. A coach can sense impending disaster. You have that sick feeling in the pit of your stomach.

We had a history of coming back from poor starts. In those instances we had made adjustments to improve our execution. In this case, we were getting knocked all over the field physically. I said to myself, "We worked them too goddamned hard."

We were only down, 20–3, so anything could happen. But, we played as sluggishly at the start of the second half as we'd played in the first.

Joe had all kinds of problems, the main one being the pressure put on him by the pass rush. We couldn't execute anything. Even the simplest play would blow up in our face.

It became obvious that something had to be done. In Joe's first two series of the second half, he was sacked twice and could not complete a pass for a first down. Much of the problem came from breakdowns in our pass protection, especially on the left side. The stark reality hit me: I would have to go with Steve Young. His spontaneous running might break that Viking pass rush and turn the game around. Meanwhile, I would have Joe on the sideline, and if he returned, we'd know exactly what to do.

I replaced Joe in the third quarter. It killed me to do it. When he came to the sideline, I hugged him but couldn't allow myself to get maudlin. I simply said, "We're going with Steve." Later in the game, I attempted to explain to Joe, but it wasn't going to help much.

My job was to try to win the football game. At that point, I had to go with my professional judgment. I had to go with my gut feeling. If I couldn't make a tough decision like this, then I was derelict in my duty. I wouldn't allow myself to get sentimental. I'd have to live with the results. It was an all-or-nothing situation.

Steve performed admirably, but he wasn't able to turn the tide. The Vikings won the game, 36–24.

That was as bitter and difficult a loss as we've ever had, but it was one you could almost see coming. There really wasn't much I could do about it as the game progressed. I'd plead guilty for us being overtrained and stale. All of us would plead guilty for spending so much of ourselves on the Rams game.

There was absolute suffering. We were in a state of shock, still not believing what had just happened. How were we to know we'd be in the Super Bowl the next year? When you get that close, you figure it's now or never.

We had had three frustrating years. We'd lost to the Giants in '85 in the playoffs. We'd been absolutely destroyed by the Giants the next year. Now, we had been shocked by Minnesota. Those playoff losses were all taken extremely hard by Eddie. Each loss got progressively worse. I'm sure Eddie was asking himself, "Why do we continue to fall short? There must be something I can do about it. There's fault somewhere and Bill's in charge."

All that we'd accomplished had become of little consequence. True, we had been bitterly disappointed by this loss, but we'd had a great season under trying circumstances. The season would have had to be considered a success, but we had reached the point where anything short of the Super Bowl was not considered a successful year and therefore was not acceptable.

Our inability to regain the premiere position in the NFL (in '86) should not necessarily reflect failure. I often related it to a climbing expedition assaulting Mount Everest. The 49ers' standard of performance over the years has established a base camp within striking distance of the summit. Each year (in '85, '86, and '87) we would make our assault and unfortunately be stopped short. We regained the summit in 1988. Often our opposition would take a run at it only to fall short and be driven back to the village far below. Even though we didn't reach the summit, we were close. Each year we were in the playoffs and had our shot.

18

The Quarterback Controversy

As the 1988 season began, we moved from our tired, inadequate Redwood City facility to a new location in Santa Clara. The Santa Clara facility is the finest for a sports team anywhere in the world. In the past, we had been forced to practice on two fifty-yard fields, with cramped meeting and locker room quarters. Now we had a "state of the art" camp, featuring three complete fields, including one with an artificial surface. We had spent years designing it to be both functional and beautiful. Ed had dedicated it to the memory of his mother, Marie P. DeBartolo, and he had spared nothing. Marie was gracious, energetic, loving—a very special person.

In leaving behind the nostalgia of our antiquated Redwood City quarters for this thoroughly contemporary structure, I reminded myself of the sense of comfort and affluence that had adversely affected other teams, such as Dallas, who had relocated to new, plush facilities. The Cowboys have never been the same. They say you lose that hungry, hard-bitten mind set in these "executive" surroundings. This tendency really concerned me; we weren't going to let it happen to us, and in the final analysis it didn't. But I guess I acted miserably in the process. On the management side, I didn't want anyone on the staff to feel they had "arrived" just because they had an individual office instead of a tin desk in the corner. Luxury and convenience can bring complacency, and I rode everyone hard to avoid that.

Despite the new practice location and my high hopes for the team, the season began on an off-note. In the summer of 1988, we played an exhibition game in London, against the Miami Dolphins. Early in the week, after practice, Miami coach Don Shula and I were asked for impromptu interviews on the sideline.

The question asked both of us was, "What are your main concerns going into 1988?"

Don talked first to the reporters, and he concentrated on his team's problems, which were quite extensive. Meanwhile, I was very happy with my team. We had no serious concerns, and I expected us to be contenders, if not champions. So, as I was interviewed, I talked at length about the 49er positives. When I was asked if I had any worries, I blurted out, "We may have a quarterback controversy." The moment I said it, I thought, "Uh-oh. This could be a problem." Shula looked at me with a faint smile. He knew, as I did, that I had opened the door for the media. It was an unfortunate choice of words—I really should have said that we had a legitimate competition between Joe Montana and Steve Young—but though the original error was mine, the media can be faulted for fabricating a controversy later.

The problem, I'm convinced, started with our loss to Minnesota in the playoffs following the '87 season. After that, everybody was sensitive to anything that might go wrong with the 49ers. It seemed, though we'd won 13 games in the regular season and had the best record in the NFL, that there was a chink in our armor. Throughout the '88 season, there was more scrutiny by the press. Many writers were looking for something to demonstrate that the team was collapsing, or that something was inherently wrong with the 49ers. The cause could be how I handled the players or our style of football or perhaps team dissension.

Meanwhile, Steve Young had shown that he had the ability to be the 49er quarterback. Whenever he'd played as a 49er, he'd been not only productive but exciting.

Once we'd become established as a championship-level NFL team, all our quarterbacks had played well. When Matt Cavanaugh had had to replace Joe Montana, he'd done well. Jeff Kemp played well when Montana was sidelined by back surgery. Even Mike Moroski had won one game for us before Joe came back in '86.

Steve Young was in a different category, a talent comparable to Montana. As good a runner as Joe has been and as spontaneous and instinctive as he has been, Steve is even better. Steve's speed is around 4.5 for 40 yards and he is considered to be possibly the best running quarterback ever.

Steve would quickly revert to his running if a play didn't develop exactly as planned, so his passing game hadn't developed as it should have. It took a full year for him to acquire the necessary knowledge, but in the process, he was such a threat that, when placed in a game, he could make things happen. His passing improved so much that, following his first season with us, I was obliged to say that he was in competition with Montana for the quarterback job.

That was consistent with my general philosophy: that any player who had played well should be given a chance to compete for a starting job. For instance, Dwight Clark was an excellent receiver, possibly a Hall of Fame player, but Mike Wilson played very well behind him. So, when training camp began, I never ruled out Mike as a potential starter. Well, I never ruled Steve Young out, either.

But that was clearly not the same as saying that Young would be our starting quarterback.

Steve had really begun to mature and develop as a quarterback. He was acquiring the discipline of our passing offense and the knowledge and expertise of our system, so he could function well on the field. He adapted well and played skillfully in the preseason games, but Joe was our quarterback. I continued to emphasize that. We were pleased and gratified with Steve Young's progress, but Joe Montana was our quarterback.

Though Young performed better in the '88 preseason than Montana did, Joe was our quarterback when the season started. Joe had nothing to prove; he would be ready. And, despite all the "controversy" during the season, I started Joe whenever he was healthy (and occasionally, when he wasn't completely healthy) and substituted for him only in extreme circumstances, when Steve's spontaneous running might pull out a game.

Joe Montana had been the key performer in our previous success, and we all believed in him. Undoubtedly, he was one of the truly great players in NFL history. He had mastered our offensive system and directed it brilliantly. Of all my quarterbacks, he had been the most successful at directing my offense. It was ludicrous to think I'd want to bench him if he could play.

I regularly said these things to the media about Joe. But whenever anything positive was said about Young, it was considered almost as heresy on my part because it might reflect on Joe Montana and his status.

In fact, my only concern about Montana was his health. Joe is a courageous man who has often played despite injuries or illness, but he is obviously more effective when he's healthy. We had the luxury of having the equivalent of two starting quarterbacks, so I could rest Joe when he was hurt and still feel confident that we could win the game with Steve. My goal was to have Joe healthy for the stretch run and the playoffs, and that worked. Joe played as well as he ever has in the final games of the season and the postseason, right through that dramatic last drive in the '89 Super Bowl.

If I had listened to critics, I would have played Joe even when he was injured and ill during the '88 season. Most likely, he would not then have been healthy when we needed him most.

Ironically, George Seifert used the same approach with Joe in his first year as head coach. Because of injuries, Montana actually missed the equivalent of four full games in 1989. But nobody criticized Seifert for not playing Montana. Nor did any writer or broadcaster suggest that George was somehow phasing out Montana.

More than anything else, that confirmed my belief that I had stepped down at the right time. By resigning as coach, I had defused the "quarterback controversy" because George understandably had some breathing room with the media I no longer had after ten years on the job.

We had other complications as we started that year. We were rebuilding; in fact, I had anticipated that this team would reach its peak in '89. We were moving players like Harris Barton, Jesse Sapolu, and Jeff Bregel into the offensive line, and trying to get rookies Dan Stubbs and Pierce Holt into the defensive line, while moving Charles Haley from defensive line to a combination linebacker-lineman role, hoping to increase his effectiveness as a pass rusher.

Then, we were hit by injuries, with those to Keena Turner and Ronnie Lott being the most damaging. Because Don Griffin and Tim McKyer had held out, demanding new contracts, they were late in reporting, and they were not in competitive condition for our opener in New Orleans. We were extremely vulnerable on defense.

In New Orleans, Joe hurt his elbow when he banged it on the hard artificial turf. He played well and we won, but his elbow was badly swollen after the game and into the next week. Steve began to get all the practice time. Joe also had suffered from dysentery, which caused him to lose six or seven pounds and weakened him considerably.

We started Steve the next Sunday against the Giants in New York, because Joe had been able to practice only on Saturday, twenty-four hours prior to kickoff.

Steve was somewhat skittish because of the pressure being applied by that great Giants defense. The score was tied at halftime, 10–10, but Steve had been tentative in his passing and had reverted to his running tactics too often. That was not successful against a Giants team that was so powerful and quick.

At halftime, I replaced Steve with Joe, who had thrown well warming up before the game. I thought, if anyone could win, he could. Joe too had problems, but he pulled out a great victory with a beautiful 78-yard pass to Jerry Rice on our last play, with only 42 seconds left in the game (see Diagram F, page 271). This was vintage Montana.

It was a play we had prepared to use against the Giants' "prevent defense." New York had dominated defensively for several years, using a pass coverage that featured two deep safeties. We had felt that we could get Rice past the cornerback, before the safety could get to him. This again was a credit to our planning, because we had the play best suited against that defense and used it at the right time. Denny Green had calmly reminded me of this play, the 76 All Go, as the series began. I acknowledged it, saying we'd wait until third down, when the safeties would be at their deepest. There was less than a minute remaining. This would have to be it. We weren't going to get another shot. Joe threw a perfect strike to Jerry, who was able to outsprint the Giants' safety the rest of the way. It was one of the most beautifully executed passes I have seen, and with all that pressure.

But Joe had yet to play up to standard because he continued to suffer from his elbow problem and the dysentery lingered.

Our third game was a shocking upset by Atlanta. Apparently we relaxed after that great win against the Giants. We came back and played an excellent game against Seattle, Joe's best of the early season. He hit Jerry over the head of the weak safety twice for spectacular touchdowns. Our offense really got into gear, gaining 580 yards in a 38–7 victory. We had a lackluster performance against Detroit, winning unimpressively, 20–13. Wayne Fontes' defense gave us fits.

Then, we had an agonizing game against the Denver Broncos at Candlestick.

We had not beaten the Broncos since I had been head coach,

playing them three times in the regular season and five times in exhibitions.

The most frustrating loss came in a game in Denver in 1985, when a snowball thrown from the stands distracted Matt Cavanaugh, holding for Ray Wersching on a field-goal attempt. Ray missed the kick, and we lost, 17–16.

I blamed myself, because I had kept Montana, our best holder, on the sideline because I didn't want to risk an injury to him. Joe was a little quicker with his hands and not affected by distraction, but that game is a prime example of how the weather and noise—the Denver fans are as loud as any in the NFL—can disrupt concentration and execution.

Weather was a factor in this game, too; the second half was played in a brutal wind, probably the worst I've ever seen at Candlestick. It completely changed the game, which went into overtime. Denver won the toss and took the wind, and that really decided the outcome.

With the wind in our faces, we had no chance of a good kickoff return, then found it impossible to throw effectively, so I substituted Steve, hoping his spontaneous running ability could get us out of a hole. If we had to punt, Denver would be immediately in field-goal position. But Steve threw an interception. He misread the coverage and threw to the wrong receiver, and that interception cost us the game.

If I were to do it again, I'd still make the same substitution. There was no way Joe or anybody could have thrown effectively into that wind.

We were more emotionally primed for this game than any other in the entire season, again demonstrating that execution and standard of performance are more critical factors than emotion. Too often, if emotion is the basis of play, frustration can set in and players can overreact with grievous errors.

Following a solid 24–21 win over an excellent Rams team, in which Roger Craig had a field day, we played the Bears in Chicago, a showdown game. It was certainly the game of the week in the NFL, the Monday night game, two powers contesting in what became a preview of the NFC championship game.

We moved the ball very well early and scored on a 23-yard pass from Montana to Rice midway through the first quarter. Our defense was playing superbly against a good Chicago offense.

But as the game went on, our pass protection began to break down, and Joe took some terrible punishment. He had never recovered his full strength from the dysentery, and that began to show. In the fourth quarter, Joe had lost the zip in his arm. Toward the end of the game, I substituted Steve, again hoping a run would make the difference. It didn't, and we lost, 10–9.

The next day, while visiting with our medical and training staff and with Denny Green and Mike Holmgren, I decided that if Joe didn't get some rest now, it might affect his play all year. When I was questioned at the weekly press conference that day, I said that Steve Young might get more playing time.

I was speaking honestly and directly, and I again stated that Joe was our starting quarterback. Unfortunately, I hadn't had a chance to visit with Joe about this before I spoke to the media.

The many reporters who cover the 49ers stampeded to find Joe Montana and caught him, misrepresenting what I had said. Joe was told he was being replaced by Steve Young. Fatigued, frustrated by the loss, embarrassed because Young had replaced him in the waning moments of games, Joe responded emotionally.

After I heard that, I immediately had a meeting with Joe. It was cordial; we have never had harsh words at any time. I apologized in a sense and reminded him of my feelings about him and what I anticipated for the rest of the year. I reassured him that he was still an outstanding performer and I expected him to continue to be the class of the league. But at the same time, I felt he was not physically up to par, almost exhausted.

Joe didn't completely agree with that, but ironically, when he got up to leave, his back went into spasms. Team doctor Michael Dillingham saw him immediately and told Joe to stay out of practice. Within forty-eight hours, he was scratched for the upcoming game.

So, though my remarks may have been untimely, my judgment was accurate.

The quarterback controversy continued. Some wrote that I had replaced Joe with Steve, without mentioning that Joe had been ruled out by Mike Dillingham, the team physician.

Steve's play against the Vikings was an example of the way he'd played with the 49ers. Certainly he didn't function as smoothly as Joe did and he made some mistakes early that were maddening to me, but he also showed the great spontaneity that had impressed us so much originally.

In the first half, he simply could not get untracked. He was looking too much at the pass rush, which left him unprepared to throw the ball downfield. I had designed a play on which Chris Doleman was supposed to be blocked to the outside. Steve would then step up into the pocket and throw to the right side. But when he saw Doleman coming, he tried to circle around him to the left side. He got sacked once because of that, and on other plays, he wasn't in position to throw the ball to the right side because Doleman was between him and his receivers.

But in the second half, Steve settled down and played well, directing a 97-yard drive to start the half and later completing a pass to John Taylor that became a 73-yard touchdown. And then, just two minutes before the end, he demonstrated his great running ability with a spectacular 49-yard run in which he seemingly went through the entire Vikings defense before he staggered across the goal line.

It was a great victory for the 49ers. We had, in a sense, redeemed ourselves against a Minnesota team that had shocked us in the playoffs the previous year. But it only intensified the quarterback controversy, as writers began to speculate that Joe was being phased out and Steve was replacing him.

At my Monday press conference, one writer asked me if Steve would be the starter for the rest of the season if he played well against Phoenix. I replied that anything was possible but that neither I nor anybody in the organization expected that. The writer quoted me only as saying that "anything's possible," which created an entirely different impression of what I had said.

Using that quote, a columnist who had not been at the press conference wrote that it was unfair that Steve was being handed the job!

Meanwhile, still another columnist interviewed Joe, who said he was sure the 49ers were trying to trade him. By this time, it was three weeks past the trading deadline, so he couldn't have been traded, but the columnist was either unaware of this or chose to ignore it.

By the end of the week, the doctors said Joe could play in a limited role but that we must not allow him to strain his back. I decided that if the prognosis was so guarded, I should give Joe at least another full week of rest. He dressed for the Phoenix game, but I had no intention of playing him.

So, Steve played against Phoenix. He did extremely well. We had a 23–0 lead midway in the third quarter, but then the wheels began to come off.

Don Griffin was just coming back from an injury, and the Cardinals quarterback, Neil Lomax, picked on him for a 35-yard touchdown pass to Roy Green. Don had jumped into a bump-and-run defense, on almost his first play back, and he was beaten for the touchdown.

We had given up a lot of yardage because our other cornerback, Tim McKyer, was also injured and an inexperienced Darryl Pollard had to play corner. Darryl later went on to play well for the 49ers in the 1989 season, but at this time, he had just been with the team for a couple of weeks and really wasn't prepared to play. He was out of position in our zone defense at critical times, and Lomax just kept hitting his receivers to get his team back into the game.

We had been noted for being able to control the ball at the end of the game to save a win, but we failed to do it this time. The last time we had the ball, we got one first down but couldn't get the second we needed to run out the clock.

There were two strategic errors in that last drive. The first was when I called a run by Roger Craig that stretched the defense to the outside. I had failed to account for the fact that the weak safety was playing close to the line in what was really a short-yardage defense. He nailed Roger for a loss.

We had one play remaining. Steve Young, talking to me on the sideline, was sure he could outrun defensive end Freddie Joe Nunn on a quarterback keeper. On third-and-three, we thought he made the first down—and the films later confirmed that he clearly had—but the official called Steve out of bounds about six inches short of the first down.

Regardless of the accuracy of the official's ruling, I wish I could have called back those two plays. First, we should have had Roger going over the top. Second, if Steve had kept the ball, we should have had him run to the right. We normally liked to have Steve run to his left, because he's a lefthander and the ball would be in his left hand, which gives him more control. But in this case, the defensive end wouldn't have been as alert. Steve had previously run that play to his left for a first down, so Nunn was ready for it. The other end wouldn't have been.

When we failed to make the first down, we punted and Phoenix picked apart our zone defense. With one play remaining, the Cardinals again went after Darryl Pollard, hitting Green for a 9-yard touchdown to beat us, 24–23. I was especially disturbed by that play because I didn't think an inexperienced defensive back should have been in a bump-and-run situation with Green, one of the best receivers in the league. I have never been so enraged after a game. I was out of control for a few minutes in the locker room. No question the heat was on; everyone was feeling it. I was upset at certain players, totally disturbed at our tactics on the final play. More than anything else I was upset at myself.

During the game, I had been hit by two players running full speed while I was looking the other way. I was knocked into the air and suffered two cracked ribs.

Flying home on the plane, I was in real distress with my cracked ribs, and such a terrible loss didn't help. I had always been critical of other teams that could not protect a lead, and now it had happened to us. That was one of the toughest losses in our history. We had thoroughly dominated a game and then lost it.

And again, we heard about the "quarterback controversy." Some writers questioned whether Young should have played, while I was certain that Joe had not been ready. At that point, it seemed that the story had a life of its own. The media had not had this kind of "continuing saga" for a long time, one with so many possibilities. They could continue to go to each quarterback and to the coach— and even to the fans; one newspaper ran a poll asking readers who should be starting.

I found it ironically humorous that after all my experience in developing successful quarterbacks, I was now not only being second-guessed but heavily criticized for my judgment in handling the position.

I don't think this affected the team. The players had been conditioned over time to ignore these kinds of sensational things. We'd been through this before, whether it was Jack Reynolds retiring or Fred Dean's contract problems.

I think the team understood it better. Players were working very closely with both Joe Montana and Steve Young. Joe was an established veteran and respected leader, so the bulk of the team's support and sympathy was his. But I don't think anybody would have dismissed Steve as not being an important member of the 49ers or as unable to compete with Joe for the job.

Those things have less effect on a team than people might think. You'll hear people say "Your morale must be low" because of different problems, but so often, players are primarily concerned with their own performances. They aren't distracted, unless a player is being mistreated or the team as a whole is depressed and disillusioned because of the direction the organization is taking. But that never occurred. I would refer to this ongoing scenario when appropriate. I probably didn't need to. I asked players to respond privately if they chose.

Joe started the next game because he'd been given medical clearance, but it soon became apparent that he wasn't completely ready. He was beginning to regain his strength, but he did not play with conviction. Nor did the rest of the team. We were humiliated by the Raiders, a 9–3 loss in which we gained only 219 yards. That was our lowest point in several years. Our defense played well, so it can't be said that the team collapsed. But that was the worst offensive game I could remember, maybe the worst we had in my career as 49ers coach.

In an evenly matched game the offense must sustain itself through a continuous series of first downs. This allows the defensive unit to retain its quick, explosive response. It's almost impossible for the defense to sustain a fierce, violent tempo if they're on the field for long periods of time. You can only block so many punches.

We were still in shock from the Phoenix game. We were in much the same state as we were after the loss to Atlanta in '83. When you lose that way, especially on the last play of the game, it can affect you, permeating your entire organization.

I credit the Raiders for spending considerable time throughout the season preparing for us and playing very well, but we were absolutely flat and unable to generate anything.

We had a key play late in the game when tight end Ron Heller was called for holding. I thought it was a bad call, but when you get one like that and don't recover from it, it's an indication that the team is not primed to play football. In other games, we recovered from similar penalties, but we just couldn't in this one. In the '89 Super Bowl, Randy Cross was called for being downfield on a pass play, but the team just kept going. But any setback can be devastating to a team that isn't in a positive state of mind and isn't concentrating. My response following the Cardinal game could very well have been too severe. A coach can only go so far with a negative stance. I was embarrassed; so was everyone who had built the organization.

We felt that if we hit one big play, we could win the game. We had special plays that could take advantage of their free safety, Vann McElroy. An excellent support man, he would commit himself early to the run. With a good run fake, we could get down the middle and make a big play, which we'd been doing regularly with Jerry Rice. But we'd either miss the pass or the protection would break down.

After the game, one of their defensive coaches claimed that he knew what we were going to do from the way we lined up. There was no question that they had our number but they must have lost the keys in the ensuing weeks, because they failed to make the playoffs.

So often, when you upset someone, you have the choice of taking pride in a great team effort or saying that you were smarter than the other team. But you'd like to think you can do it regularly, and the Raiders couldn't in the next few weeks, so that particular coach's claims of superior strategy had a hollow ring.

In the hour after the Raiders game, I was escorted by two security guards as I went to my box to meet my family. I was accosted by two young men who decided that, here and now, they were going to run me out of San Francisco. In my agitated state of mind, I responded. I was on the verge of sustaining my second loss of the day, but fortunately, the security guards intervened before anything physical could happen. I'd had a stark example of how bitter some of the fans had become.

As I left the field, the weight of this loss seemed to be more staggering than any other I'd experienced. The cumulative stress over the years was taking its toll.

I had never been able to wax philosophical about losing. Even the first year, I couldn't say, "Well, that's the breaks. In time, we'll win." Each year, it became tougher to lose, not easier. You can only attack that part of your nervous system so many times. Toward the end, every loss was a mortifying experience. There would be a terrible hurting.

It's not anger or depression. Being depressed would mean you're giving up, so you fight your way through that. The worst thing is losing two in a row, because you start thinking, "Will we ever win another game? Maybe we'll lose ten in a row." We had lost to the Raiders with Joe Montana and I thought, "If Joe is back and we can't win, what the hell's happened to us?"

You get to the point where you don't want to be in a position where you can take another loss. That sick feeling that consumes you seems to affect you more and more as the years pass. The only criterion for success for the 49ers had become winning the Super Bowl. When that's the only criterion, the coach is very aware of how something can go wrong, as when we lost to Minnesota in the playoffs after the '87 season.

Paul Brown always said, sometimes you don't know what you don't know. There are those who sail smoothly through life because they aren't sensitive enough to realize the implications of what's happening. They'll never suffer burnout. People such as myself often internalize too much, and consequently, suffer more.

A season for a coaching staff can be like a prolonged voyage in a cramped submarine. The tight quarters of the typical coaches' office complex. The never-ending schedule of meetings. Staff members must contend with tedious long hours through a six-month season, and in the process must make vital decisions as to personnel, strategy, and tactics. They must reach an accord and demonstrate a solid front in presenting a plan and preparing the team for each week's contest. Naturally, there will be some disagreement; hopefully it will only be a small degree of difference. Egos are involved, for each coach will be exerting every bit of his knowledge on the task.

There is a combination of work and pressure that does the damage. The game was on my mind every minute of every day. I would be out to dinner with my wife on Friday night, and suddenly I'd fall silent, staring into space. "You've clicked in again, haven't you?" Geri would say. I'd work at it, break out for about thirty minutes and seem quite normal, but then I'd fall back into almost a trance. I could be replaying my mistakes of the previous week or "playing" the next game. I could envision my call, and actually see the play develop. Then I'd think, "Ah, hell, you screwed up again." One time when I had my arm around Geri's shoulder, I was unconsciously drawing a play with my finger on her shoulder. When it appeared that I had finished, she said, "Did it work?"

Now, when you think about six straight months of that and absolute agony after every loss, after twenty years in the NFL, you begin to wonder. The highs didn't make up for the lows; winning the Super Bowl barely compensated for that loss to the Raiders. John Robinson and I often philosophized about head coaching. "When you win, it's only a zero; when you lose, it's a minus." As soon as you win, you're worried about the next game. Only after the season could I look back and say, "We were 10–6. That's not bad." During the season, I couldn't reflect on anything.

I put more pressure on myself because I felt that, if I was going to be the head coach, I should still draw up plays and call them, and still put together the offense. I personally drew up every pass play the team used for ten years. It was a ritual that took me well into the morning hours every week. In retrospect, I could have delegated more with the same results.

But I'm not sure I would have gotten as much satisfaction and gratification had I delegated more responsibility. I didn't get enough satisfaction from only motivating the team and orchestrating the overall plan. I had to do the "football," the specific planning and the strategy. If I had delegated my role as offensive coordinator, as other coaches often do, I'd have felt left out and of little value.

Others didn't spot it, but as each year passed, my emotions got closer to the surface. I'm sure it was the wear and tear over the years, the stress and strain. By 1988, in any public situation, sentiment might cause me to break down. The drama of the moment could set me off. I dealt with that by quickly cutting things off. People thought that I was being an impersonal, calculating SOB, a complete contrast to the way I actually felt.

When I left the field after the Raider game, I knew I didn't want to feel that way again, but first, I had to deal with the potential problems in my relationship with Ed DeBartolo, Jr.

Our relationship had not been quite the same since the Minnesota loss. Eddie was distressed by that loss because everybody had assumed we were back on top. None of us came back quickly, including Ed and myself, so as we struggled through the '88 season, our relationship seemed guarded, because neither of us knew what the future held. It was a tenuous time. Just as I was, Ed, too, was having a tough time dealing with losses. He didn't like that feeling, either.

So, after the Raiders game, we agreed that we'd meet at our practice facility in Santa Clara and confidentially review everything.

Ed was concerned. The bottom line for Ed now had become the

Super Bowl. We had tasted the championship twice before, and he knew that was what he wanted.

Ed and I had a relaxed but businesslike conversation. He wanted to talk about what had happened to the 49ers. I certainly did, too, because we no longer had firm, positive feelings about our direction. Some doubts had begun to surface.

I explained how I thought things were going, without making excuses. I had a better grasp of the situation because Ed, living in Youngstown, was able to attend some games, but if we lost, that would be his only exposure to the team. I was aware of the injuries and Joe Montana's status, and having been a coach in the NFL for twenty years, I realized there was an ebb and flow to a game and to a season. The stronger teams and the ones with more determination work through bad times. Teams with less character and commitment will fall apart; they can't sustain themselves.

I felt we still had a reasonable chance to win it all, because we were only two games behind the division-leading Saints. But Ed was extremely disappointed, having seen his team lose three straight years in the playoffs and now going through a 6–5 season. It was up to me to be forthright and direct and, in a sense, tender a resignation that would go into effect whenever he chose. It was important that Ed have all avenues open for the future.

In the previous forty-eight hours, I had given this considerable thought, so I formulated some options: I would continue as coach for the rest of the season, but at the end of the year, I could resign to become general manager, or I could resign and remain as consultant to Ed, or I could just leave the organization entirely. There was also the possibility that I could remain as coach after the '88 season, if he agreed, but I was leaning strongly toward retirement.

None of these options was presented because Ed had directly requested them. He wasn't forcing me out or demanding a resignation from me. But he was concerned, and, most likely, had his doubts. I'm sure there were those who had suggested that I just didn't have it anymore or that the game had passed me by. So, he was getting mixed reviews on me from people close to him. I'm sure it was said, "Eddie, with all that material you should be winning." Of course, I had directed the acquiring of that material.

But once we visited, we didn't have to remind each other that we had a great feeling for one another and had been through a lot together, and that our commitment to each other ran a lot deeper than just football. That conversation cleared the air because he no longer had to worry—he had the destiny of his team firmly in his hands and could make whatever moves he felt were necessary.

We embraced and together rededicated ourselves to bring this team back; together we would make the best of a difficult situation. From that point on, there was no uneasiness between us. We went about our work.

I was relaxed after our conversation. I had removed myself from the position of a coach under pressure, trying to justify every decision he made and explaining his failures under the weight of holding his job.

I could now concentrate on the games, rather than my status as a coach. I was able again to focus myself openly and freely on the team's progress.

Had we continued to lose, it could have been the beginning of a difficult era for the 49ers, because the press en masse was fully committed to covering the team. But we had a standard of play that we had established over the years and it was to carry us through those emotional, turbulent times.

The comeback from that low point was directly correlated to the character of the team. An emotional plea from the coach wouldn't be enough. I think I was forceful with the team, but it was the organization's character—built over the previous ten years—that really revealed itself in the next game, and for the remainder of the season.

The veterans who had experienced both triumph and failure pulled themselves together. They called a team meeting, without coaches, and reminded their teammates what they were playing for—the world championship. Player-held team meetings often can be an exercise in hollow rhetoric, but in this case, our tough, competitive, driven veterans took charge.

They came out practicing hard, concentrating, not allowing themselves to succumb to desperation and frustration. Beginning the day after the Raiders loss, practices were very spirited, with total concentration. That was a tribute to the squad's state of mind and the standard of performance we had developed. We simply would not allow ourselves to cave in.

I took deep pride in the fact that the team had such character that players would not concede the season, that they refused to allow it to become unraveled because they had played poorly. We were true champions, and we rededicated ourselves. All of this internal upheaval was occurring when we were 6–5. Most teams would have been quite pleased with this record.

Often in the NFL, you'll see teams start fast but then come apart when they lose a couple of games. That can result from a lack of ownership support, or from a coach ridiculing his players. At no point did I ridicule the players. I offered as much support as I could, and reminded them that they'd get firm, assertive direction.

On Monday night, I had called a meeting with our coaching staff and told them I was meeting the next day with Eddie, and that they shouldn't assume that we had permanent status, that the owner was concerned. But more importantly, each man was asked to give an appraisal of where we were and what it would take to turn this season around. We spoke about specific players, about our tactics, and about the approach that would best motivate the squad. After this process was completed, I bluntly told everyone in the room what I expected. I wanted up-beat, positive, active coaching. I asked that they remind themselves of how they'd approached their work in their first week of coaching, and that that was the kind of enthusiasm we had to have. We opened a few bottles of wine and reminded each other of our past successes and how they'd been achieved. In a sense, we all pledged ourselves to doing the best job possible. At this point, I became somewhat emotional and abruptly had to leave the room. We had been considered the best staff in football and had built this team from the depths to become the dominant force in the 1980s. Together we would recover and bring it back.

We did not play with great execution in our Monday night game against the Redskins, but we played with great intensity. That didn't surprise me. I'd been concerned until I saw the atmosphere in our locker room. Fred von Appen grabbed me and said, "This team is ready."

It was stone quiet until I said, "Everybody up." Then, the place exploded.

Both of our teams were cornered at 6–5. They were the world champions from the previous year, and their owner, Jack Kent Cooke, had called his team "the team of the '80s." We had compiled the best season record in '87. But now, we were both struggling. This game would decide which of us would recover and which would continue on a downhill slide that might not stop.

Of all the coaches I competed against over the years, I felt the strongest rivalry with Joe Gibbs. It was a rivalry based on respect. Joe was a true contemporary, because we became head coaches at about the same time. Both of our teams had become great in the '80s. I admired and respected the coaching job he and his staff had done. We could not be considered the best team in football unless we could defeat the Redskins.

It was an exciting game, a spirited game, and afterward, we could feel that the adversity we had suffered would motivate us for the rest of the season. Being at 7–5 and a viable contender, and having beaten the world champions soundly, 37–21, those devastating losses we had suffered would serve as an inspiration to the team.

That Redskins game was a true test of our character and the standards we had developed over the years.

From that point, we played outstanding football. The team grew healthy. As Joe's strength and stamina returned, his timing improved. With Joe playing at his best and everybody rallying, we made a great comeback. The rest of the season, we played much as we had throughout the '84 season, with conviction and confidence and great fellowship among the players. We were almost on a crusade to take it all the way. People like Bill Romanowski, John Taylor, Jesse Sapolu, and Pierce Holt were becoming championship performers.

19

Our Two Greatest Games

Two of the very best games ever played by the 49ers came in the playoffs that year.

Before the game against the Minnesota Vikings, Billy Wilson and I met, as was our custom, for the drive to Candlestick. There'll be a lot of activity around that stadium this morning, I thought. Here we go again. Bill's going to drive, I'll just sit back and relax. The tailgaters will be there early. This has become as big as our Dallas game in '82. Forty-Niner pride is on the line, my self respect is on the line.

I wanted to say to Billy, "This is my last game at Candlestick." Instead we visited about the weather: Are we going to get the late afternoon wind? God, I hope not. Joe's got to hit people when he gets a chance. They're going to be after his ass.

I settled back, closed my eyes. Billy grew quiet. I started reflecting on all of my years of taking this ride, always with excitement and apprehension. Oh, hell, don't get sentimental. At this moment, the only thing that matters in life is beating the Vikings. Thank God we are getting another shot at them. How quickly twelve months have passed, and yet, there's been so much agonizing in the meantime. As we pulled in, I said, "Our fans are here early." Billy said, "Don't worry, coach, you'll take them apart today."

As I stood on the sideline, everything looked the same—their uniforms and ours, the weather, the crowd. It seemed like a continuation. But this time, we owned the psychological edge. We came in with the inspiration, as they had the year before.

We had in a sense settled the score earlier in the season, when Steve Young made his incredible 49-yard run, but the Vikings thought they had been beaten on a fluke, which wouldn't happen again. They were confident they could beat us. They felt they would be the world champions because they were the strongest team defensively in the NFL and also had some gifted offensive players. They had come very close the year before, narrowly losing in the NFC championship game.

But I went into this one confident that we would beat them, and beat them soundly, because of our offensive and defensive game plans. That's exactly what happened. We dominated almost from the beginning. By the time it was over, we had destroyed their famed defense in a 34–9 rout. Our entire defensive staff, George, Bill, Ray, Fred, and Tommy, had done their homework. This time we had the Vikings' number.

Our defense played brilliantly. The big concern going into the game was Anthony Carter, who had almost singlehandedly destroyed us the year before. Even our supporters wondered: How could we ever stop him? Much of our game plan depended on a zone defense, hitting him at the line of scrimmage with one defender while another took him deep. He never could get untracked. Amazingly, the Vikings didn't go to him very often, but I doubt it would have mattered, because our defense was shutting him down.

Much of their offense was predicated on special plays. If we were playing alert defense and exploded off the ball, these types of plays wouldn't have a chance to develop. So, I knew we had a chance to take them apart, and we did. To a man, our defense beat them to the punch all day.

Through the years, we had developed a high regard for Viking defensive coordinator Floyd Peters's "25 defense." Consequently, we studied it throughout the off-season, established a game plan to deal with it before training camp started, and then refined that plan as the season progressed. The premise of the defense was to attack the line of scrimmage and rush the passer on every down. Its fundamental success was a combination of the system and talent ideally suited to it. Chris Doleman and Keith Millard, in particular, were among the very best defensive linemen in football.

One example of the way we attacked the Vikings was to run right at Keith Millard, who had developed a technique of jumping around his blocker to get into the backfield. He had disrupted virtually every offense he had faced. But with that quick movement, if our guard could just keep him going in that direction, it left a momentary hole.

Then, our trapping plays worked well. We had called a successful trap with Tom Rathman the previous year in the playoff game, but because the score got out of hand, it wasn't a play we could use very often. But now, starting fresh at 0–0, we could really go after them.

Plus, their zone defense was not sound. Their cornerbacks weren't disciplined, so we could throw the ball in front of them early and then go deep on them later.

But perhaps the best strategy was to use their own strength against them. The Vikings' front four came off the ball very quickly, but that quick start also made them vulnerable to misdirection. We would start a running play in one direction and then cut back the other way, and the Vikings couldn't recover.

The strategy worked well for the entire game, but the most successful play came late in the game, when Roger Craig broke for an 80-yard touchdown. The play was designed for a short-yardage situation. They overcommitted when Roger broke to the right, so as he countered back to the left, a big hole had developed. Excellent blocks by Steve Wallace, Jesse Sapolu and John Frank made it possible for Roger to go all the way.

To that point it was the best game we had played. I'd have to go back to the Super Bowl after our '84 season, against Miami, to recall another where we executed so well.

Following our loss to the Vikings in the '87 playoff game, Minnesota coach Jerry Burns had failed to acknowledge me as we left the field. Without realizing it, he had snubbed me, which added insult to injury. After this game, I got to him immediately. He was most congratulatory, saying, "Bill, you guys will beat the Bears and go all the way."

As years passed, I found myself feeling real empathy for coaches at all levels. During the pregame warmups, just before the battle began, I would have true affinity for the opposing coaches. As I would visit briefly with different individuals, regardless of their age or the significance of their responsibilities, I would feel a kind of bond with them, a deep fraternal respect and regard. We shared a love for the game.

Our next playoff game, for the NFC championship against the Chicago Bears, was one of the real highlights of my coaching career.

We were going back to Chicago to face the team that had beaten us, 10–9. After that game, Mike Ditka said to me, "Bill, these are a great bunch of guys. They just won't quit. They knew what they had to do, and they got it done. I'm really proud of them." I acknowledged the job his team had done. Anything I had said about my team at that point would have been hollow because we were the losers. In reality, I, too, was proud of our team. It had been a great game. As I reflected while riding to the airport on the team bus, if Joe were healthy and we revised our offensive plan, we could take them apart. In the dressing room just following the first game, I had remarked, "We're going to get another shot at these guys."

With all their pride, the Bears felt unbeatable, especially in Chicago. They also thought they had our number, but we were absolutely exhilarated at the thought of returning to Chicago, unconcerned about the weather or their record or anything. This time, we would be ready. I had great confidence in our defense. George Seifert had done a great job in our earlier game, and there was no reason to think we couldn't shut the Bears down completely.

I had miscalculated in the first game by worrying too much about their pass rush, and their great front four. I had assigned the tight end and both backs as blockers to double every pass rusher they had, to keep them away from Joe. But the problem was that our pass receivers just weren't getting open. The Bears would drop into a zone defense, and with just two men going downfield, the openings weren't there. By the time a receiver got open, Joe would be getting pressure and couldn't throw accurately.

Because I was almost consumed with effectively blocking their great front four, I had departed from our basic formula of offense, going to unnecessarily restrictive pass-protection schemes. We depended too much on Jerry Rice making big plays downfield. Regularly, tough decisions must be made. The final choice will most often be made by degree. As an example: We believe we can beat their left cornerback deep, but logically we'll only get one shot. The question is, what is the best way? By play pass, by dropback, by an out-and-up? Each option can be argued equally, but the final choice had better be right. In this case it was a formula pass protection, so I was mistaken by a degree.

As the game progressed, it was evident that the Bears were beating us to the punch. We were doing too much thinking, and they began to sense the kill. That combined with Joe's weakened state, rendered us ineffectual by the fourth quarter. As the clock wound down, we were within one first down of getting into position for a long field goal to win it, but we couldn't get the job done. It was embarrassing and humiliating to have our offense physically dominated in front of the Chicago crowd. It was even more devastating because the loss ruined our chance to set an NFL record for consecutive wins on the road.

Going into the championship game, it was obvious to our offensive staff that we should go with our basic style of football and not give any special consideration to their front four. We planned for that game as if the Bears were just another team. Our offensive guards, Guy McIntyre and Jesse Sapolu, would be expected to handle Steve McMichael and Dan Hampton.

We didn't lack in confidence. We also had a psychological edge, of which the Bears weren't aware. They considered themselves unbeatable at home and thought they had our number. Chicago fans were calling them a "team of destiny." But we had the incentive of being the underdog and the confidence that we were the better team.

The weather was bad, cold and windy, and the people in Chicago, presumably including the Bears, thought a California team could not win in such weather. Much was made of the fact that the 49ers hadn't won a playoff game on the road since 1970, but in reality, the 49ers had only played four road playoff games in that period—three since I had been a coach—which was hardly a large statistical sample. Nor did it mean much in this situation. Some of our players had hardly been born the last time the 49ers had won a playoff game on the road. They weren't concerned with history. They were ready to play now.

Chicagoans have tremendous enthusiasm for their team, and the press echoed their adulation. There just weren't any critics, which was an unusual experience for us.

In the Bay Area, there were writers predicting that the 49ers would lose, because the Bears had a much better win-loss record, 14–2 to our 10–6. The Bears had already beaten us, the weather differential and the fact that it had been years since the visiting team had won a championship game—all these factors were supposed to work against us. But no Chicago writers went against their home team. Everyone predicted a Bears win by two or three touchdowns; everyone explained why they would win. There just wasn't a columnist or a TV sports-caster who didn't see it the same way, that the Bears were a team of destiny. I read column after column about how great the Bears were, that this was the greatest Bears team ever and had more dedication than even the world champion '85 team.

I had been required to take part in an NFC championship game press conference two days before the game. Upon arriving at the airport and traveling by limousine to the press conference, I had time to browse through the week's newspapers and noted that every Chicago columnist and every beat writer had declared the Bears the winner. In their minds, it was a matter of getting this game over with so they could go on to Miami for the Super Bowl. There were even predictions of the final score in Miami, such as Chicago 28, Buffalo 7.

At the press conference, I reminded the media that we were a competitive team and warned them not to be too sure of themselves. I was strongly challenged as to how I could be so positive about this team, when the 49ers had been 6–5 at one point and had had a season-long quarterback controversy. They doubted we would even make a game of it. In a television interview following the press conference, a Chicago sportscaster became quite argumentative when I spoke positively about our chances, and concluded by reminding his viewers that the 49ers must now face the "team of destiny."

In the pregame warmups, Dan Hampton was standing there in his shirt-sleeves, though it was bitterly cold. He and McMichael, hands on hips, were trying to stare us down from across the field.

We began to joke about it, how they looked. Harry Sydney exclaimed, "God, they must be cold, standing there like that." Tom Rathman looked over and said, "They'd better get back with their team." We were even more exhilarated returning to the dressing room, saying that the Bears were so contemptuous of us that they thought they could intimidate us simply by standing there with their hands on their hips, holding in their stomachs.

I've never seen a team more up for a game. We were laughing and teasing about the weather. Word had gotten around the locker room about their staring us down during the pregame warmups, and everybody was joking and laughing about it. Now, if we could only execute in those freezing conditions, with that cold wind coming off Lake Michigan.

Our rivalry with the Bears produced all sorts of sidelights. In the

41–0 beating we gave them at home in 1987, our fans had gotten on Mike Ditka so badly that he finally began to yell back at them and, after the game, threw his gum at the crowd before ducking into the tunnel leading to the dressing rooms.

Upon reading about it in the paper the next day, I called Ed McCaskey, the Bears chairman of the board, and followed up with a letter, apologizing for our fans' behavior. But the Bears fans were waiting for me when we showed up in Chicago for our regular-season game.

The Bears fans are within twenty feet of the sideline on the visiting side. In the first game an enterprising fan had a powerful bullhorn and methodically began ridiculing me. Our team and everyone in that area of the stadium could hear him. He did a beautiful job and really hit home on occasion. I knew he was right behind me, but didn't dare turn around and look. As the game progressed, I kept trying to find him out of the corner of my eye. I was wondering how I could get hold of that SOB. On reflection, it was a hilarious situation but it didn't seem funny at the time. To this day, it seems strange that the security guards standing within a few feet of him didn't step forward.

He was ready and waiting again the second time around.

I knew it was cold, because this guy's teeth were chattering and his voice was breaking, but as the game progressed, there were fewer and fewer remarks. I assumed he was in his car heading home by the end of the third quarter, because we had taken the Bears apart. On reflection, I think it was our best performance of the '80s.

I take great pride in that offensive game plan. We just attacked them. Our style of cut blocking was ideally suited to stop their tall, rangy, defensive linemen. If we could cut down Hampton and Mc-Michael at the line of scrimmage, by the end of the game they would have a terrible time getting up. Bobb McKittrick had prepared his offensive linemen masterfully.

We thought we could attack their linebackers. The key man was Mike Singletary. We had Tom Rathman in pass protection checking to see if Singletary was blitzing. Tom took Singletary head-to-head very effectively. They really punished each other, but in the process, we were moving the ball.

We had reemphasized our basic contention that short, timed passes were well suited for such weather and could be thrown and caught before the defense could respond. The Bears were not able to get close to either Joe or his receivers. Their cornerbacks just didn't have the quickness to match up with Jerry Rice, Mike Wilson, and John Taylor.

Even the weather conditions worked for us. Early in the game, Jerry Rice caught a comeback pattern with two defenders next to him, but they couldn't keep their balance as well as Jerry. He cut across the field and shocked the Bears by turning that short pass into a 61-yard touchdown.

In this game, we beat the Bears to the punch. Typical of our success was Tom Rathman breaking for 20 yards on a trap play against their nickel defense, as we were driving for a second-quarter touchdown.

The final score was 28–3 and it could have been higher. We had a fumble on one drive that otherwise probably would have been a touchdown. They just weren't stopping us.

In turn, the Bears could do nothing offensively. George Seifert and the defensive staff had put together a great game plan, and we were playing with incredible intensity. Michael Walter and Jeff Fuller, in particular, played as if they were possessed. Walter had 11 unassisted tackles and Fuller had 10 tackles and the one interception of the game. We were much quicker than the Bears. Since that time, other teams have also taken advantage of that lack of quickness.

Following the game, Mike Ditka and I met on the field. He was magnanimous in defeat and I in turn was most positive about his team and the job he had done. Much had happened since our last meeting. They had continued to win with much fanfare. We had struggled, but after weeks of frustration and turmoil that tested our character and resolve, we would be the team traveling to Miami and into history.

20

Retiring on a High Note

My meeting with Ed DeBartolo, Jr., after the Raiders game had taken the stress out of what otherwise would have been a tense situation because I knew I could smoothly retire at the end of the season. At that point, I thought I probably would, but I wanted to wait to make my final decision because I remembered 1982.

In 1982, I had expected to retire but I finally changed my mind when I was able to step away from the pressure and get good advice from my peers. Because of that, I wanted to give myself time to think about my future, without making an emotional decision under pressure. As every week passed, I continued to reflect on how I felt. Could I really step away from coaching after finally reaching the top?

More and more, I thought that, yes, I could make that decision. I never told Ed that I planned to retire, but I think he expected it, though he said publicly near the end of the season that he hoped I would continue coaching.

By Super Bowl week, I had privately decided to retire, but I didn't announce my decision because I was concerned about the team and the future of the organization. I did not want my decision to become a public spectacle, setting up a "win-one-for-the-Gipper" type of scenario. I did not want a lot of speculation about the next coach, and I especially did not want the players thinking about who their next coach might be and losing their concentration on the world championship.

I had always worked to convince our players that they were replaceable, unfortunate though that might be. Whenever anybody was injured, or when a veteran was replaced in the lineup, the new player would be expected to play just as well and we would continue without skipping a beat. I believed in that approach, so naturally I felt obligated to depart in the same way.

I didn't want to go public because it would be a distraction to everybody. I was determined not to let this become a sideshow. It was the team's game to win or lose. I didn't want my situation to be a factor in how we played, and I didn't want to divert any attention from the players.

So, there was never any question in my mind that I would hold any announcement until after the season. In fact, there was a period even after the Super Bowl before I publicly said anything. In that way, all the accolades that the players deserved went to them, without my announcement overshadowing what they had accomplished.

I know some players expected me to tell the team I was retiring, to share it with them. When I didn't, they may have felt I was insensitive and removed from them, that I did only what was in my best interests, without concern for them. In fact, my motives were totally opposite. In itself, a Super Bowl has many more distractions than a regular-season game because there are two thousand media representatives on the scene. I did not want my players to have the additional burden of having to answer questions about what life would be like without Bill Walsh.

Frankly, I don't know whether I could have told the players, anyway. During that period, I was highly emotional. I had directed the 49ers for ten years and had been in coaching for more than thirty years, and now I was ending my career by coaching for the world championship. My emotions were just under the surface.

I found myself worn thin after all we'd experienced throughout the '88 season. I knew that if I were to broach that subject with the players, it was likely that I would break down.

As time has passed, I have become aware that some players misunderstood my actions. I feel bad that there wasn't better communication at the time. The first opportunity I had to speak with the entire team was a short time later at a banquet in Youngstown, held by Eddie. I believe I expressed my feelings well, but again, I had to cut my remarks short because my emotions broke through the surface. Later, in preparing for our championship ring ceremony in San Francisco, I spoke with both a psychiatrist and a physician as to how I could make sense and complete my remarks without breaking down. In fact, I took a prescription drug in an effort to avert being forced to retire from the stage.

I considered it of paramount importance that the organization have the same format, the same approach, the same philosophy, and definitely the same system of offense. It was just as vital to retain as many people as possible, and for my replacement to come from within the organization, for continuity.

So often, teams falter because when they have a tough loss or two, there are public statements from the owner or coach, fixing blame. We never had that. Certainly, there were moments of great disappointment, such as the playoff loss to Minnesota, but there was none of this public sniping. We had a solid organization, and we cared for each other. I was determined that we maintain that feeling, and the one way to ensure this was to name my replacement from within the organization. If my successor had come from outside, it would have set the 49ers back for years. They might never have returned to that championship level.

Had Denny Green remained with the 49ers, he would have been included for consideration as my replacement. But when the head coaching job at Stanford became available, Denny was immediately interested and became the top candidate.

Because of my own experiences, I had always been very sensitive to the career needs of my coaches. I personally met with members of the Stanford administration and endorsed Denny. Of course, he got the job on his merits.

George Seifert had been the strongest candidate to replace me; with Denny at Stanford, he was the only choice. George and I had worked together for nine of my ten years with the 49ers and, before that, in my two years at Stanford. He was a bright, conscientious, and hard-working man who was ready to take on the responsibility of being a pro head coach.

I thought it would be wise to take the team through its final game before having a final determination with Eddie. If we were successful, it was likely that George would be named the head coach. Had I gone public with my decision earlier, there was always the possibility that other people would be considered, that other coaches would line up for the position, which naturally would be considered a real plum. George might have been passed over for somebody with more national recognition.

Winning the Super Bowl would certainly boost George's chances, which was another reason I wanted to concentrate on the game.

Even though I didn't announce my decision, there was still considerable speculation during Super Bowl week about my future, but I don't think that speculation distracted the team. The players were concentrating on the game. They were worried about their personal contributions to victory. Players don't think as much about outside influences as their own personal needs. I think they felt I knew what I was doing, and that it was my business.

As players took the field for pregame warmups, I purposely allowed myself a few moments of reflection. I moved away from everyone and tried to capture the moment. I thought of the significance of the last game that I would coach being for the world championship.

I was trying to sort out my feelings. I guess I was kind of maudlin. Thoughts flashed through my mind: my first game thirty-one years before, pacing the sideline as my Washington High team beat Mountain View by the crazy score of 11–0 . . . Cal and Stanford; God, was I impetuous . . . my devastation when Bill Johnson was named the head coach in Cincinnati . . . the satisfaction I had when Stanford upset UCLA, 32–28, in 1977 . . . the dejection after the Minnesota playoff loss in '87 . . . the absolute agony of losing to the Raiders this season, the satisfaction in destroying the Bears in the championship game . . . the two Super Bowls we'd won. . . . Now, we were in Miami for another Super Bowl. This would be it. My emotions were right on the surface. I started to break down, but then told myself, "Get it together. Here you go."

I had to become almost computerized to function effectively. A coach simply can't afford to indulge in the emotion of the moment. He has to be able to function smoothly, to stay in control. Players would have emotion in excess. What they needed from me was decisive direction and stability.

The game itself was one of the most frustrating I've ever coached, so much so that it was well over a year before I could bring myself to look at the film. I had no such problem with our first two Super

Bowls, especially the second, which was as close to a perfect game as one of my teams ever had, but this game was an almost constant struggle. It has been referred to as one of the most exciting Super Bowls, because we had to make a drive in the final minutes of the game to win it, but it was exciting only because of our offensive problems. I give the Cincinnati Bengals credit for playing hard and making key defensive plays when they had to, but the game should not have been that close, because we had a much stronger and more experienced team.

Our defense, led by Ronnie Lott and Kevin Fagan, stopped Cincinnati's number-one running offense and frustrated quarterback Boomer Esiason. The single constant of our team throughout the year was the effectiveness of our defense, and it proved true again in this game. But our offense was continually frustrated.

We moved the ball in big chunks. When the game was over, our offensive stats were impressive. We controlled the ball, and yet we didn't score a touchdown until the fourth quarter.

In sports, there are any number of things that can upset a team. Some of those we have no control of, such as an official's call or the bounce of a ball. Sometimes, too, it can be shaky strategy or the failure of a player to execute.

In that game, it was all of the above, and two plays in particular illustrate our problems.

We were driving in the first quarter when Mike Wilson seemed to catch a pass at the two, but instant replay showed that Mike had trapped the ball. If John Taylor had been the receiver, with his great hands, he probably would have caught the ball. But Taylor wasn't in the game because I had gone against my basic philosophy.

Mike Wilson had been a solid performer for us for many years. Usually, he was our third receiver who could be depended on to make the play when he was in the game—as he did in the 1982 Super Bowl—and he had also played well as a starter on occasion. When Dwight Clark was injured before the '83 championship game against the Redskins, Mike stepped in and played beautifully.

With Mike at the end of his career, he was not the equal of Taylor, who had the speed and athletic ability to make great plays, but because of his experience, I was still alternating Mike with Taylor. I'll always wonder about this play, whether John could have made it. Again, that makes the point: If a man is the best performer and can come up with a play that makes the difference, he's got to be on the field. Because he wasn't, we didn't make the play and we lost a chance to take command of the game early.

In the second quarter, we had an excellent, sustained drive that resulted in a fourth-and-one at the goal line. My choice was to take the field goal. In retrospect, I should have run Roger Craig on the same counterplay on which he'd gone 80 yards to score against Minnesota in our playoff game. He would have dived over the top for the necessary yardage. But at that point, in such a pressure-packed game, I thought we should get points on the board. As it happened, there was a bad snap from center and we didn't even get the field goal.

That wasn't a gross error. Other coaches have since indicated they'd have done the same. As recently as last season, I saw a game in which a coach passed up a chance for a field goal and then didn't get the touchdown—and wound up losing by a single point. But, I'd still like to have that call back. We would have scored the touchdown.

The last drive was a culmination of many years of establishing not only our system of football but a style that emphasized precision and skill to reduce the risk factor.

Players must execute. They just can't depend on emotion to win. It didn't matter how much we wanted to win the game. The bottom line was: Could we execute a series of plays almost flawlessly? If any one play had been disastrous, it would have cost us the game and the championship. It's the standard of performance that is the difference when the opponent is equally motivated.

Only through years of repetition and experience with those plays can each player complete consecutive assignments without someone making the kind of error that ends the drive. If you want something too badly, you can throw yourself out of sync trying to make a play that isn't really achievable. The fabled "superhuman effort" often becomes unproductive desperation.

We kept our basic offense on the field, with our tight end and two running backs. There was enough time—3:10 when we got the ball— that we did not have to throw on every down. We wanted our tight end in the game to block for the run, and both backs who could carry the ball, block, or be used as receivers. The tight end can often be a better short- to medium-range target than a wideout.

This tactic forced the Bengals to stay in their basic defense. They realized we would run well if they went to their nickel defense, so they had to stay in a defense that could handle both the run and the pass.

We used plays that Joe Montana and his teammates had perfected. In that kind of situation, with the pressure that's on the team, you want to have familiar plays that men are confident they can execute, rather than trying high-risk plays and depending on great individual effort. In this circumstance, we were going to depend heavily on our "standard of performance."

We put together a series that I felt confident Joe, with his poise and spontaneity, would execute. These were plays we had selected to attack the basic Bengal defense. They were high percentage plays that would result in steady gains if properly executed.

The clock was a factor, but after all the practice we'd had, we knew our team could function in that time. The hours we'd given this, going all the way back to training camp, would now pay dividends.

We were well aware that if at any time a blocker had been called for holding, it could have been fatal. It took tremendous concentration and poise on our pass protectors' parts to be disciplined enough to avoid a penalty while at the same time holding off Cincinnati linemen who were desperately trying to get to Joe. At that point, all of us were fighting not to succumb to the intense stress and pressure.

We depended heavily on Joe being willing to throw the ball away if necessary or changing the call at the line of scrimmage if there was an unexpected change in the defense.

Joe got the play call from me on the sideline, but if the clock was running, he would immediately go without a huddle and call a play that we had prepared for that situation. It was the two-minute offense, which we ran as well as anybody, because Montana is so cool under pressure and because we had practiced it so often that it was almost second nature.

My goal was to get within field-goal range. At that point, we would take a shot at a touchdown and, if that failed, kick the field goal to tie the game and take our chances in overtime. I was confident that Mike Cofer could kick the field goal if we needed it.

We had some real advantages: Jerry Rice was capable of making big plays, and Roger Craig had been through this so many times that he knew what to do, including protecting the ball to avoid fumbling. And, of course, Joe had taken us on a successful drive in nearly the same circumstances in our championship game against Dallas eight years earlier.

I made one call in that sequence that could have stopped our drive. I had called a fake screen to Craig. Randy Cross would pull down the line as if it were a screen pass. Roger would start to the outside but then stop and break back to the middle. We call that our "fake screen left, halfback check middle."

It took perfect timing, but was ideally suited to their defense, and I remember telling Bobb McKittrick and Mike Holmgren, "Grab your . . . We're going to go for it."

Two problems arose on that play, inadvertently. Roger was knocked off balance by the Bengals' defensive end, which ruined his release. At the same instant, Cross was knocked across the line by the Cincinnati nose tackle and couldn't get back. When we finally threw to Roger, Randy was still downfield and the head linesman spotted it. This was not a subjective, phantom call; I had no problem accepting it.

Following that misadventure with the fake screen, we were forced to go downfield; it was now second-and-twenty. We knew what we wanted for that situation: I had informed Joe earlier that Jerry Rice would be open on a "deep over."

Jerry had made all his breaks to the outside, so I felt that if he broke into the middle, the secondary would be deep and to the outside. The linebackers had to be conscious of Roger Craig coming out of the backfield, so the opening was there for Jerry. He broke across the field and Joe had good protection, but what was also important was that Jerry broke a tackle and made a 27-yard play out of what we had thought would be a 20-yard gain at best.

We had always reminded our players who handled the ball that they were really an extension of the other ten men. If the ball was approaching Jerry Rice in flight, he would remind himself almost instinctively that ten other people had sacrificed so much to get the ball to him. Those who are advancing the ball are responsible to their teammates to get the most out of it. A Harris Barton or a Fred Quillan blocking are doing their job just as Jerry does his.

This case illustrated this teamwork perfectly. It was a pinpoint pass by Montana, precise pass routes run by other receivers, and great pass protection.

At this point, we were close enough for a field goal, but we also had enough time to work methodically for a touchdown. We moved closer to the goal line with a pass to Roger Craig that was almost automatic, with Roger starting to the outside and then curling into the middle to catch the ball in front of the linebackers.

Joe called a time-out with thirty-nine seconds remaining, and we discussed two things: our next call and our final strategy. We would go for the end zone twice. If those plays failed, we would then kick the field goal.

The call would be "20 halfback curl X up." Roger would run the same pattern as he had on the previous play, occupying the linebackers, and John Taylor would break open behind him, after first faking a move to the outside.

As Joe returned to the field, the last thing I said was, "Don't force it. We'll have another shot."

That play was designed specifically for the coverage the Bengals used. Inside their own fifteen, they locked their linebackers on the tight end and running backs and had their safeties double-cover the wide receivers in combination with the cornerbacks. It was a common defense, and the Bengals used it automatically. They had never been hurt with it.

I didn't realize until later that Roger Craig had lined up and run his pattern to the wrong side. But, the linebackers still responded to Roger, and in the meantime, John had run a perfect pattern. The safety had bit on his fake, so there was nobody in the middle. Joe threw a perfect strike for the touchdown (see Diagram G, page 272).

I took real pride in having a play that I had designed over a period of years work for the winning touchdown in a Super Bowl.

Throughout all this, Joe was just brilliant, even surviving one misadventure. At one point in the drive, after completing a pass to Roger Craig, he brought his team to the line without a huddle. Because of the tremendous crowd noise, he spent so much energy barking out the play that he hyperventilated. His only recourse was to throw the ball away, rather than to take a chance with a bad pass. As the play developed, he almost passed out. He then turned to me and gestured for a time-out. Not realizing he was having a problem, I waved him off. As Joe got into the huddle, he began to recover. He continued on, and the rest is history.

Of course, I was excited and exhilarated by the game, that we had won the world championship. We'd been written off by many people and had struggled to overcome our earlier frustrations. The character, the inner confidence, that had been developed and cultivated over ten years had been the difference. We had conditioned ourselves to deal with adversity and when it hit, we overcame it. We arrived at and won this game so differently from the other two. To this day, I take great satisfaction in that accomplishment. We played the season "our way," and reached the summit. We "beat people to the punch." We established a standard of performance where each man was an extension of his teammates. We prepared for every contingency and throughout all of this there was a single thrust—sacrifice for your team, because you infinitely care.

We took great pride in playing like a "precision machine." We weren't obsessed with individually attracting attention. We could thrive in the volatile, sometimes cruel arena of the National Football League with class, dignity and mutual respect. I take pride in the fact that every man who wore a 49er uniform could be proud of his participation, even if it was a brief training camp episode. I believe each man profited in every sense with his 49er experience. How fortunate I was to have touched these men and their families—the players, coaches, management staff, the ownership. From Washington High School in 1957 to San Francisco in 1988, hundreds of people had endured so much to share victory and defeat with men they grew to love. And, Jeff Fuller, I do love you.

Now I had to address my retirement. I had no second thoughts. I had almost forced myself to tell enough friends privately that I was stepping away so that I couldn't change my mind.

The next question was: When would I make the announcement? Many writers thought I would make it in the press conference the morning after the game, but I was not prepared to say anything until I met with Ed DeBartolo, Jr.

That meeting came in Carmel on Wednesday. Both Carmen Policy and my attorney, Steven Kay, also took part. The meeting was relaxed, upbeat, and cordial. Throughout my years with the 49ers, Carmen Policy was the most honest, direct, and astute person with whom I associated. He also became a close friend. Ed and Carmen asked if I would stay, with a considerable raise in salary. But my decision had been made, and I told them it was time to make the move. Both Eddie and Carmen had complete appreciation for my decision. It was agreed that I would remain as director of football operations for an indefinite period.

That was just my first step. Next, I wanted to feel certain that George Seifert would be the head coach, and to establish a hierarchy within the organization with John McVay as the administrative head in California. Ed was in total agreement. George was his choice.

The timing of all this was important, because I couldn't commit the position to George until I could be sure it would be offered to him. Meanwhile, he was beginning to interview for other jobs, and I couldn't discourage him. Until Ed was prepared to complete the changeover, we didn't want to distract George from his own career decisions.

I did feel that, even if he was offered another job, George would talk to us first, so we had a little time. But it was getting close because, even as we talked, George was on a plane to Cleveland. Fortunately, he had to make a connection in Dallas. While he was there, he phoned his wife, Linda. We had told her that we wanted George to return immediately to discuss becoming the next 49ers coach, so she rather enthusiastically told him to "get home fast."

There was only one question remaining: How would we make the public announcement? If I had made known my retirement independently, there would have been more attention focused on me. But I wanted a smooth transition, so we announced my retirement and that George would replace me at the same press conference.

One of the basic tenets in establishing the organization was to make it so solid that it could survive anyone's departure, including mine. I take real pride in the team continuing to thrive, winning the Super Bowl the following year with George Seifert as coach. In all honesty, the team was revitalized; it was to become one of the best teams in NFL history.

I'm no longer a part of the 49ers organization, but thoughts of the team are with me daily.

About a year after I stepped away, Keith Fahnhorst, our team captain during our most notable achievements, called and said he was flying in from Minneapolis on business and asked if I had time to get together. It was great hearing from him. We agreed to meet for lunch. I picked Keith up in Redwood City, near our old training camp, the place from which we had transformed the team from the dregs to the top.

We drove to our usual spot, a coffee shop where players and coaches had often gathered in the past, but there was a glitzy new building in its place. Keith said, "Good God, even the Copper Shield is gone."

We looked around and found another place to eat and reminisce. So, we sat and covered a span of several years together, talking about what everyone was doing, who was doing well, who may have been having problems adjusting to life outside football. We recalled some of our great moments and then began to talk about today's team, teasing each other about how much they'd missed both of us.

We found ourselves saying the old familiar things. "It'll never be the same without us," and "These new guys don't have the same attitude." We talked about how so many of the new players don't realize the pain and sacrifices that others had endured to get the 49ers where they are. They only know the 49ers as world champions. Somehow they assume it's always been this way.

Keith said, "Bill, I really miss it." I looked him in the eye and said, "I'm having a tough time myself." We both got sort of emotional.

As we waved good-bye, I headed up Jefferson Street. I found myself turning into the old complex, thinking, "Why don't I take one last look?" As I circled through the parking lot, looking at the deserted field and the weathered building, memories flashed through my mind—the personalities, the laughs, the glory. Driving out I said to myself, "God, I wish this was 1979 again."

I swallowed hard. Don't look back.

Appendix

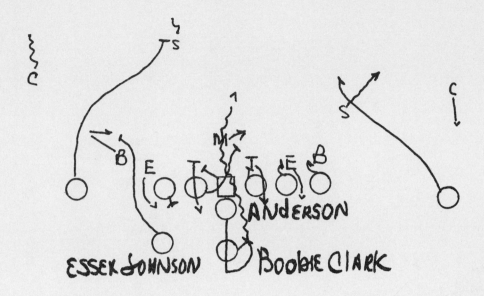

A. Wraparound or Slow Draw
Bengal offense, 1975
20 yards vs. Cleveland

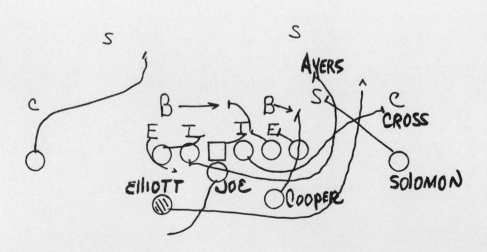

B. Red Right–18 Bob—Sweep that took apart Dallas nickel
defense
NFC Championship Game, 1981

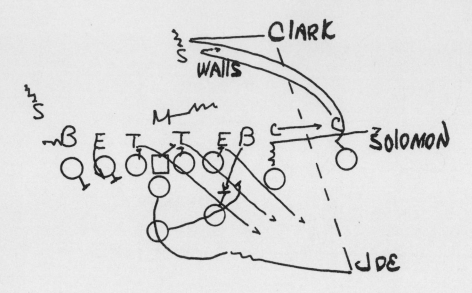

C. Brown Left Slot–Sprint Right Option
The Catch, NFC Championship, 1981
Solomon covered; Clark is the alternate

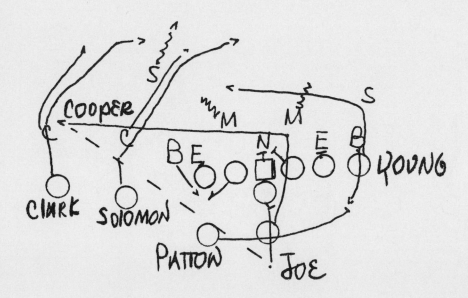

D. Brown Right Slot–Fox 2 FB Cross
Touchdown vs. Cincinnati
Super Bowl XVI

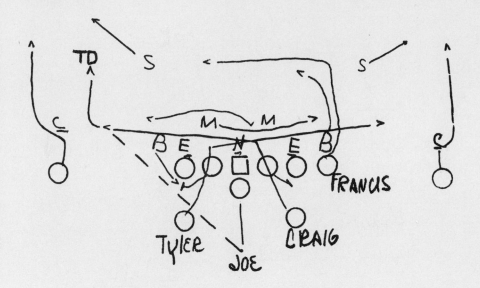

E. Red Right–20 Bingo Cross
   Miami linebackers attempting to cover Roger Craig and
      Wendell Tyler
   TD—San Francisco
   Super Bowl XIX

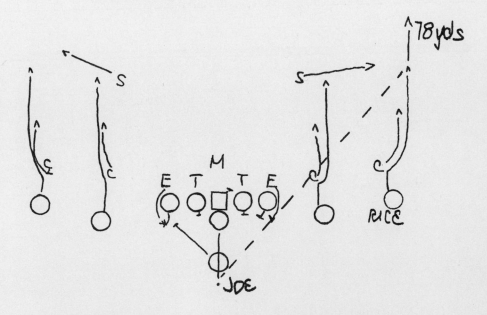

F. Winning touchdown with 42 seconds remaining to beat the
   Giants 20–17, in 1988

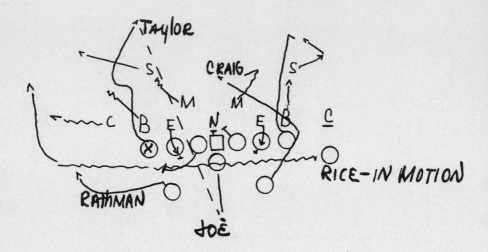

G.   Red Right Tight–F left–20 HB Curl–X up
Touchdown, 34 seconds remaining
Super Bowl XXIII